# The Complete

# *Cuisinart Air Fryer Oven*

# COOKBOOK

600 Healthy and Delicious Air Fryer Oven Recipes That Perfect for Beginners and Advanced Users| with Pro Tips & Illustrated Instructions to Master Your Air Fryer Oven

By Irene Barrett

Dear Readers,

We are glad that you purchased this book, your opinion is very important to us. If you have any comments and suggestions on this cookbook, we sincerely invite you to send us an email for feedback.

With your participation, we will grow faster and better.

After receiving your email, we will upgrade the product according to your needs and give you an e-book of 50 recipes as a gift.

We are committed to continuous growth and progress, providing readers with cookbooks that help create a better kitchen life and a healthy body.

I wish you happy every day.

Company contact email: Healthrecipegroup@outlook.com

# Table of Content

## Chapter 4 Poultry · 41

## Chapter 5 Fish and Seafood     61

## Chapter 6 Meats     79

## Chapter 7 Casseroles, Frittatas and Quiches            99

## Chapter 8 Wraps and Sandwiches            108

## Chapter 9 Appetizers and Snacks     119

## Chapter 10 Desserts 133

## Chapter 11 Fast and Easy Everyday Favorites 145

## Chapter 12 Holiday Specials — 157

## Chapter 13 Sauces for Air Fryer Recipes — 165

## Appendix 1: Measurement Conversion Chart — 169

## Appendix 2: Cuisinart Air Fryer Oven Time Table — 170

## Appendix 3: Recipes Index — 172

# Introduction

If there is one thing that makes your kitchen complete, it is a quick and efficient multipurpose cooking appliance- just like the Cuisinart air fryer oven. This air fryer oven comes with so many cooking options and a large cooking capacity which helps you create an entire menu at home using one single appliance. It not only air fries but also lets you toast, bake and broil a variety of food portions perfectly. To meet the needs of all its customers, Cuisinart has launched an entire series of Air fryer ovens tagged as TOA (Toaster Oven Air Fryer), which has different models, including TOA 60, 70, 65 and 90. The TOA 65 and 90s are the digital variants which come with a control panel having a display screen, a dial and buttons to select different cooking modes. Whereas TOA 60 and 70 are Toaster oven air fryers with no digital screen and four dials to adjust the cooking functions. The great thing is that all these models are super simple to use and easy to understand.

If you are a foodie who loves to enjoy healthy home-cooked meals, then this cookbook is definitely for you! There are recipe ideas that will let you get the best out of your Cuisinart air fryer oven and its variety of cooking modes. Since I am a health enthusiast and I care about the health of my family, I used this air fryer oven to create a variety of oil-free recipes. So while compiling this cookbook, I made sure to add as many healthy recipes as I could. With all sorts of meat, poultry, vegetarian, seafood, breakfast, snacks and dessert recipes in this cookbook, you will get to enjoy a complete doze of flavors and nutrients.

Cuisinart's Air Fryer Oven is a stainless steel multi cooker which comes with several cooking options- bake, convection bake, air fry, toast, warm, convection broil and broil. A rack, baking/drip pan, air fry basket and, in some models, a grill are all included in the package. The limited three-year warranty covers the button and knob-based LED interface. When I first heard about Cuisinart's TOA-65 Air Fryer Toaster Oven, I had my doubts. I couldn't picture keeping it out of a cabinet to toast a bagel or air fry onion rings since it was too big, roughly 17 x 22 x 16 inches. However, when I used each of its seven cooking modes, I forgot about the size because every setting, from toasting bread to air-frying French fries, was perfect. I also discovered that you could also use it for roasting a tiny chicken when your oven is full of cake, or you can quickly broil a cheese sandwich for your kids.

The TOA-65 is the epitome of clever practicality and adaptability in a multicooker. The majority of the features function well, the preprogrammed settings make sense, and the user-friendly interface makes it simple to use, so specialized equipment for each unique task is not required. This compact but powerful device won me over and now sits next to the kettle.

## Cuisinart Toa 60 Vs Toa 65

The interface is where the TOA-60 and TOA-65's designs differ the most. The TOA-60 model has four knobs that may be turned to change the temperature, time, settings, and function.

The TOA-65 has a digital interface with buttons that let you change the settings and functions, set the timer, and adjust the temperature. Functionality-wise, the TOA-65 offers more precise cooking options than the TOA-60. The TOA-60 knob can toggle in 50-degree increments, whereas TOA-65 sets a precise temperature in five-degree increments.

Moreover, I used both, and the TOA-65 fared better than the TOA-60 on nearly every test when we evaluated the cooking capabilities. The TOA-65 produces super crispy air-fried frozen fries, golden-brown Toast, excellently cooked poultry, and well-baked cookies. On the other hand, I discovered that the TOA-60 fried to a higher degree. Before the cooking durations were up, parts of the chicken, cookies, and fries started to burn. And I also discovered that the toast settings did not consistently produce well-cooked Toast as we had anticipated. The TOA-65 costs more than the TOA-60.

## Who Ought to Buy a Cuisinart Toa-60?

The Cuisinart TOA-65 Air Fryer Toaster Oven is something I would never have thought of purchasing, but after using it, I've changed my opinion. This equipment made it so much easier for me to quickly bake a few cookies or make a quesadilla for my kids' dinner. There are several good reasons why I shouldn't use the stovetop or oven. I can also dehydrate and air fry. The TOA-65 is ideal for you if you enjoy using kitchen appliances but wish to streamline your work and keep your kitchen clean. It's also your best option if you wish you had a second oven or didn't have one at all. It is efficient, small, and a powerhouse. It does deserve a spot on the countertop.

## Specifications

The specification of the Cuisinart air fryer oven is important to look into, as they let you understand the appliance better. Since Cuisinart TOA 60 is the most commonly used model due to its fair price and 7 cooking options, I am about to discuss a few of its highlighting features:

**The Power Light:** When the oven is being used, the indicator light will switch on and stay lit.

Dial for the ON/Oven Timer. With the exception of the Toast function, it is used to set the desired time. The unit is turned on, and the cooking cycle is started by the oven timer. After the timer runs out, the unit is powered off.

**Simple Interior:** The coating on the oven's sides creates a surface that is simple to clean.

**Automatic Door Switch for Safety:** The oven has a Safety Auto Off button that automatically turns the power off when the oven door is opened. Please remember to close the oven door while cooking or Air frying.

**An Extendable Crumb Tray:** The crumb tray is placed in this oven. For simple cleaning, the crumb tray slides out from the front bottom of the Air fryer Toaster Oven.

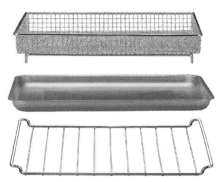

**Air Fryer Basket:** To achieve the best cooking results, use the Air fryer Basket with the Air fry setting. Always use the Air fryer Basket nestled inside the baking pan.

**Oven Rack:** Suitable for usage in Position 1 (bottom) and Position 2 (top). The rack stops halfway out of the oven when it is in Position 2. The front of the oven rack can be raised and slid out of Position 2 to be removed.

**A Drip Tray or Baking Pan:** It comes with a baking pan and drip tray for your convenience. When roasting or baking, use only the baking pan without the air fryer basket. When air frying, use a baking pan with the air fryer basket.

**Cord Storage:** The oven also has a space to roll and store the power cord at the back. In this way, the power cord remains protected when the oven is not in use.

## How to Use the Appliance?

After bringing this appliance home, here is what you need to do. Unbox it, and remove all the stickers and packing material. Keep the cooking accessories aside. Now your air fryer toaster oven should be placed on a flat surface. Move your air fryer oven away from the wall and any items on the countertop by 2 to 4 inches (5 to 10 cm) before using it. Never use on heat-sensitive surfaces. The top of the oven should not be used to store objects. If they are, remove everything prior to starting your oven. Keep it away from the reach of young kids. Pull the power cord out. Check that the crumb tray is in its proper location and that the oven is empty. Connect the power cord to the wall outlet. Switch it on and try testing its cooking functions with some test food. Here is how you can use it in different cooking modes:

## Convection Broil or Broil:

To broil in rack Position 2, place the air fryer basket on top of the baking pan. Select either Broil or Convection Broil on the Function Dial. Select toast/broil on the temperature dial. The

oven will then turn on and start to broil when the ON/Oven Timer dial is set to the proper cooking time. The power light will start to shine. When the cycle is over, the timer will beep once, and the oven will turn off when the timer beeps.

Turn the ON/Oven Timer dial to the OFF position to stop the broiling. Use the Air fryer Basket fitted within the Baking Pan to broil for the finest results. Never broil anything in a glass baking dish. Food should be watched carefully while broiling since it can quickly turn black. Fit the provided baking pan or oven rack into the appropriate rack position. Select Broil using the function dial. The temperature should be set using the Temperature Dial.

Then, to turn on the oven and start broiling, turn the ON/Oven Timer dial to the chosen cooking time (it is advised to pre-heat the oven for 5 minutes before baking). Add this to the overall baking time). The power light will start to shine. When the cycle is over, the timer will sound once, and the oven will turn off when the timer beeps. Turn the ON/Oven Timer dial to the OFF position to halt baking.

## Convection Bake or Bake:

For delicate baked products like custards, cakes, and eggs, choose Bake. Position 1 is best for baking most baked products and larger things, while Position 2 is best for baking most egg dishes and custards. Placing the Baking Pan in Position 1 of the oven for cooking fresh pizza. Pizza should be placed immediately on the rack in Position 1 if it is frozen. The pan can be in Position 1 for large foods like chicken or other meats.

Select Convection Bake as the function. The temperature should be set using the Temperature Dial. Then, to start the oven and start baking, turn the ON/Oven Timer dial to the desired cooking time (it is advised to pre-heat the oven for 5 minutes before baking). Add this to the overall baking time). The power indicator will turn on. When the cycle is over, the timer will sound once, and the oven will turn off when the timer beeps.

For baking, set the pan in Position 2. The pan can be in Position 1 for large foods like chicken or other meats. Turn the ON/Oven Timer dial to the OFF position to stop the Convection Bake function.

When using the convection mode, most baking recipes advise lowering the temperature by 25 degrees F (5 °C). Always check the status of the food 10 minutes before the recommended cooking time. For roasts and poultry, as well as the majority of baked dishes that demand even browning, such as scones and pies, choose Convection Bake.

## Warm Mode:

Insert the baking pan or oven rack provided in position 2 of the rack. Select Warm mode using the function dial. Then, to start the oven and start warming, turn the ON/Oven Timer Dial to the appropriate time. The power light will start to light. When the cycle is over, the timer will sound once, and the oven will turn off when the timer beeps. Turn the ON/Oven Timer dial to the OFF position to halt warming.

## Toasting:

Toast in Position 2 of the oven rack. Place two objects that need to be toasted in the centre of the oven rack. Two toasts should be placed in front and two in the back, evenly spaced apart. Six objects should be distributed evenly, three in front and three behind. Select Toast using the Function Dial. Select Toast/Broil on the temperature dial. To switch on the oven and start toasting, turn the ON/Toast Timer Dial to the desired shade setting, from light to dark, within the marked settings. The power light on the oven will come on. The alarm will sound and then expire. Turn the ON/Toast Timer dial to the OFF position to end toasting.

## Air Fry:

The Air fryer Basket should be placed on the baking pan. In rack Position 2, insert the Air fryer basket. Select Air fry using the function dial. Set the temperature dial to the desired setting. Then, to switch on the oven and start Air frying, set the ON/Oven Timer dial to the desired cooking time. The power light on the oven will turn on. When the cycle is over, the timer will beep once, and the oven will turn off when the timer beeps.

Turn the ON/Oven Timer dial to the OFF position to discontinue Air frying. A healthier option for frying is Air frying. You can Air fry a lot of meals that can be fried without using a lot of oil. Compared to deep-fried dishes, air-fried items will taste fresher and less oily. Most types of oils work well for Air frying. For a flavour that is fuller, olive oil is preferred.

For a light flavour, vegetable, canola, or grapeseed oil is advised. Oil should be evenly and liberally sprayed onto food to get the crispiest, golden results. Foods that are air-fried can be coated in a variety of ways. Breadcrumbs, seasoned breadcrumbs, panko breadcrumbs, cornflakes, potato chip crumbs, graham cracker crumbs, quinoa, various flours, etc., are a few examples of varied crumb mixes.

While larger products, like chicken cutlets, should be turned halfway through cooking to achieve quick, even cooking and browning, most foods don't need to be turned over during cooking. Toss the food midway through cooking when you are Air frying a lot of food that fills the pan to guarantee even cooking and coloring. For things that cook more rapidly, like bacon and chips, use higher temperatures; for meals that take longer to cook, such as breaded chicken, use lower temperatures.

If foods are sliced into the same size pieces, they will cook more uniformly. For simple cleanup, line the baking tray with aluminium foil. Please be aware that most foods release water while they cook. Condensation may form while cooking large quantities of food for an extended length of time, which could leave moisture on your surface.

## Cleaning and Maintenance

The Cuisinart air fryer oven has nonstick interior sides and a convenient pull-out crumb tray that serves its purpose. The outside requires only a fast wipe-down and drying after being cleaned with a microfiber cloth dampened with a light soap solution. While the baking/drip pan and air fryer basket could be easily cleaned in the dishwasher, the oven rack and crumb tray had to be hand-washed.

Prior to cleaning, always let the oven cool completely. Never leave the oven plugged into an outlet. The use of abrasive cleansers will harm the finish, so avoid using them. Simply use a clean, moist towel to wipe the exterior and completely dry it. Before cleaning, apply the cleaning solution on a cloth rather than the toaster oven itself. Use a moist cloth and a mild liquid soap solution or a spray to clean interior walls. Never use corrosive or aggressive abrasives. These might damage the oven's surface. Never clean the inside of an oven with steel wool pads, etc. Use a nylon scouring pad, nylon brush, or hot, sudsy water to hand-wash the oven rack, baking pan, air fryer basket, and crumb tray. Do not wash them in a dishwasher. Always clean the top interior of your oven after cooking fatty items. Your oven will function perfectly if you do this on a regular basis.

Slide out the Crumb Tray and toss the crumbs into the trash to remove them. Put the tray in hot, sudsy water or use nonabrasive cleansers to remove baked-on grease. Never use the oven if the Crumb Tray isn't there. Use the cleats for storing cords on the oven's back.

## FAQs about the Air Fryer Oven

### 1. How Does the Digital Toaster Oven Air Fryer from Cuisinart Operate?

To "fry" healthier versions of French fries and other food favorites, the Cuisinart Digital Toaster Oven Air fryer employs a fan and heater to guide high-heat airflow at an extreme velocity around food. According to Cuisinart, this is accomplished with little noise. This appliance can bake, broil, roast, toast, make bagels, reheat, warm, and cook two things at once. You may braise or slow-cook food in it at low temperatures, use the dehydrator or proofing features, or bake pizza in it like a convection oven.

### 2. What Does the Cuisinart Digital Air Fryer Oven Come with?

The oven rack, baking pan, mesh air fryer basket, and removable crumb tray is included with the Cuisinart Digital Toaster Oven Air fryer. The only dishwasher-safe items are the baking pan and the air fryer basket. Each product box also contains a user guide and a collection of recipes. Additionally, the device has a built-in quick-reference guide with operating instructions. The control panel has a big LCD screen and a glass so you can see how your cooking is coming along.

### 3. What Is the Capacity of the Cuisinart Air Fryer Oven?

This air fryer oven is large enough to Bake a 12-inch pizza, toast 6 bread pieces, roast a 4-pound chicken, or cook 3-pounds of chicken wings.

### 4. What Are the Different Temperature and Time Settings for Commonly Cooked Food Items?

The following table shows the temperature, cooking function and time that needs to be adjusted for the given categories of food:

| Food | Function | Amount (MAX) | Time | Temperature |
|---|---|---|---|---|
| Bacon | Air fry | 8 slices | 8-10 minutes | 400°F (204°C) |
| Chicken wings | Air fry | 2 lbs. (20 wings) | 20-25 minutes | 400°F (204°C) |
| Frozen shrimp, mozzarella etc | Air fry | 1½ lbs. (28 mozzarella sticks) | 5-7 minutes | 400°F (204°C) |
| Frozen chicken nuggets | Air fry | 1 lb. (34 nuggets) | 10 minutes | 400°F (204°C) |
| Frozen fish sticks | Air fry | 12 oz. (20 sticks) | 8 minutes | 400°F (204°C) |
| Frozen fries | Air fry | 1-2 lbs. | 15-25 minutes | 450°F (232°C) |
| Frozen steak fries | Air fry | 1-2 lbs. | 15-25 minutes | 450°F (232°C) |
| Hand cut fries | Air fry | 2 lbs. | 15-20 minutes | 400°F (204°C) |
| Hand-cut steak fries | Air fry | 2 lbs. | 15-20 minutes | 400°F (204°C) |
| Shrimp | Air fry | 1 lb. (16 large shrimp) | 8-10 minutes | 375°F (190°C) |
| Tortilla chips | Air fry | 6,5-inch tortillas cut into quarters | 5-6 minutes | 400°F (204°C) |

## Get Ready for the Recipes

Are you ready to set your Cuisinart air fryer oven up and start cooking some delicious meals for the table? This cookbook is your one-stop shop to find all the best-suited recipes to cook in your Cuisinart oven. Whether you want to broil cheese sandwiches, toast the morning bread, bake some pizza or air fry crispy chicken wings, you can do it all using your 7-in-one Cuisinart air fryer oven. In this cookbook, you will find recipes for your daily routine and for all the special festivities. So, go ahead! Give them a try, and let us know which ones you liked the most through your valuable feedback.

## Fried Toast Sticks with Maple Dip

Prep time: 10 minutes | Cook time: 6 minutes | Serves 4

| | |
|---|---|
| Cooking spray | ½ cup milk |
| 2 eggs | ¾ cup crushed cornflakes |
| 6 slices sandwich bread, | ½ tsp. pure vanilla extract |
| each slice cut into 4 | ⅛ tsp. salt |
| strips | Maple syrup, for dipping |

1. Preheat the air fryer oven to 390ºF (200ºC).
2. Beat together the eggs, milk, salt, and vanilla in a small bowl.
3. Place crushed cornflakes on a plate or in a shallow dish.
4. Dip bread strips in egg mixture, shake off excess, and roll in cornflake crumbs.
5. Spray both sides of bread strips lightly with cooking spray.
6. Arrange bread strips in the air fryer basket in a single layer.
7. Place the air fryer basket onto the baking pan, and slide the baking pan into Rack Position 2, select Air Fry and set time to 6 minutes.
8. Repeat steps 6 and 7 to air fry the remaining French toast sticks.
9. Serve warm with maple syrup.

## Classic Vanilla Soufflé

Prep time: 10 minutes | Cook time: 22 minutes | Serves 4

| | |
|---|---|
| Cooking spray | ¼ cup flour |
| 4 egg yolks | 1 ounce (28 g) sugar |
| 6 egg whites | 1 tsp. vanilla extract |
| 1 cup milk | 1 tsp. cream of tartar |
| ⅓ cup butter, melted | |

1. In a bowl, mix the butter and flour until the mixture is smooth.
2. Add the milk into a saucepan over medium-low heat. Place the sugar and let dissolve before raising the heat to boil the milk.
3. Put the flour and butter mixture and stir rigorously for about 7 minutes to eliminate any lumps. Make sure the mixture thickens. Turn off the heat and let cool for 15 minutes.
4. Preheat the air fryer oven to 320ºF (160ºC). Spritz 6 soufflé dishes lightly with cooking spray.
5. Add the egg yolks and vanilla extract in a separate bowl and beat them together by using a fork. Pour in the milk and mix well to incorporate everything.
6. In a smaller bowl, combine the egg whites and cream of tartar with a fork. Gently fold into the egg yolks-milk mixture before putting in the flour mixture. Take equal amounts to the 6 soufflé dishes.
7. Put the soufflé dishes in the baking pan. Slide the baking pan into Rack Position 1, select Convection Bake and set time to 15 minutes.
8. Serve hot.

## Crispy Avocado Quesadillas

Prep time: 10 minutes | Cook time: 11 minutes | Serves 4

| | |
|---|---|
| Cooking spray | and thinly sliced |
| 4 flour tortillas | 2 tbsps. skim milk |
| 4 eggs | Salt and ground black |
| 2 ounces (57 g) Cheddar | pepper, to taste |
| cheese, grated | 4 tbsps. salsa |
| ½ small avocado, peeled | |

1. Preheat the air fryer oven to 270ºF (132ºC).
2. Beat together the eggs, milk, salt and pepper.
3. Spritz a baking pan with cooking spray and pour in the egg mixture.
4. Slide the baking pan into Rack Position 1, select Convection Bake and set time to 8 minutes, stirring every 1 to 2 minutes, until eggs are scrambled to the liking. Remove from the heat and set aside.
5. Spritz one side of each tortilla lightly with cooking spray. Flip over.
6. Divide eggs, cheese, salsa, and avocado evenly among the tortillas, covering only half of each tortilla.
7. Fold each tortilla in half and press down lightly. Turn the temperature of the air fryer oven to 390ºF (199ºC).
8. Arrange 2 tortillas in the air fryer basket. Then place the air fryer basket onto the baking pan, and slide the baking pan into Rack Position 2, select Air Fry and set time to 3 minutes, until cheese melts and outside feels slightly crispy. Repeat this process with the remaining two tortillas.
9. Cut each cooked tortilla into halves. Serve hot.

## Buttermilk Biscuits

Prep time: 5 minutes | Cook time: 5 minutes | Makes 12 biscuits

2 cups all-purpose flour, plus more for dusting the work surface
¾ cup buttermilk
6 tbsps. cold unsalted butter, cut into 1-tbsp. slices
2 tsps. sugar
1 tbsp. baking powder
¼ tsp. baking soda
1 tsp. salt

1. Preheat the air fryer oven to 360ºF (182ºC). Grease the baking pan lightly with olive oil.
2. Combine the flour, baking powder, baking soda, sugar, and salt in a large mixing bowl, and mix well.
3. Cut in the butter with a fork, until the mixture resembles coarse meal.
4. Pour in the buttermilk and mix until smooth.
5. Dust more flour on a clean work surface. Turn the dough out onto the work surface and roll it out until it is approximately ½ inch thick.
6. With a 2-inch biscuit cutter, cut out the biscuits. Arrange the uncooked biscuits in the greased baking pan in a single layer.
7. Slide the baking pan into Rack Position 1, select Convection Bake and set time to 5 minutes. Remove the cooked biscuits from the air fryer oven to a platter.
8. Repeat steps 6 and 7 to cook the remaining biscuits.
9. Serve hot.

## Avocado, Pepper and Egg Burrito

Prep time: 10 minutes | Cook time: 4 minutes | Serves 4

4 low-sodium whole-wheat flour tortillas
**Filling:**
1 hard-boiled egg, chopped
2 hard-boiled egg whites, chopped
1 ripe avocado, peeled, pitted, and chopped
1 red bell pepper, chopped
1 (1.2-ounce / 34-g) slice low-sodium, low-fat American cheese, torn into pieces
3 tbsps. low-sodium salsa, plus additional for serving (optional)
**Special Equipment:**
4 toothpicks (optional), soaked in water for at least 30 minutes

1. Preheat the air fryer oven to 390ºF (199ºC).
2. Make the filling: In a medium bowl, combine the egg, egg whites, avocado, red bell pepper, cheese, and salsa and stir until blended well.
3. Assemble the burritos: Place the tortillas on a clean work surface and spread ¼ of the prepared filling in the middle of each tortilla, leaving about 1½-inch on each end unfilled. Gently fold in the opposite sides of each tortilla and roll up. Secure with toothpicks through the center, as needed.
4. Take the burritos to the air fryer basket. Then place the air fryer basket onto the baking pan, and slide the baking pan into Rack Position 2, select Air Fry and set time to 4 minutes, or until the burritos are crisp and golden brown.
5. Let cool for about 5 minutes and serve with salsa, if desired.

## Banana Churros with Oatmeal

Prep time: 15 minutes | Cook time: 15 minutes | Serves 2

**For the Churros:**
Cooking spray
2 tsps. oil (sunflower or melted coconut)
1 large yellow banana, peeled, cut in half lengthwise, then cut in half widthwise
2 tbsps. whole-wheat
pastry flour
1 tsp. water
1 tbsp. coconut sugar
½ tsp. cinnamon
⅛ tsp. sea salt
**For the Oatmeal:**
¾ cup rolled oats
1½ cups water

To make the churros:
1. Place the 4 banana pieces in a medium-size bowl and put the flour and salt. Stir carefully. Pour in the oil and water. Stir gently until evenly combined. You may need to press some coating onto the banana pieces.
2. Spray the air fryer basket lightly with the cooking spray. Arrange the banana pieces in the air fryer basket. Place the air fryer basket onto the baking pan, and slide the baking pan into Rack Position 2, select Air Fry and set time to 5 minutes. Remove, gently turn over, and air fry for 5 minutes more or until browned.
3. Add the coconut sugar and cinnamon in a medium bowl and stir to combine well. Once the banana pieces are nicely browned, spray with the oil and put in the cinnamon-sugar bowl. Toss gently by using a spatula to coat the banana pieces evenly with the mixture.
To make the oatmeal:
4. When the bananas are cooking, make the oatmeal. Bring the oats and water to a boil in a medium pot, then lower the heat. Simmer, stirring frequently, until all the water is absorbed, about 5 minutes. Divide the oatmeal into two bowls.
5. Place the coated banana pieces on the oatmeal and serve immediately.

## Walnut and Apple Muffins

Prep time: 15 minutes | Cook time: 10 minutes | Makes 8 muffins

1 egg
1 cup flour
¾ cup unsweetened applesauce
⅓ cup sugar
¼ cup chopped walnuts
¼ cup diced apple
2 tbsps. pancake syrup, plus 2 teaspoons

2 tbsps. melted butter, plus 2 teaspoons
1 tsp. baking powder
1 tsp. cinnamon
¼ tsp. ginger
¼ tsp. nutmeg
½ tsp. vanilla extract
¼ tsp. baking soda
¼ tsp. salt

1. Preheat the air fryer oven to 330ºF (166ºC).
2. Stir together the flour, sugar, baking powder, baking soda, salt, cinnamon, ginger, and nutmeg in a large bowl.
3. Beat egg until frothy. Add syrup, butter, applesauce, and vanilla in a small bowl, and mix well.
4. Place egg mixture into dry ingredients and stir just until moistened.
5. Gently stir in the nuts and diced apple.
6. Divide batter evenly among 8 parchment paper-lined muffin cups.
7. Arrange 4 muffin cups in baking pan. Slide the baking pan into Rack Position 1, select Convection Bake and set time to 10 minutes.
8. Repeat with the remaining 4 muffins or until toothpick inserted in center comes out clean.
9. Serve hot.

## Muffins with Nuts and Seeds

Prep time: 15 minutes | Cook time: 10 minutes | Makes 8 muffins

Cooking spray
1 egg
½ cup whole-wheat flour, plus 2 tbsps.
½ cup buttermilk
¼ cup brown sugar
½ cup grated carrots
¼ cup chopped pecans
¼ cup chopped walnuts
¼ cup oat bran
2 tbsps. flaxseed meal

2 tbsps. melted butter
1 tbsp. pumpkin seeds
1 tbsp. sunflower seeds
½ tsp. pure vanilla extract
½ tsp. baking soda
½ tsp. baking powder
¼ tsp. salt
½ tsp. cinnamon
**Special Equipment:**
16 foil muffin cups, paper liners removed

1. Preheat the air fryer oven to 330ºF (166ºC).
2. Stir together the flour, bran, flaxseed meal, sugar, baking soda, baking powder, salt, and cinnamon in a large bowl.
3. Beat together the buttermilk, butter, egg, and vanilla in a medium bowl. Pour into flour mixture and stir just until the dry ingredients moisten. Do not beat.
4. Gently stir in nuts, carrots, and seeds.
5. Double up the foil cups so you have 8 total and spray with cooking spray.
6. Arrange 4 foil cups in the baking pan and divide half the batter evenly among them.
7. Slide the baking pan into Rack Position 1, select Convection Bake and set time to 10 minutes, until a toothpick inserted in center comes out clean.
8. Repeat step 7 to bake the remaining 4 muffins.
9. Serve hot.

## Cheesy Ham and Grit Fritters

Prep time: 15 minutes | Cook time: 20 minutes | Serves 6 to 8

Cooking spray
4 cups water
1 cup quick-cooking grits
2 cups grated Cheddar cheese, divided
1 cup finely diced ham
1 egg, beaten

2 cups panko bread crumbs
2 tbsps. butter
1 tbsp. chopped chives
¼ tsp. salt
Salt and freshly ground black pepper, to taste

1. In a saucepan, bring the water to a boil. Whisk in the grits and ¼ tsp. salt, and cook for about 7 minutes until the grits are tender. Turn off the heat and stir in the butter and 1 cup of the grated Cheddar cheese. Take the grits to a bowl and allow them to cool for 10 to 15 minutes.
2. Stir the ham, chives and the rest of the cheese into the grits and sprinkle with salt and pepper to taste. Place the beaten egg and refrigerate the mixture for about 30 minutes.
3. Place the panko bread crumbs in a shallow dish. Measure out ¼-cup portions of the grits mixture and form them into patties. Coat the patties evenly with the panko bread crumbs, patting them with the hands so the crumbs adhere to the patties. You will have about 16 patties. Spray both sides of the patties lightly with cooking spray.
4. Preheat the air fryer oven to 400ºF (204ºC).
5. In batches of 5 or 6, put the fritters in the air fryer basket. Then place the air fryer basket onto the baking pan, and slide the baking pan into Rack Position 2, select Air Fry and set time to 8 minutes. With a flat spatula, flip the fritters over and air fry for 4 minutes more.
6. Serve warm.

## Mushroom and Spinach Frittata

Prep time: 10 minutes | Cook time: 20 minutes | Serves 2

Cooking spray
4 large eggs
4 ounces (113 g) baby bella mushrooms, chopped
1 cup (1 ounce / 28-g) baby spinach, chopped
½ cup (2 ounces / 57-g) shredded Cheddar cheese
⅓ cup (from 1 large)

chopped leek, white part only
¼ cup halved grape tomatoes
1 tbsp. 2% milk
¼ tsp. dried oregano
¼ tsp. garlic powder
½ tsp. kosher salt
Freshly ground black pepper, to taste

1. Preheat the air fryer oven to 300ºF (149ºC). Spray a baking pan with cooking spray.
2. In a large bowl, whisk the eggs until frothy. Place the mushrooms, baby spinach, cheese, leek, tomatoes, milk, garlic powder, oregano, salt, and pepper and stir until well blended. Add the mixture into the prepared baking pan.
3. Slide the baking pan into Rack Position 1, select Convection Bake and set time to 20 minutes, until the center is puffed up and the top is golden brown.
4. Allow the frittata to rest for 5 minutes before slicing to serve.

## Yellow Cornmeal and Ham Muffins

Prep time: 10 minutes | Cook time: 6 minutes | Makes 8 muffins

2 tbsps. canola oil
1 egg, beaten
¾ cup yellow cornmeal
½ cup milk
½ cup shredded sharp

Cheddar cheese
½ cup diced ham
¼ cup flour
1½ tsps. baking powder
¼ tsp. salt

1. Preheat the air fryer oven to 390ºF (199ºC).
2. Stir together the cornmeal, flour, baking powder, and salt in a medium bowl.
3. Add the oil, egg, and milk to the dry ingredients and mix well.
4. Stir in the shredded cheese and diced ham.
5. Divide batter evenly among 8 parchment paper-lined muffin cups.
6. Arrange 4 filled muffin cups in the baking pan. Slide the baking pan into Rack Position 1, select Convection Bake and set time to 5 minutes.
7. Turn the temperature to 330ºF (166ºC) and bake for about 1 minute or until a toothpick inserted in center

of the muffin comes out clean.
8. Repeat steps 6 and 7 to select Bake with Convection, and cook the remaining muffins.
9. Serve hot.

## Cinnamon Cinnamon Rolls

Prep time: 10 minutes | Cook time: 9 minutes | Serves 8

1 pound (454 g) frozen bread dough, thawed
¾ cup brown sugar
¼ cup butter, melted
1½ tbsps. ground cinnamon

**Cream Cheese Glaze:**
1¼ cups powdered sugar
4 ounces (113 g) cream cheese, softened
2 tbsps. butter, softened
½ tsp. vanilla extract

1. Let the bread dough come to room temperature on the counter. Roll the dough into a 13-inch by 11-inch rectangle on a lightly floured surface. Position the rectangle so the 13-inch side is facing you. Brush the melted butter the dough all the sides, leaving a 1-inch border uncovered along the edge farthest away from you.
2. In a small bowl, combine the brown sugar and cinnamon. Scatter the mixture evenly over the buttered dough, keeping the 1-inch border uncovered. Roll the dough into a log, starting with the edge closest to you. Roll the dough tightly, rolling evenly, and push out any air pockets. When you get to the uncovered edge of the dough, press the dough onto the roll to seal it together.
3. Slice the log into 8 pieces, cutting slowly with a sawing motion so you don't flatten the dough. Turn the slices on their sides and use a clean kitchen towel to cover. Allow the rolls to sit in the warmest part of the kitchen for 1½ to 2 hours to rise.
4. To make the glaze, put the cream cheese and butter in a microwave-safe bowl. Soften the mixture in the microwave for about 30 seconds at a time until it is easy to stir. Gradually put the powdered sugar and stir to combine well. Place the vanilla extract and whisk until smooth. Set it aside.
5. When the rolls have risen, preheat the air fryer oven to 350ºF (177ºC).
6. Take 4 of the rolls to the baking pan. Slide the baking pan into Rack Position 1, select Convection Bake and set time to 5 minutes. Turn the rolls over and bake for 4 minutes more. Repeat with the remaining 4 rolls.
7. Allow the rolls to cool for 2 minutes before glazing. Brush large dollops of cream cheese glaze on top of the warm cinnamon rolls, allowing some glaze to drip down the side of the rolls. Serve hot.

## Yellow Squash and Mushroom Toast

Prep time: 10 minutes | Cook time: 10 minutes | Serves 4

| | |
|---|---|
| 1 tbsp. olive oil | 1 red bell pepper, cut into |
| 4 slices bread | strips |
| 1 small yellow squash, | ½ cup soft goat cheese |
| sliced | 2 green onions, sliced |
| 1 cup sliced button or | 2 tbsps. softened butter |
| cremini mushrooms | |

1. Spritz the air fryer basket with the olive oil and preheat the air fryer oven to 350ºF (177ºC).
2. Place the mushrooms, red pepper, green onions, and squash inside the air fryer basket, give them a good stir. Put the air fryer basket onto the baking pan, and slide the baking pan into Rack Position 2, select Air Fry and set time to 7 minutes, stirring once during the cooking time.
3. Take the vegetables and set them aside.
4. Evenly spread the butter on the slices of bread and take them to the air fryer oven, butter-side up. Brown for about 3 minutes.
5. Remove the toast from the air fryer oven and place the goat cheese and vegetables on top. Serve hot.

## Corn Frittata with Avocado Dressing

Prep time: 10 minutes | Cook time: 20 minutes | Serves 2 or 3

| | |
|---|---|
| 6 large eggs, lightly | Kosher salt and freshly |
| beaten | ground black pepper, to |
| ½ cup cherry tomatoes, | taste |
| halved | **Avocado Dressing:** |
| ½ cup corn kernels, | 1 ripe avocado, pitted |
| thawed if frozen | and peeled |
| ½ cup shredded | 2 tbsps. fresh lime juice |
| Monterey Jack cheese | ¼ cup olive oil |
| ¼ cup milk | 1 scallion, finely chopped |
| 1 tbsp. finely chopped | 8 fresh basil leaves, |
| fresh dill | finely chopped |

1. Place the tomato halves in a colander and lightly sprinkle with salt. Set aside for about 10 minutes to drain well. Pour the tomatoes into a large bowl and fold in the eggs, milk, corn and dill. Season with salt and pepper and stir until mixed well.
2. Preheat the air fryer oven to 300ºF (149ºC).
3. Put the egg mixture into a baking pan. Slide the baking pan into Rack Position 1, select Convection Bake and set time to 15 minutes.
4. Sprinkle the cheese on top. Turn the air fryer oven

temperature to 315ºF (157ºC) and continue to cook for 5 minutes more, or until the frittata is puffy and set.
5. Meanwhile, make the avocado dressing: In a medium bowl, mash the avocado with the lime juice until smooth. Mix in the olive oil, basil and scallion and stir until well incorporated.
6. Allow the frittata to cool for about 5 minutes and serve alongside the avocado dressing.

## Cheesy Broccoli and Bacon Bread Pudding

Prep time: 15 minutes | Cook time: 48 minutes | Serves 2 to 4

| | |
|---|---|
| ½ pound (227 g) thick cut | 1½ cups grated Swiss |
| bacon, cut into ¼-inch | cheese |
| pieces | 3 eggs |
| 3 cups brioche bread, cut | 1 cup milk |
| into ½-inch cubes | 2 tbsps. butter, melted |
| 1 cup frozen broccoli | ½ tsp. salt |
| florets, thawed and | Freshly ground black |
| chopped | pepper, to taste |

1. Preheat the air fryer oven to 400ºF (204ºC).
2. Put the bacon in the air fryer basket. Place the air fryer basket onto the baking pan, and slide the baking pan into Rack Position 2, select Air Fry and set time to 8 minutes, stirring a few times to make it air fry evenly. Transfer the bacon and set it aside on a paper towel.
3. Air fry the bread cubes for about 2 minutes to dry and toast lightly.
4. Butter a cake pan. In a large bowl, combine all the remaining ingredients and toss well. Take the mixture to the buttered cake pan, cover with aluminum foil and refrigerate the bread pudding overnight, or for at least 8 hours.
5. Take the cake pan from the refrigerator an hour before you are ready to bake and allow it to sit on the countertop to come to room temperature.
6. Preheat the air fryer oven to 330ºF (166ºC). Gently fold the ends of the aluminum foil over the top of the cake pan. Then take the covered cake pan to the air fryer oven.
7. Air fry for about 20 minutes. Take the foil and air fry for another 20 minutes. If the top browns a little too much before the custard has set, simply return the foil to the pan. When a skewer inserted into the center comes out clean, the bread pudding has cooked through.
8. Serve right away.

## Simple Egg and Bacon Bread Cups

Prep time: 10 minutes | Cook time: 8 minutes | Serves 4

4 (3-by-4-inch) crusty rolls
5 eggs
4 thin slices Gouda or Swiss cheese mini wedges
3 strips precooked

bacon, chopped
2 tbsps. heavy cream
½ tsp. dried thyme
Pinch of salt
Freshly ground black pepper, to taste

1. Preheat the air fryer oven to 330ºF (166ºC).
2. Cut the tops off the rolls on a clean work surface. With your fingers, remove the insides of the rolls to make bread cups, leaving a ½-inch shell. Put a slice of cheese onto each roll bottom.
3. In a medium bowl, whisk together the eggs and heavy cream until well combined. Gently fold in the bacon, thyme, salt and pepper and stir well.
4. Scrape the egg mixture into the prepared bread cups.
5. Take the bread cups to the baking pan. Slide the baking pan into Rack Position 1, select Convection Bake and set time to 8 minutes, until the eggs are cooked to your preference.
6. Serve hot.

## Soft Pretzels

Prep time: 10 minutes | Cook time: 6 minutes | Makes 24 pretzels

2½ cups all-purpose flour
2 tsps. yeast
1 cup water, warm
1 tsp. sugar
1 tsp. salt

2 tbsps. butter, melted, plus more as needed
1 cup boiling water
1 tbsp. baking soda
Coarse sea salt, to taste

1. In a small bowl, combine the yeast and warm water. Mix the sugar, salt and flour in the bowl of a stand mixer. With the mixer running and using the dough hook, drizzle in the yeast mixture and melted butter. Knead dough for about 10 minutes until smooth and elastic. Shape the dough into a ball and allow to rise for 1 hour.
2. Punch the dough down to release any air and divide the dough evenly into 24 portions.
3. Roll each portion into a skinny rope with both hands on the counter and rolling from the center to the ends of the rope. Spin the rope into a pretzel shape (or tie the rope into a knot) and arrange the tied pretzels on a parchment lined baking sheet.
4. Preheat the air fryer oven to 350ºF (177ºC).

5. In a shallow bowl, combine the boiling water and baking soda and whisk to dissolve. Allow the water to cool so you can put the hands in it. Working in batches, dip the pretzels (top side down) into the baking soda mixture and allow them to soak for 30 seconds to a minute. Then remove the pretzels gently and return them (top side up) to the baking sheet. Scatter the coarse salt on the top.
6. Work in batch. Slide the baking sheet into Rack Position 1, select Convection Bake and set time to 3 minutes. Turn over and cooking for another 3 minutes. Once the pretzels are finished, brush them generously with the melted butter and serve them warm.

## Curried Potato Bread Rolls

Prep time: 15 minutes | Cook time: 20 minutes | Serves 5

1 tbsp. olive oil
5 large potatoes, boiled and mashed
8 slices bread, brown sides discarded
2 small onions, chopped
2 green chilies, deseeded and chopped

2 sprigs curry leaves
1 bunch coriander, chopped
½ tsp. turmeric powder
½ tsp. mustard seeds
Salt and ground black pepper, to taste

1. Preheat the air fryer oven to 400ºF (204ºC).
2. In a bowl, place the mashed potatoes and season with salt and pepper. Set it aside.
3. In a skillet, fry the mustard seeds in olive oil over a medium-low heat, stirring frequently, until they sputter.
4. Place the onions and cook until they turn soft. Put the curry leaves and turmeric powder and stir well. Cook for another 2 minutes until fragrant.
5. Remove the pan from the heat and combine well with the potatoes. Mix in the green chilies and coriander.
6. Wet the bread slightly and drain of any excess liquid.
7. Scoop a small amount of the potato mixture into the center of the bread and enclose the bread around the filling, sealing it entirely. Continue until the rest of the bread and filling is used up. Coat each bread roll with some oil and take to the baking pan.
8. Slide the baking pan into Rack Position 1, select Convection Bake and set time to 15 minutes, carefully flipping the rolls at the halfway point to ensure each roll is cooked evenly.
9. Serve right away.

Baked Ricotta Spinach Omelet, page 21

Delicious Coffee Donuts, page 21

Fluffy Banana Bread, page 16

Cheesy Ham and Bell Pepper Omelet, page 20

## Fluffy Banana Bread

Prep time: 10 minutes | Cook time: 22 minutes |
Makes 3 loaves

3 ripe bananas, mashed
1½ cups all-purpose flour
1 cup sugar
1 large egg

4 tbsps. (½ stick)
unsalted butter, melted
1 tsp. baking soda
1 tsp. salt

1. Spray the insides of 3 mini loaf pans with cooking spray.
2. Mix the bananas and sugar in a large mixing bowl.
3. In a separate large mixing bowl, combine the egg, flour, butter, baking soda, and salt and mix well.
4. Place the banana mixture to the egg and flour mixture. Combine well.
5. Distribute the batter evenly among the prepared pans.
6. Preheat the air fryer oven to 310ºF (154ºC). Place the mini loaf pans in the baking pan.
7. Slide the baking pan into Rack Position 1, select Convection Bake and set time to 22 minutes. The loaf has cooked through, when a toothpick inserted into the center comes out clean.
8. When the loaves are cooked through, take the pans from the oven. Turn out the loaves onto a wire rack to let cool.
9. Enjoy!

## Orange Rolls

Prep time: 15 minutes | Cook time: 8 minutes |
Makes 8 rolls

Butter-flavored cooking spray
3 ounces (85 g) low-fat cream cheese
1 can (8 count) organic crescent roll dough
¼ cup chopped walnuts
¼ cup dried cranberries
¼ cup shredded, sweetened coconut

1 tbsp. low-fat sour cream or plain yogurt
2 tsps. sugar
¼ tsp. pure vanilla extract
¼ tsp. orange extract
**Orange Glaze:**
½ cup powdered sugar
1 tbsp. orange juice
¼ tsp. orange extract
Dash of salt

1. Cut a circular piece of parchment paper slightly smaller than the bottom of the baking pan. Set it aside.
2. Combine the cream cheese, sugar, sour cream or yogurt, and vanilla and orange extracts in a small bowl. Stir until smooth.
3. Preheat the air fryer oven to 300ºF (149ºC).
4. Separate crescent roll dough into 8 triangles and divide cream cheese mixture evenly among them. Starting at wide end, spread cheese mixture to within 1 inch of point.
5. Scatter nuts and cranberries evenly over cheese mixture.
6. Starting at wide end, roll up triangles, then scatter with coconut, pressing in lightly to make it stick. Spritz tops of rolls with butter-flavored cooking spray.
7. Put parchment paper in baking pan, and arrange 4 rolls on top, spaced evenly.
8. Slide the baking pan into Rack Position 1, select Convection Bake and set time to 8 minutes, until rolls are golden brown and cooked through.
9. Repeat steps 7 and 8 to bake the remaining 4 rolls. You can use the same piece of parchment paper twice.
10. Stir together ingredients for glaze in a small bowl and drizzle over warm rolls. Serve right away.

## White Chocolate Banana and Walnut Bread

Prep time: 10 minutes | Cook time: 30 minutes |
Serves 4

¼ cup cocoa powder
1½ ripe bananas
1 large egg, whisked
¼ cup vegetable oil
½ cup sugar
6 tbsps. plus 2 tsps. all-purpose flour, divided
6 tbsps. chopped white

chocolate
6 tbsps. chopped walnuts
3 tbsps. buttermilk or plain yogurt (not Greek)
½ tsp. vanilla extract
¼ tsp. baking soda
½ tsp. kosher salt

1. Preheat the air fryer oven to 310ºF (154ºC).
2. In a medium bowl, mix together the cocoa powder, 6 tbsps. of the flour, salt, and baking soda.
3. In another medium bowl, mash the bananas with a fork until smooth. Gently fold in the egg, oil, buttermilk, sugar, and vanilla, and whisk until thoroughly combined. Put the wet mixture to the dry mixture and stir until well incorporated.
4. In a third bowl, combine the white chocolate, walnuts, and the remaining 2 tbsps. of flour and toss to coat well. Add this mixture to the batter and stir until well incorporated. Place the batter into a baking pan and smooth the top by using a spatula.
5. Slide the baking pan into Rack Position 1, select Convection Bake and set time to 30 minutes. Check the bread for doneness: The bread is done, if a toothpick inserted into the center of the bread comes out clean.
6. Transfer the bread from the air fryer oven and allow to cool on a wire rack for 10 minutes before serving.

## Baked Egg Pumpkin

Prep time: 10 minutes | Cook time: 10 minutes | Serves 2

1 tbsp. olive oil
2 eggs
½ cup milk
2 cups flour
1 cup pumpkin purée

2 tbsps. cider vinegar
2 tsps. baking powder
1 tbsp. sugar
1 tsp. cinnamon powder
1 tsp. baking soda

1. Preheat the air fryer oven to 300ºF (149ºC).
2. Crack the eggs into a bowl and beat with a whisk. Mix with the milk, flour, cider vinegar, sugar, pumpkin purée, baking powder, cinnamon powder, and baking soda, combining well.
3. Grease a baking pan lightly with olive oil. Put the mixture in the baking pan. Slide the baking pan into Rack Position 1, select Convection Bake and set time to 10 minutes.
4. Serve hot.

## Chicken and Apple Breakfast Sausages

Prep time: 15 minutes | Cook time: 10 minutes | Makes 8 patties

1 pound (454 g) ground chicken breast
1 Granny Smith apple, peeled and finely chopped
1 egg white

⅓ cup minced onion
2 garlic cloves, minced
2 tbsps. apple juice
3 tbsps. ground almonds
⅛ tsp. freshly ground black pepper

1. Preheat the air fryer oven to 330ºF (166ºC).
2. In a medium mixing bowl, combine all the ingredients except the chicken and stir well.
3. Place the chicken breast to the apple mixture and mix with your hands until well incorporated.
4. Distribute the mixture evenly into 8 equal portions and shape into patties. Put the patties in the air fryer basket. You may need to work in batches depending on the size of your air fryer basket.
5. Place the air fryer basket onto the baking pan, and slide the baking pan into Rack Position 2, select Air Fry and set time to 10 minutes, until a meat thermometer inserted in the center of the chicken reaches at least 165ºF (74ºC).
6. Transfer from the air fryer oven to a plate and repeat the step 5 with the remaining patties.
7. Allow the chicken to cool for 5 minutes and serve warm.

## Healthy Blueberry Breakfast Cobbler

Prep time: 5 minutes | Cook time: 15 minutes | Serves 4

Cooking spray
½ cup blueberries
⅓ cup whole-wheat pastry flour
⅓ cup unsweetened nondairy milk
¼ cup granola

2 tbsps. maple syrup
¾ tsp. baking powder
½ tsp. vanilla
Dash sea salt
Nondairy yogurt, for topping (optional)

1. Preheat the fryer to 347ºF (175ºC). Spray a baking pan lightly with cooking spray.
2. In a medium bowl, mix together the baking powder, flour, and salt. Pour in the milk, maple syrup, and vanilla and whisk to combine well.
3. Scrape the mixture into the prepared pan. Sprinkle the blueberries and granola on top.
4. Slide the baking pan into Rack Position 1, select Convection Bake and set time to 15 minutes, until the top starts to brown and a knife inserted in the center comes out clean.
5. Allow the cobbler to cool for 5 minutes and serve with a drizzle of nondairy yogurt.

## Breakfast Bacon Casserole

Prep time: 10 minutes | Cook time: 14 minutes | Serves 4

Cooking spray
6 eggs
6 slices bacon
¾ cup shredded Cheddar cheese

½ cup chopped green bell pepper
½ cup chopped onion
Salt and pepper, to taste

1. In a skillet over medium-high heat, place the bacon and cook each side for 4 minutes until evenly crisp. Transfer the bacon from the heat to a paper towel-lined plate to drain. Crumble it into small pieces and set it aside.
2. In a medium bowl, whisk the eggs with the salt and pepper.
3. Preheat the air fryer oven to 400ºF (204ºC). Spray a baking pan lightly with cooking spray.
4. Arrange the whisked eggs, crumbled bacon, green bell pepper, and onion in the prepared pan. Slide the baking pan into Rack Position 1, select Convection Bake and set time to 6 minutes.
5. Sprinkle the Cheddar cheese all over and Bake for another 2 minutes.
6. Let sit for 5 minutes and serve on plates.

## Scrambled Eggs with Spinach and Tomato

Prep time: 10 minutes | Cook time: 10 minutes | Serves 2

2 tbsps. olive oil
4 eggs, whisked
1 medium tomato, chopped
5 ounces (142 g) fresh spinach, chopped
½ cup of fresh basil, roughly chopped
1 tsp. fresh lemon juice
½ tsp. coarse salt
½ tsp. ground black pepper

1. Grease a baking pan lightly with the olive oil, tilting it to spread the oil around. Preheat the air fryer oven to 280ºF (138ºC).
2. Combine the remaining ingredients in the baking pan, except the basil leaves, whisking well until everything is entirely mixed.
3. Slide the baking pan into Rack Position 1, select Convection Bake and set time to 10 minutes.
4. Sprinkle with fresh basil leaves before serving.

## Crispy Asparagus and Cheese Strata

Prep time: 10 minutes | Cook time: 15 to 19 minutes | Serves 4

Cooking spray
6 asparagus spears, cut into 2-inch pieces
4 eggs
½ cup grated Havarti or Swiss cheese
2 slices whole-wheat bread, cut into ½-inch
cubes
3 tbsps. whole milk
2 tbsps. chopped flat-leaf parsley
1 tbsp. water
Pinch salt
Freshly ground black pepper, to taste

1. Preheat the air fryer oven to 330ºF (166ºC).
2. Place the asparagus spears and 1 tbsp. of water in a baking pan. Slide the baking pan into Rack Position 1, select Convection Bake and set time to 4 minutes until crisp-tender. Remove the asparagus from the pan and drain on paper towels. Spray the pan lightly with cooking spray.
3. Arrange the bread and asparagus in the pan.
4. In a medium mixing bowl, whisk together the eggs and milk until creamy. Gently fold in the cheese, parsley, salt, and pepper and stir to combine well. Pour this mixture into the baking pan.
5. Bake for about 11 to 14 minutes or until the eggs are set and the top is lightly browned.
6. Allow to cool for 5 minutes before slicing and serving.

## Spicy Potatoes with Peppers

Prep time: 10 minutes | Cook time: 35 minutes | Serves 4

1½ tbsps. extra-virgin olive oil
1 pound (454 g) red potatoes, cut into ½-inch dices
1 large green bell pepper, cut into ½-inch dices
1 large red bell pepper,
cut into ½-inch dices
1 medium onion, cut into ½-inch dices
¾ tsp. sweet paprika
¾ tsp. garlic powder
1¼ tsps. kosher salt
Freshly ground black pepper, to taste

1. Preheat the air fryer oven to 350ºF (177ºC).
2. In a large mixing bowl, mix together the oil, potatoes, bell peppers, onion, salt, paprika, garlic powder and black pepper and toss to coat well.
3. Take the potato mixture to the air fryer basket. Then place the air fryer basket onto the baking pan, and slide the baking pan into Rack Position 2, select Air Fry and set time to 35 minutes, until the potatoes are nicely browned. Stir the mixture three times during the cooking time.
4. Transfer the potato mixture to a plate and serve hot.

## Vegetable Frittata

Prep time: 10 minutes | Cook time: 10 minutes | Serves 4

1 tsp. olive oil
1 egg
6 egg whites
½ cup chopped red bell pepper
⅓ cup grated carrot
⅓ cup minced onion
⅓ cup 2% milk
1 tbsp. shredded Parmesan cheese

1. Preheat the air fryer oven to 350ºF (177ºC).
2. Mix together the carrot, red bell pepper, onion, and olive oil in a baking pan and stir to combine well.
3. Slide the baking pan into Rack Position 1, select Convection Bake and set time to 5 minutes, until the veggies are tender. Stir once during the cooking time.
4. Meantime, whisk together the egg, egg whites, and milk in a medium bowl until a creamy consistency is achieved.
5. When the veggies are done, place the egg mixture over the top. Sprinkle with the Parmesan cheese.
6. Select Bake with Convection, and cook for another 5 minutes, or until the eggs are set and the top is golden around the edges.
7. Let the frittata cool for about 5 minutes before slicing and serving.

## Bell Peppers and Spinach Omelet

Prep time: 10 minutes | Cook time: 13 minutes | Serves 2

2 tsps. canola oil
4 eggs, whisked
1 red bell pepper, deseeded and chopped
1 green bell pepper, deseeded and chopped
1 white onion, finely chopped
½ cup Halloumi cheese, shaved
½ cup baby spinach leaves, roughly chopped
3 tbsps. plain milk
1 tsp. melted butter
Kosher salt and freshly ground black pepper, to taste

1. Preheat the air fryer oven to 350ºF (177ºC).
2. Grease a baking pan lightly with canola oil.
3. Add the remaining ingredients in the baking pan and stir well.
4. Slide the baking pan into Rack Position 1, select Convection Bake and set time to 13 minutes.
5. Serve hot.

## Maple Oat and Banana Bread Pudding

Prep time: 10 minutes | Cook time: 18 minutes | Serves 4

Cooking spray
2 medium ripe bananas, mashed
½ cup low-fat milk
2 slices whole-grain bread, cut into bite-sized cubes
¼ cup quick oats
2 tbsps. maple syrup
2 tbsps. peanut butter
1 tsp. vanilla extract
1 tsp. ground cinnamon

1. Preheat the fryer to 350ºF (177ºC). Spray the air fryer basket with cooking spray.
2. In a large mixing bowl, mix the bananas, milk, maple syrup, peanut butter, vanilla, and cinnamon and stir until entirely incorporated.
3. Place the bread cubes to the banana mixture and stir until thoroughly coated. Gently fold in the oats and stir to combine well.
4. Take the mixture to the air fryer basket. Wrap the air fryer basket in aluminum foil.
5. Then place the air fryer basket onto the baking pan, and slide the baking pan into Rack Position 2, select Air Fry and set time to 12 minutes.
6. Take off the foil and cook for another 6 minutes, or until the pudding has set.
7. Allow the pudding to cool for 5 minutes before serving.

## Coconut Brown Rice and Date Porridge

Prep time: 5 minutes | Cook time: 23 minutes | Serves 1 or 2

1 cup canned coconut milk
½ cup cooked brown rice
4 large Medjool dates, pitted and roughly chopped
¼ cup unsweetened shredded coconut
¼ cup packed dark brown sugar
¼ tsp. ground cardamom
½ tsp. kosher salt
Heavy cream, for serving (optional)

1. Preheat the air fryer oven to 375ºF (191ºC).
2. Add all the ingredients except the heavy cream in a baking pan and stir until well blended.
3. Slide the baking pan into Rack Position 1, select Convection Bake and set time to 23 minutes, until the porridge is thick and creamy. Stir the porridge halfway through the cooking time.
4. Transfer the porridge from the air fryer oven and ladle the porridge into bowls.
5. Serve warm with a drizzle of the cream, if desired.

## Pecorino and Kale Baked Eggs

Prep time: 5 minutes | Cook time: 10 minutes | Serves 2

¼ cup olive oil
4 large eggs
1 cup roughly chopped kale leaves, stems and center ribs removed
¼ cup grated pecorino cheese
1 garlic clove, peeled
3 tbsps. chopped pitted mixed olives
3 tbsps. whole almonds
2 tbsps. heavy cream
Kosher salt and freshly ground black pepper, to taste

1. In a small blender, add the kale, pecorino, olive oil, garlic, almonds, salt, and pepper and blitz until well incorporated.
2. Preheat the air fryer oven to 300ºF (149ºC).
3. One at a time, crack the eggs in a baking pan. Spread the kale pesto on top of the egg whites. Top the yolks with the cream and swirl together the yolks and the pesto.
4. Slide the baking pan into Rack Position 1, select Convection Bake and set time to 10 minutes, until the top begins to brown and the eggs are set.
5. Let the eggs cool for about 5 minutes. Sprinkle the olives on top and serve right away.

## Tasty Baby Pancake with Mixed Berries

Prep time: 10 minutes | Cook time: 12 minutes | Serves 4

1 tbsp. unsalted butter, at room temperature
1 egg
2 egg whites
1 cup sliced fresh strawberries
½ cup fresh raspberries
½ cup fresh blueberries
½ cup 2% milk
½ cup whole-wheat pastry flour
1 tsp. pure vanilla extract

1. Preheat the air fryer oven to 330ºF (166ºC). Grease a baking pan lightly with the butter.
2. In a medium mixing bowl, beat together the egg, egg whites, milk, pastry flour and vanilla with a hand mixer, until well incorporated.
3. Slide the baking pan into Rack Position 1, select Convection Bake and set time to 12 minutes, or until the pancake puffs up in the center and the edges are golden brown.
4. Let the pancake cool for about 5 minutes and serve topped with the berries.

## Walnut Pancake

Prep time: 10 minutes | Cook time: 20 minutes | Serves 4

3 tbsps. melted butter, divided
1 cup flour
1 egg, beaten
¾ cup milk
½ cup roughly chopped walnuts
2 tbsps. sugar
1½ tsps. baking powder
1 tsp. pure vanilla extract
¼ tsp. salt
Maple syrup or fresh sliced fruit, for serving

1. Preheat the air fryer oven to 330ºF (166ºC). Grease a baking pan lightly with 1 tbsp. of melted butter.
2. In a medium bowl, mix together the flour, sugar, baking powder, and salt. Place the milk, beaten egg, the remaining 2 tbsps. of melted butter, and vanilla and stir until the batter is sticky but slightly lumpy.
3. Slowly put the batter into the greased baking pan and sprinkle with the walnuts.
4. Slide the baking pan into Rack Position 1, select Convection Bake and set time to 20 minutes, until golden brown and cooked through.
5. Allow the pancake to cool for 5 minutes and serve topped with the maple syrup or fresh fruit, if desired.

## Air Fried Sourdough Croutons with Thyme

Prep time: 5 minutes | Cook time: 6 minutes | Makes 4 cups

1 tbsp. olive oil
4 cups cubed sourdough bread, 1-inch cubes
1 tsp. fresh thyme leaves
¼ tsp. salt
Freshly ground black pepper, to taste

1. In a bowl, combine all the ingredients.
2. Preheat the air fryer oven to 400ºF (204ºC).
3. Toss the bread cubes in a baking pan. Slide the baking pan into Rack Position 1, select Convection Bake and set time to 6 minutes, stirring once or twice during the cooking time.
4. Serve hot.

## Cheesy Ham and Bell Pepper Omelet

Prep time: 5 minutes | Cook time: 19 to 20 minutes | Serves 2

4 large eggs
¾ cup shredded sharp Cheddar cheese
¼ cup diced ham
¼ cup chopped bell
pepper, green or red
¼ cup chopped onion
2 tbsps. milk
1 tsp. butter
⅛ tsp. salt

1. Preheat the air fryer oven to 390ºF (199ºC).
2. Place the ham, bell pepper, onion, and butter in the air fryer basket and mix well.
3. Then place the air fryer basket onto the baking pan, and slide the baking pan into Rack Position 2, select Air Fry and set time to 1 minutes. Stir and continue to cook for another 4 to 5 minutes until the veggies are soft.
4. Meanwhile, whisk together the milk, eggs, and salt in a bowl.
5. Pour the egg mixture over the veggie mixture. Turn the temperature to 360ºF (182ºC) and slide the baking pan into Rack Position 1, select Convection Bake and set time to 13 minutes, until the top is lightly golden browned and the eggs are set.
6. Sprinkle the omelet with the shredded cheese. Select Bake with Convection, and cook for 1 minute more until the cheese has melted.
7. Allow the omelet to cool for about 5 minutes before serving.

# Baked Ricotta Spinach Omelet

Prep time: 10 minutes | Cook time: 10 minutes | Serves 1

1 tsp. olive oil
3 eggs
¼ cup chopped spinach

1 tbsp. ricotta cheese
1 tbsp. chopped parsley
Salt and ground black pepper, to taste

1. Lightly grease a baking pan with olive oil. Preheat the air fryer oven to 330ºF (166ºC).
2. In a bowl, use a fork to beat the eggs and sprinkle with salt and black pepper.
3. Arrange the ricotta, spinach, and parsley and put in the baking pan. Slide the baking pan into Rack Position 1, select Convection Bake and set time to 10 minutes, until the egg is set.
4. Enjoy!

# Delicious Coffee Donuts

Prep time: 5 minutes | Cook time: 6 minutes | Serves 6

1 cup flour
¼ cup sugar
¼ cup coffee
1 tbsp. aquafaba

1 tbsp. sunflower oil
1 tsp. baking powder
½ tsp. salt

1. Combine the sugar, salt, flour, and baking powder in a large bowl.
2. Place the aquafaba, coffee, and sunflower oil and mix until a dough is formed. Let the dough to rest in and the refrigerator.
3. Preheat the air fryer oven to 400ºF (204ºC).
4. Transfer the dough from the fridge and divide up, kneading each section into a doughnut.
5. Arrange the doughnuts inside the air fryer basket. Then place the air fryer basket onto the baking pan, and slide the baking pan into Rack Position 2, select Air Fry and set time to 6 minutes.
6. Serve right away.

# Chapter 3 Vegetables

## Spinach and Carrot Stuffed Tomatoes

Prep time: 10 minutes | Cook time: 16 to 18 minutes | Serves 4

2 tsps. olive oil
4 medium beefsteak tomatoes, rinsed
2 cups fresh baby spinach
1 medium onion, chopped
½ cup grated carrot
¼ cup crumbled low-sodium feta cheese
1 garlic clove, minced
½ tsp. dried basil

1. Preheat the air fryer oven to 350ºF (177ºC).
2. Cut a thin slice off the top of each tomato on a cutting board. Scoop out a ¼- to ½-inch-thick tomato pulp and arrange the tomatoes upside down on paper towels to drain. Set them aside.
3. Stir together the garlic, carrot, onion, and olive oil in a baking pan. Slide the baking pan into Rack Position 1, select Convection Bake and set time to 4 minutes, until the carrot is crisp-tender.
4. Take the pan from the oven and stir in the spinach, feta cheese, and basil.
5. Scoop ¼ of the vegetable mixture into each tomato and take the stuffed tomatoes to the oven.
6. Bake for 12 to 14 minutes until the filling is hot and the tomatoes are lightly caramelized.
7. Allow the tomatoes to cool for 5 minutes and serve warm.

## Spicy Tofu, Carrot and Cauliflower Rice

Prep time: 10 minutes | Cook time: 22 minutes | Serves 4

½ block tofu, crumbled
1 cup diced carrot
½ cup diced onions
2 tbsps. soy sauce
1 tsp. turmeric
**Cauliflower:**
1½ tsps. toasted sesame oil
3 cups cauliflower rice
½ cup frozen peas
½ cup chopped broccoli
2 tbsps. soy sauce
2 garlic cloves, minced
1 tbsp. minced ginger
1 tbsp. rice vinegar

1. Preheat the air fryer oven to 370ºF (188ºC).
2. Combine together the tofu, carrot, onions, soy sauce, and turmeric in the air fryer basket and stir until well incorporated.
3. Then place the air fryer basket onto the baking pan, and slide the baking pan into Rack Position 2, select Air Fry and set time to 10 minutes.
4. Meanwhile, combine all the ingredients for the cauliflower in a large bowl, and toss well.
5. Remove the baking dish and pour the cauliflower mixture to the tofu and stir to combine well.
6. Take the air fryer basket back to the air fryer oven and continue cooking for about 12 minutes, or until the vegetables are cooked to your preference.
7. Let rest for 5 minutes before serving.

## Beet Roast with Chermoula

Prep time: 15 minutes | Cook time: 25 minutes | Serves 4

**Chermoula:**
½ cup extra-virgin olive oil
1 cup packed fresh cilantro leaves
½ cup packed fresh parsley leaves
6 cloves garlic, peeled
2 tsps. ground cumin
2 tsps. smoked paprika
1 tsp. ground coriander
Pinch of crushed saffron
(optional)
½ to 1 tsp. cayenne pepper
Kosher salt, to taste
**Beets:**
3 medium beets, trimmed, peeled, and cut into 1-inch chunks
2 tbsps. chopped fresh cilantro
2 tbsps. chopped fresh parsley

1. Combine the cilantro, parsley, garlic, paprika, cumin, coriander, and cayenne in a food processor. Pulse until coarsely chopped. Add the saffron, if using, and process until well combined. With the food processor running, gradually add the olive oil in a steady stream; process until the sauce is uniform. Sprinkle with salt.
2. Preheat the air fryer oven to 375ºF (191ºC).
3. Drizzle the beets with ½ cup of the chermoula to coat in a large bowl. Place the beets in the baking pan. Slide the baking pan into Rack Position 2, select Roast and set time to 25 minutes, until the beets are tender.
4. Take the beets to a serving platter. Scatter with the chopped cilantro and parsley and serve hot.

# Cauliflower Roast with Cilantro-Yogurt Sauce

Prep time: 15 minutes | Cook time: 20 minutes | Serves 4

**Cauliflower:**
3 tbsps. vegetable oil
5 cups cauliflower florets
½ tsp. ground coriander
½ tsp. ground cumin
½ tsp. kosher salt
**Sauce:**
½ cup Greek yogurt or

sour cream
¼ cup chopped fresh cilantro
1 jalapeño, coarsely chopped
4 cloves garlic, peeled
2 tbsps. water
½ tsp. kosher salt

1. Preheat the air fryer oven to 400ºF (204ºC).
2. Combine the cauliflower, oil, cumin, coriander, and salt in a large bowl. Toss to coat well.
3. Place the cauliflower in the baking pan. Slide the baking pan into Rack Position 2, select Roast and set time to 20 minutes, stirring halfway through the cooking time.
4. Meanwhile, combine the yogurt, cilantro, jalapeño, garlic, and salt in a blender. Blend, adding the water as needed to keep the blades moving and to thin the sauce.
5. At the end of cooking time, take the cauliflower to a large serving bowl. Pour the sauce over and toss to coat well. Serve right away.

# Cauliflower Rice with Mushroom and Water Chestnuts

Prep time: 15 minutes | Cook time: 40 minutes | Serves 8

Cooking spray
1 tbsp. peanut oil
1 tbsp. sesame oil
1 large head cauliflower, rinsed and drained, cut into florets
2 (8-ounce / 227-g) cans mushrooms
1 (8-ounce / 227-g) can

water chestnuts
¾ cup peas
1 egg, beaten
½ lemon, juiced
2 garlic cloves, minced
4 tbsps. soy sauce
1 tbsp. minced fresh ginger

1. Preheat the air fryer oven to 350ºF (177ºC).
2. Mix the peanut oil, sesame oil, soy sauce, minced ginger, lemon juice, and minced garlic to combine well.
3. In a food processor, pulse the cauliflower florets in small batches to break them down to resemble rice grains. Pour them into the air fryer basket.

4. Drain the chestnuts and roughly chop them. Pour the chestnuts into the air fryer basket. Then place the air fryer basket onto the baking pan, and slide the baking pan into Rack Position 2, select Air Fry and set time to 20 minutes.
5. In the meantime, drain the mushrooms. Place the mushrooms and the peas to the air fryer oven and continue to air fry for an additional 15 minutes.
6. Lightly spray a frying pan lightly with cooking spray. Prepare an omelet with the beaten egg, ensuring it is firm. Spread on a cutting board and slice it up.
7. When the cauliflower is ready, throw in the omelet. Slide the baking pan into Rack Position 1, select Convection Bake and set time to 5 minutes. Serve warm.

# Healthy Vegetarian Meatballs

Prep time: 15 minutes | Cook time: 18 minutes | Serves 3

2 tbsps. olive oil
2 cups cooked chickpeas
1 cup rolled oats
½ cup grated carrots
½ cup sweet onions
½ cup roasted cashews

Juice of 1 lemon
2 tbsps. soy sauce
1 tbsp. flax meal
1 tsp. cumin
1 tsp. garlic powder
½ tsp. turmeric

1. Preheat the air fryer oven to 350ºF (177ºC).
2. Mix together the olive oil, carrots, and onions in the air fryer basket and stir to combine well.
3. Then place the air fryer basket onto the baking pan, and slide the baking pan into Rack Position 2, select Convection Broil and set time to 6 minutes.
4. Meanwhile, place the oats and cashews in a food processor or blender and pulse until coarsely ground. Take the mixture to a large bowl. Put the chickpeas, lemon juice, and soy sauce to the food processor and pulse until smooth. Transfer the chickpea mixture to the bowl of oat and cashew mixture.
5. Transfer the carrots and onions from the oven to the bowl of chickpea mixture. Place the flax meal, garlic powder, cumin, and turmeric and stir to incorporate well.
6. Spoon tablespoon-sized portions of the veggie mixture and roll them into balls with your hands. Take the balls to the baking pan in a single layer.
7. Turn the temperature to 370ºF (188ºC). Slide the baking pan into Rack Position 1, select Convection Bake and set time to 12 minutes, until golden through. Flip the balls halfway through the cooking time.
8. Serve hot.

## Cheesy Rice and Onion Stuffed Bell Peppers

Prep time: 5 minutes | Cook time: 16 to 17 minutes | Serves 4

4 red bell peppers, tops sliced off
2 cups cooked rice
1 onion, chopped
1 cup crumbled feta cheese
¾ cup tomato sauce
¼ cup sliced Kalamata olives
1 tbsp. Greek seasoning
2 tbsps. chopped fresh dill, for serving
Salt and black pepper, to taste

1. Preheat the air fryer oven to 360ºF (182ºC).
2. Microwave the bell peppers for about 1 to 2 minutes until soft.
3. When ready, take the red bell peppers to a plate to let cool.
4. In a medium bowl, mix together the cooked rice, feta cheese, onion, kalamata olives, tomato sauce, Greek seasoning, salt, and pepper and stir until combined well.
5. Distribute the rice mixture evenly among the red bell peppers and transfer to a greased baking pan.
6. Slide the baking pan into Rack Position 1, select Convection Bake and set time to 15 minutes, or until the rice is heated through and the vegetables are tender.
7. Transfer the bell peppers from the oven and sprinkle with the dill. Serve hot.

## Asparagus and Potato Platter with Cheese Sauce

Prep time: 5 minutes | Cook time: 26 to 28 minutes | Serves 5

Cooking spray
2 tbsps. olive oil
1 bunch asparagus, trimmed
4 medium potatoes, cut into wedges
Salt and pepper, to taste
**Cheese Sauce:**
¼ cup buttermilk
¼ cup crumbled cottage cheese
1 tbsp. whole-grain mustard
Salt and black pepper, to taste

1. Preheat the air fryer oven to 400ºF (204ºC). Spray the air fryer basket lightly with cooking spray.
2. Place the potatoes in the air fryer basket. Then place the air fryer basket onto the baking pan, and slide the baking pan into Rack Position 2, select Convection Broil and set time to 20 minutes, until golden brown.

Flip halfway through the cooking time.
3. When ready, transfer the potatoes from the oven to a platter. Cover the potatoes with foil to keep warm. Set them aside.
4. Arrange the asparagus in the basket and drizzle with the olive oil. Season with salt and pepper.
5. Broil for 6 to 8 minutes, flipping once or twice during the cooking, or until the asparagus are cooked to your desired crispiness.
6. Meanwhile, make the cheese sauce: in a small bowl, stir together the cottage cheese, buttermilk, and mustard. Season with salt and pepper as needed.
7. Take the asparagus to the platter of potatoes and drizzle with the cheese sauce. Serve hot.

## Herbed Broiled Veggies

Prep time: 15 minutes | Cook time: 20 minutes | Makes 3 cups

**Glaze:**
2 tbsps. raw honey
2 tsps. minced garlic
¼ tsp. dried oregano
¼ tsp. dried marjoram
¼ tsp. dried basil
⅛ tsp. dried thyme
⅛ tsp. dried sage
⅛ tsp. dried rosemary
½ tsp. salt
¼ tsp. ground black pepper
**Veggies:**
3 tbsps. olive oil
3 to 4 medium red potatoes, cut into 1- to 2-inch pieces
1 small zucchini, cut into 1- to 2-inch pieces
1 (10.5-ounce / 298-g) package cherry tomatoes, halved
1 small carrot, sliced into ¼-inch rounds
1 cup sliced mushrooms

1. Preheat the air fryer oven to 380ºF (193ºC).
2. In a small bowl, combine the honey, garlic, marjoram, basil, oregano, sage, rosemary, thyme, salt, and pepper and stir to mix well. Set it aside.
3. In a large bowl, add the red potatoes, zucchini, carrot, cherry tomatoes, and mushroom. Drizzle with the olive oil and toss to coat well.
4. Put the veggies into the air fryer basket. Then place the air fryer basket onto the baking pan, and slide the baking pan into Rack Position 2, select Convection Broil and set time to 15 minutes.
5. When ready, take the broiled veggies to the large bowl. Pour the honey mixture over the veggies, tossing to coat well.
6. Spread out the veggies evenly in the air fryer basket.
7. Turn the temperature to 390ºF (199ºC) and broil for another 5 minutes, or until the veggies are soft and glazed. Serve hot.

## Chili Black Bean and Tomato

Prep time: 15 minutes | Cook time: 23 minutes | Serves 6

1 tbsp. olive oil
3 cans black beans, drained and rinsed
2 cans diced tomatoes
1 medium onion, diced
1 cup vegetable broth
3 garlic cloves, minced

2 chipotle peppers, chopped
2 tsps. chili powder
2 tsps. cumin
1 tsp. dried oregano
½ tsp. salt

1. In a skillet over a medium heat, fry the garlic and onions in the olive oil for about 3 minutes.
2. Place the remaining ingredients, stirring frequently and scraping the bottom to prevent sticking.
3. Preheat the air fryer oven to 400ºF (204ºC).
4. Take a baking pan and put the mixture inside. Arrange a sheet of aluminum foil on top.
5. Slide the baking pan into Rack Position 1, select Convection Bake and set time to 20 minutes.
6. When ready, plate up and serve right away.

## Quick Parmesan Asparagus Fries

Prep time: 15 minutes | Cook time: 6 minutes | Serves 4

Cooking spray
12 ounces (340 g) fresh asparagus spears, woody ends trimmed
2 egg whites
¼ cup plus 2 tbsps.

grated Parmesan cheese, divided
¾ cup panko bread crumbs
¼ cup water
¼ tsp. salt

1. Preheat the air fryer oven to 390ºF (199ºC).
2. Whisk together the egg whites and water until slightly foamy in a shallow dish. Thoroughly mix ¼ cup of Parmesan cheese, bread crumbs, and salt in a separate shallow dish.
3. Dip the asparagus in the egg white, then roll in the cheese mixture to coat well.
4. Arrange the asparagus in the air fryer basket in a single layer, leaving space between each spear. You may need to work in batches to avoid overcrowding.
5. Spray the asparagus lightly with cooking spray. Then place the air fryer basket onto the baking pan, and slide the baking pan into Rack Position 2, select Air Fry and set time to 6 minutes, until golden brown and crisp. Repeat with the remaining asparagus spears.
6. Sprinkle with the remaining 2 tbsps. of cheese and serve hot.

## Spicy Baked Tofu

Prep time: 5 minutes | Cook time: 10 minutes | Serves 2

6 ounces (170 g) extra firm tofu, pressed and cubed
1 tbsp. soy sauce
1 tbsp. water

⅓ tsp. garlic powder
⅓ tsp. onion powder
⅓ tsp. dried oregano
⅓ tsp. dried basil
Black pepper, to taste

1. Whisk together the soy sauce, water, garlic powder, onion powder, oregano, basil, and black pepper in a large mixing bowl. Place the tofu cubes, stirring to coat, and allow them to marinate for about 10 minutes.
2. Preheat the air fryer oven to 390ºF (199ºC).
3. Arrange the tofu in the baking pan. Slide the baking pan into Rack Position 1, select Convection Bake and set time to 10 minutes, until crisp. Flip the tofu halfway through the cooking time.
4. Transfer the tofu from the oven to a plate and serve warm.

## Chickpea, Fig and Arugula Salad

Prep time: 15 minutes | Cook time: 20 minutes | Serves 4

2 tbsps. extra-virgin olive oil, plus more for greasing
3 cups arugula rocket, washed and dried
1½ cups cooked chickpeas

8 fresh figs, halved
4 tbsps. balsamic vinegar
1 tsp. crushed roasted cumin seeds
Salt and ground black pepper, to taste

1. Preheat the air fryer oven to 375ºF (191ºC).
2. Cover the air fryer basket with aluminum foil. Grease the air fryer basket with olive oil. Put the figs in the air fryer basket. Then place the air fryer basket onto the baking pan, and slide the baking pan into Rack Position 2, select Air Fry and set time to 10 minutes.
3. Combine the chickpeas and cumin seeds in a bowl.
4. Transfer the air fried figs from the air fryer oven and replace with the chickpeas. Air fry for about 10 minutes. Leave to cool.
5. At the same time, prepare the dressing. In a small bowl, mix the balsamic vinegar, olive oil, salt and pepper.
6. Combine the arugula rocket with the cooled figs and chickpeas in a salad bowl.
7. Top with the sauce and Toss well to coat. Serve warm.

## Easy Broiled Asparagus

Prep time: 5 minutes | Cook time: 10 minutes | Serves 4

2 tbsps. olive oil
1 pound (454 g) asparagus, woody ends trimmed

1 tbsp. balsamic vinegar
2 tsps. minced garlic
Salt and freshly ground black pepper, to taste

1. Preheat the air fryer oven to 400ºF (204ºC).
2. Toss the asparagus with the olive oil, balsamic vinegar, garlic, salt, and pepper in a large shallow bowl, until thoroughly coated.
3. Place the asparagus in the air fryer basket. Then place the air fryer basket onto the baking pan, and slide the baking pan into Rack Position 2, select Convection Broil and set time to 10 minutes. Flip the asparagus with tongs halfway through the cooking time.
4. Serve hot.

## Mediterranean Air Fried Vegetables

Prep time: 10 minutes | Cook time: 6 minutes | Serves 4

6 tbsps. olive oil
1 large zucchini, sliced
1 cup cherry tomatoes, halved
1 parsnip, sliced
1 carrot, sliced

1 green pepper, sliced
1 tsp. garlic purée
1 tsp. mixed herbs
1 tsp. mustard
Salt and ground black pepper, to taste

1. Preheat the air fryer oven to 400ºF (204ºC).
2. In a bowl, combine all the ingredients, making sure to coat the vegetables well.
3. Put in the air fryer basket. Then place the air fryer basket onto the baking pan, and slide the baking pan into Rack Position 2, select Air Fry and set time to 6 minutes, ensuring the vegetables are soft and browned.
4. Serve right away.

## Soy Green Beans with Sesame Seeds

Prep time: 5 minutes | Cook time: 8 minutes | Serves 4

4 tsps. toasted sesame oil, divided
12 ounces (340 g) trimmed green beans
1 tbsp. reduced-sodium

soy sauce or tamari
½ tbsp. Sriracha sauce
½ tbsp. toasted sesame seeds

1. Preheat the air fryer oven to 375ºF (191ºC).
2. In a small bowl, whisk together the soy sauce, Sriracha sauce, and 1 tsp. of sesame oil until smooth.
3. In a large bowl, toss the green beans with the remaining sesame oil until evenly coated.
4. Arrange the green beans in the air fryer basket in a single layer. You may need to work in batches to avoid overcrowding.
5. Then place the air fryer basket onto the baking pan, and slide the baking pan into Rack Position 2, select Air Fry and set time to 8 minutes, until the green beans are lightly charred and tender. Flip halfway through the cooking time.
6. Transfer the green beans from the oven to a platter. Repeat the step 4 to 5 with the remaining green beans.
7. Pour the prepared sauce over the top of green beans and toss well. Scatter with the toasted sesame seeds. Serve warm.

## Lush Broiled Veggies Salad

Prep time: 5 minutes | Cook time: 20 minutes | Serves 2

2 tbsps. olive oil, divided
1 potato, chopped
1 carrot, sliced diagonally
1 cup cherry tomatoes
A handful of arugula
A handful of baby spinach
½ small beetroot, sliced
¼ onion, sliced

Juice of 1 lemon
3 tbsps. canned chickpeas, for serving
Parmesan shavings, for serving
½ tsp. turmeric
½ tsp. cumin
¼ tsp. sea salt

1. Preheat the air fryer oven to 370ºF (188ºC).
2. In a large bowl, combine the potato, carrot, cherry tomatoes, beetroot, onion, turmeric, cumin, salt, and 1 tbsp. of olive oil and toss until well coated.
3. Place the veggies in the air fryer basket. Then place the air fryer basket onto the baking pan, and slide the baking pan into Rack Position 2, select Convection Broil and set time to 20 minutes, flipping halfway through.
4. Allow the veggies to cool for 5 to 10 minutes in the oven.
5. Arrange the arugula, baby spinach, lemon juice, and remaining 1 tbsp. of olive oil in a salad bowl and stir to combine well. Mix in the broiled veggies and toss well.
6. Sprinkle the chickpeas and Parmesan shavings on top and serve right away.

## Stuffed Mushrooms with Pesto

Prep time: 10 minutes | Cook time: 15 minutes | Serves 6

1 tbsp. olive oil
1 pound (454 g) baby bella mushroom, stems removed
1 cup basil
½ cup cashew, soaked

overnight
½ cup nutritional yeast
2 cloves garlic
1 tbsp. lemon juice
Salt, to taste

1. Preheat the air fryer oven to 400ºF (204ºC).
2. Prepare the pesto. Blend the basil, cashew nuts, nutritional yeast, lemon juice, garlic and olive oil in a food processor to combine well. Season with salt as desired.
3. Turn the mushrooms cap-side down and lay the pesto on the underside of each cap.
4. Take to the air fryer basket. Then place the air fryer basket onto the baking pan, and slide the baking pan into Rack Position 2, select Air Fry and set time to 15 minutes.
5. Serve hot.

## Balsamic Glazed Beets

Prep time: 5 minutes | Cook time: 10 minutes | Serves 2

**Beet:**
2 tbsps. olive oil
2 beets, cubed
2 springs rosemary, chopped

Salt and black pepper, to taste
**Balsamic Glaze:**
⅓ cup balsamic vinegar
1 tbsp. honey

1. Preheat the air fryer oven to 400ºF (204ºC).
2. In a mixing bowl, mix the beets, olive oil, rosemary, salt, and pepper and toss until the beets are well coated.
3. Arrange the beets in the air fryer basket. Then place the air fryer basket onto the baking pan, and slide the baking pan into Rack Position 2, select Air Fry and set time to 10 minutes, until the beets are crisp and browned at the edges. Flip halfway through the cooking time.
4. Meanwhile, make the balsamic glaze: In a small saucepan, place the balsamic vinegar and honey and bring to a boil over medium heat. When the sauce starts to boil, reduce the heat to medium-low heat and simmer until the liquid is reduced by half.
5. When ready, transfer the beets from the oven to a platter. Add the balsamic glaze over the top and serve hot.

## Two-Cheese Cabbage Wedges

Prep time: 5 minutes | Cook time: 20 minutes | Serves 4

4 tbsps. melted butter
1 head cabbage, cut into wedges
1 cup shredded Parmesan cheese

½ cup shredded Mozzarella cheese
Salt and black pepper, to taste

1. Preheat the air fryer oven to 380ºF (193ºC).
2. Coat the melted butter over the cut sides of cabbage wedges and scatter both sides with the Parmesan cheese. Sprinkle with salt and pepper to taste.
3. Arrange the cabbage wedges in the air fryer basket. Then place the air fryer basket onto the baking pan, and slide the baking pan into Rack Position 2, select Air Fry and set time to 20 minutes, flipping the cabbage halfway through, or until the cabbage wedges are lightly browned.
4. Take the cabbage wedges to a plate and top with the Mozzarella cheese. Serve warm.

## Cheesy Beef Stuffed Bell Peppers

Prep time: 10 minutes | Cook time: 30 minutes | Serves 4

1 pound (454 g) ground beef
1 can diced tomatoes and green chilies
4 green bell peppers

1 cup shredded Monterey jack cheese, divided
1 tbsp. taco seasoning mix

1. Preheat the air fryer oven to 350ºF (177ºC).
2. In a skillet over high heat, cook the ground beef for about 8 minutes. Make sure it is cooked through and browned all over. Drain the fat.
3. Stir in the diced tomatoes and green chilies, and the taco seasoning mix. Let the mixture cook for a further 4 minutes.
4. At the same time, slice the tops off the green peppers and remove the seeds and membranes.
5. When the meat mixture is completely cooked, scoop equal amounts of it into the peppers and place the Monterey jack cheese on top. Then put the peppers into the air fryer basket. Then place the air fryer basket onto the baking pan, and slide the baking pan into Rack Position 2, select Air Fry and set time to 15 minutes.
6. The peppers are ready when they are tender, and the cheese is bubbling and brown. Serve hot.

## Creamy Spinach

Prep time: 10 minutes | Cook time: 15 minutes |
Serves 4

Vegetable oil spray
1 (10-ounce / 283-g)
package frozen spinach,
thawed and squeezed
dry
½ cup grated Parmesan
cheese

½ cup chopped onion
4 ounces (113 g) cream
cheese, diced
2 cloves garlic, minced
½ tsp. ground nutmeg
1 tsp. kosher salt
1 tsp. black pepper

1. Preheat the air fryer oven to 350ºF (177ºC). Spray a heatproof pan lightly with vegetable oil spray.
2. Combine the spinach, onion, garlic, cream cheese, nutmeg, salt, and pepper in a medium bowl. Transfer this mixture to the prepared pan.
3. Slide the pan into Rack Position 1, select Convection Bake and set time to 10 minutes. Open and stir to thoroughly combine the cream cheese and spinach.
4. Scatter the Parmesan cheese on top and bake for another 5 minutes, or until the cheese has melted and browned.
5. Serve warm.

## Crispy Cauliflower Tater Tots

Prep time: 15 minutes | Cook time: 16 minutes |
Serves 12

1 pound (454 g)
cauliflower, steamed and
chopped
½ cup nutritional yeast
½ cup bread crumbs
1 onion, chopped
3 tbsps. flaxseed meal
3 tbsps. water
1 tbsp. oats

1 tbsp. desiccated
coconuts
1 tsp. minced garlic
1 tsp. chopped parsley
1 tsp. chopped oregano
1 tsp. chopped chives
Salt and ground black
pepper, to taste

1. Preheat the air fryer oven to 390ºF (199ºC).
2. Wring the cauliflower with a paper towel to drain any excess water out of it.
3. Combine the cauliflower with the remaining ingredients, save the bread crumbs in a bowl. With the hands, shape the mixture into several small balls.
4. Coat the balls in the bread crumbs and take them to the air fryer basket. Then place the air fryer basket onto the baking pan, and slide the baking pan into Rack Position 2, select Air Fry and set time to 6 minutes. Increase the temperature to 400ºF (204ºC) and then air fry for another 10 minutes.
5. Serve hot.

## Brussels Sprouts with Chili Sauce

Prep time: 5 minutes | Cook time: 20 minutes |
Serves 2

8 ounces (227 g)
Brussels sprouts,
trimmed (large sprouts
halved)
¼ cup Thai sweet chili
sauce
2 small shallots, cut into
¼-inch-thick slices
2 tbsps. black vinegar or

balsamic vinegar
2 tsps. lightly packed
fresh cilantro leaves, for
garnish
½ tsp. hot sauce
Kosher salt and freshly
ground black pepper, to
taste

1. In a large bowl, place the chili sauce, vinegar, and hot sauce and whisk to combine well.
2. Put the shallots and Brussels sprouts and toss to coat well. Sprinkle with the salt and pepper to taste. Take the Brussels sprouts and sauce to a metal cake pan.
3. Slide the pan into Rack Position 2, select Roast and set time to 20 minutes, until the Brussels sprouts are crisp-tender and the sauce has reduced to a sticky glaze. Stir twice during the cooking time.
4. Scatter the cilantro on top for garnish and serve hot.

## Appetizing Tofu

Prep time: 15 minutes | Cook time: 20 minutes |
Serves 2

½ block firm tofu, pressed
to remove excess liquid
and cut into cubes
2 green onions, chopped
1 tbsp. sugar
1 tbsp. soy sauce
3 tsps. lime juice

2 tsps. apple cider
vinegar
1 tsp. ground ginger
1 tsp. garlic powder
1 tsp. cornstarch
Toasted sesame seeds,
for garnish

1. Thoroughly combine the apple cider vinegar, sugar, soy sauce, lime juice, ground ginger, and garlic powder in a bowl.
2. Cover the tofu with this mixture and let marinate for at least 30 minutes.
3. Preheat the air fryer oven to 400ºF (204ºC).
4. Take the tofu to the air fryer basket, keeping any excess marinade for the sauce. Then place the air fryer basket onto the baking pan, and slide the baking pan into Rack Position 2, select Air Fry and set time to 20 minutes, until crispy.
5. At the same time, thicken the sauce with the cornstarch over a medium-low heat.
6. Top the cooked tofu with the sauce, green onions, and sesame seeds. Serve hot.

## Authentic Ratatouille

Prep time: 15 minutes | Cook time: 16 minutes | Serves 2

2 tbsps. olive oil
1 zucchini, thinly sliced
2 Roma tomatoes, thinly sliced
2 yellow bell peppers, sliced

2 garlic cloves, minced
2 tbsps. herbes de Provence
1 tbsp. vinegar
Salt and black pepper, to taste

1. Preheat the air fryer oven to 390ºF (199ºC).
2. In a large bowl, place the tomatoes, zucchini, bell peppers, garlic, olive oil, herbes de Provence, and vinegar and toss until the vegetables are evenly coated. Season with salt and pepper and toss again. Put the vegetable mixture into a baking dish.
3. Slide the baking pan into Rack Position 2, select Roast and set time to 8 minutes. Stir and continue cooking for about 8 minutes until soft.
4. Allow the vegetable mixture to rest for 5 minutes in the oven before removing and serving.

## Mascarpone Mushrooms with Noodles

Prep time: 10 minutes | Cook time: 15 minutes | Serves 4

Vegetable oil spray
4 cups sliced mushrooms
4 cups cooked konjac noodles, for serving
8 ounces (227 g) mascarpone cheese
1 medium yellow onion, chopped
½ cup grated Parmesan

cheese
¼ cup heavy whipping cream or half-and-half
2 cloves garlic, minced
1 tsp. dried thyme
1 tsp. kosher salt
1 tsp. black pepper
½ tsp. red pepper flakes

1. Preheat the air fryer oven to 350ºF (177ºC). Spritz a baking pan lightly with vegetable oil spray.
2. Combine the mushrooms, onion, garlic, cream, mascarpone, thyme, salt, black pepper, and red pepper flakes in a medium bowl. Stir to combine well. Transfer the mixture to the prepared pan.
3. Slide the baking pan into Rack Position 1, select Convection Bake and set time to 15 minutes, stirring halfway through the baking time.
4. Divide the pasta evenly among four shallow bowls. Scoop the mushroom mixture evenly over the pasta. Scatter with Parmesan cheese and serve warm.

## Dill Baby Carrots

Prep time: 5 minutes | Cook time: 12 minutes | Serves 4

2 tbsps. olive oil
1 pound (454 g) baby carrots
1 tbsp. honey

1 tsp. dried dill
Salt and black pepper, to taste

1. Preheat the air fryer oven to 350ºF (177ºC).
2. Add the carrots in a large bowl. Place the olive oil, dill, honey, salt, and pepper and toss to coat well.
3. Put the carrots in the air fryer basket. Then place the air fryer basket onto the baking pan, and slide the baking pan into Rack Position 2, select Convection Broil and set time to 12 minutes, until crisp-tender. Stir the carrots once during the cooking time.
4. Serve hot.

## Blistered Shishito Peppers with Dipping Sauce

Prep time: 10 minutes | Cook time: 6 minutes | Serves 4

**Dipping Sauce:**
1 cup sour cream
1 green onion (white and green parts), finely chopped
1 clove garlic, minced
2 tbsps. fresh lemon juice
**Peppers:**
1 tbsp. vegetable oil

1 tsp. toasted sesame oil
8 ounces (227 g) shishito peppers
½ tsp. toasted sesame seeds
¼ to ½ tsp. red pepper flakes
Kosher salt and black pepper, to taste

1. Stir all the ingredients for the dipping sauce to combine in a small bowl. Cover and refrigerate until serving time.
2. Preheat the air fryer oven to 400ºF (204ºC).
3. Toss the peppers with the vegetable oil in a medium bowl. Place the peppers in the air fryer basket. Then place the air fryer basket onto the baking pan, and slide the baking pan into Rack Position 2, select Air Fry and set time to 6 minutes, or until peppers are lightly charred in spots, stirring the peppers halfway through the cooking time.
4. Take the peppers to a serving bowl. Drizzle with the sesame oil and toss to coat well. Sprinkle with salt and pepper to taste. Scatter with the red pepper and sesame seeds and toss again.
5. Serve hot with the dipping sauce.

Honey Eggplant with Yogurt, page 35

Breaded Zucchini Chips, page 33

Healthy Tahini Kale, page 35

Dill Baby Carrots, page 30

## Creamy Corn Egg Casserole

Prep time: 5 minutes | Cook time: 15 minutes | Serves 4

Nonstick cooking spray
2 cups frozen yellow corn
1 egg, beaten
½ cup grated Swiss or Havarti cheese
½ cup light cream
¼ cup milk
3 tbsps. flour
2 tbsps. butter, cut into cubes
Pinch salt
Freshly ground black pepper, to taste

1. Preheat the air fryer oven to 320ºF (160ºC). Spray a baking pan lightly with nonstick cooking spray.
2. In a medium bowl, stir together the remaining ingredients except the butter until well incorporated.
3. Take the mixture to the prepared baking pan and sprinkle with the butter cubes.
4. Slide the baking pan into Rack Position 1, select Convection Bake and set time to 15 minutes, until the top is golden brown and a toothpick inserted in the center comes out clean.
5. Allow the casserole to cool for 5 minutes before slicing into wedges and serving.

## Mini Prosciutto Mushroom Pizza

Prep time: 10 minutes | Cook time: 5 minutes | Serves 3

3 tbsps. olive oil
3 portobello mushroom caps, cleaned and scooped
12 slices prosciutto
3 tbsps. tomato sauce
3 tbsps. shredded Mozzarella cheese
Pinch of salt
Pinch of dried Italian seasonings

1. Preheat the air fryer oven to 330ºF (166ºC).
2. Coat both sides of the portobello mushrooms with a drizzle of olive oil, then season with salt and the Italian seasonings on the insides.
3. By using a knife, spread the tomato sauce evenly over the mushroom, before putting the Mozzarella on top.
4. Arrange the portobello in the air fryer basket.
5. Then place the air fryer basket onto the baking pan, and slide the baking pan into Rack Position 2, select Convection Broil and set time to 1 minutes. Remove from the air fryer oven and adding the prosciutto slices on top.
6. Air fry for an additional 4 minutes.
7. Serve hot.

## Zucchinis and Carrots

Prep time: 10 minutes | Cook time: 45 minutes | Serves 4

¼ cup olive oil
4 zucchinis, sliced thickly
4 carrots, cut into chunks
2 potatoes, peeled and cubed
1 head broccoli, cut into florets
1 tbsp. dry onion powder
Salt and ground black pepper, to taste

1. Preheat the air fryer oven to 400ºF (204ºC).
2. In the air fryer basket, mix all the ingredients and combine well.
3. Then place the air fryer basket onto the baking pan, and slide the baking pan into Rack Position 2, select Air Fry and set time to 45 minutes, ensuring the vegetables are tender and the sides have browned before serving.

## Stuffed Squash with Grape Tomatoes and Pepper

Prep time: 5 minutes | Cook time: 30 minutes | Serves 4

2 tsps. olive oil, divided
1 pound (454 g) butternut squash, ends trimmed
6 grape tomatoes, halved
1 poblano pepper, cut
into strips
¼ cup grated Mozzarella cheese
Salt and black pepper, to taste

1. Preheat the air fryer oven to 350ºF (177ºC).
2. On a flat work surface, cut the squash in half lengthwise with a large knife. This recipe just needs half of the squash. Spoon out the flesh to make room for the stuffing. Brush the squash half lightly with 1 tsp. of olive oil.
3. Arrange the squash half in the air fryer basket. Then place the air fryer basket onto the baking pan, and slide the baking pan into Rack Position 2, select Convection Broil and set time to 15 minutes.
4. At the same time, thoroughly combine the tomatoes, poblano pepper, remaining 1 tsp. of olive oil, salt, and pepper in a bowl.
5. Remove the basket and scoop the tomato mixture into the squash. Take the squash back to the air fryer oven and broil for 12 minutes until the tomatoes are tender.
6. Sprinkle the Mozzarella cheese on top and continue cooking for 3 minutes, or until the cheese is melted.
7. Let rest for 5 minutes before serving.

## Yogurt Oatmeal Stuffed Peppers

Prep time: 15 minutes | Cook time: 6 minutes | Serves 2 to 4

| | |
|---|---|
| 2 cups cooked oatmeal | 2 tbsps. cooked chick |
| 2 large bell peppers, halved lengthwise, deseeded | peas |
| | 1 tsp. ground cumin |
| | ½ tsp. paprika |
| ¼ cup yogurt | ½ tsp. salt or to taste |
| 2 tbsps. cooked kidney beans | ¼ tsp. black pepper powder |

1. Preheat the air fryer oven to 355ºF (179ºC).
2. Place the bell peppers, cut-side down, in the air fryer basket. Then place the air fryer basket onto the baking pan, and slide the baking pan into Rack Position 2, select Air Fry and set time to 2 minutes.
3. Remove the peppers from the air fryer oven and allow to cool.
4. Combine the remaining ingredients in a bowl.
5. Distribute the mixture evenly and use each portion to stuff a pepper.
6. Take the stuffed peppers back to the air fryer oven and continue to air fry for about 4 minutes.
7. Serve warm.

## Breaded Zucchini Chips

Prep time: 5 minutes | Cook time: 14 minutes | Serves 4

| | |
|---|---|
| Cooking spray | 2 tbsps. grated Parmesan |
| 2 egg whites | cheese |
| 2 medium zucchinis, sliced | ¼ tsp. garlic powder |
| | Salt and black pepper, to |
| ½ cup seasoned bread crumbs | taste |

1. Preheat the air fryer oven to 400ºF (204ºC). Spray the air fryer basket lightly with cooking spray.
2. Beat the egg whites with salt and pepper in a bowl. In a separate bowl, thoroughly combine the Parmesan cheese, bread crumbs, and garlic powder.
3. Dredge the zucchini slices in the egg white, then coat in the bread crumb mixture.
4. Put the zucchini slices in the air fryer basket. Then place the air fryer basket onto the baking pan, and slide the baking pan into Rack Position 2, select Air Fry and set time to 14 minutes, flipping the zucchini halfway through.
5. Transfer the zucchini from the oven to a plate and serve warm.

## Breaded Golden Pickles

Prep time: 10 minutes | Cook time: 15 minutes | Serves 4

| | |
|---|---|
| Cooking spray | 2 tbsps. cornstarch plus |
| 14 dill pickles, sliced | 3 tbsps. water |
| ¼ cup flour | ½ tsp. paprika |
| 6 tbsps. panko bread crumbs | ⅛ tsp. baking powder |
| | Pinch of salt |

1. Preheat the air fryer oven to 400ºF (204ºC).
2. Drain any excess moisture out of the dill pickles on a paper towel.
3. Combine the flour, baking powder and salt in a bowl.
4. Throw in the cornstarch and water mixture and mix well with a whisk.
5. In a shallow dish, add the panko bread crumbs along with the paprika. Mix thoroughly.
6. Dip the pickles in the flour batter, then coat in the bread crumbs. Spray all the pickles lightly with the cooking spray.
7. Transfer to the air fryer basket. Then place the air fryer basket onto the baking pan, and slide the baking pan into Rack Position 2, select Air Fry and set time to 6 minutes, until golden brown.
8. Serve hot.

## Herbed Falafel

Prep time: 15 minutes | Cook time: 15 minutes | Serves 8

| | |
|---|---|
| Cooking spray | 3 cloves garlic |
| 2 cups chickpeas, drained and rinsed | 3 tbsps. flour |
| | 1 tbsp. juice from freshly squeezed lemon |
| 1 tsp. cumin seeds | |
| ¼ cup chopped parsley | ½ tsp. coriander seeds |
| ¼ cup chopped coriander | ½ tsp. red pepper flakes |
| ½ onion, diced | ½ tsp. salt |

1. Fry the cumin and coriander seeds over medium heat in a pan until fragrant.
2. Grind with a mortar and pestle.
3. Add all the ingredients, except for the cooking spray, in a food processor and blend until a fine consistency is achieved.
4. With your hands, mold the mixture into falafels and spray with the cooking spray.
5. Preheat the air fryer oven to 400ºF (204ºC).
6. Take the falafels to the air fryer basket in one layer.
7. Place the air fryer basket onto the baking pan, and slide the baking pan into Rack Position 2, select Air Fry and set time to 15 minutes, serving when they turn golden brown.

## Simple Potato Croquettes

Prep time: 15 minutes | Cook time: 15 minutes | Serves 10

| | |
|---|---|
| 2 tbsps. vegetable oil | 1 flax egg |
| 2 cups boiled potatoes, mashed | 1 tbsp. flour |
| ¼ cup nutritional yeast | 2 tbsps. chopped chives |
| ¼ cup bread crumbs | Salt and ground black pepper, to taste |

1. Preheat the air fryer oven to 400ºF (204ºC).
2. Combine the nutritional yeast, potatoes, flax egg, flour, and chives in a bowl. Season with salt and pepper as desired.
3. Mix the vegetable oil and bread crumbs in a separate bowl to achieve a crumbly consistency.
4. Form the potato mixture into small balls and dip each one into the bread crumb mixture.
5. Arrange the croquettes inside the air fryer basket. Then place the air fryer basket onto the baking pan, and slide the baking pan into Rack Position 2, select Air Fry and set time to 15 minutes, ensuring the croquettes turn golden brown.
6. Serve hot.

## Lush Vegetable Salad

Prep time: 15 minutes | Cook time: 10 minutes | Serves 4

| | |
|---|---|
| 1 tbsp. extra-virgin olive oil | 6 cloves garlic, crushed |
| 6 plum tomatoes, halved | ½ lemon, juiced |
| 2 large red onions, sliced | 1 tbsp. baby capers |
| 4 long red peppers, sliced | 1 tsp. paprika |
| 2 yellow peppers, sliced | Salt and ground black pepper, to taste |

1. Preheat the air fryer oven to 420ºF (216ºC).
2. In a large bowl, place the tomatoes, onions, peppers, and garlic and cover with the extra-virgin olive oil, paprika, and lemon juice. Season with salt and pepper as desired.
3. Line the inside of the air fryer basket with aluminum foil. Add the vegetables inside, then place the air fryer basket onto the baking pan, and slide the baking pan into Rack Position 2, select Air Fry and set time to 10 minutes.
4. Transfer the vegetables to a salad bowl and serve with the baby capers.

## Thyme Maitake Mushrooms

Prep time: 5 minutes | Cook time: 15 minutes | Serves 2

| | |
|---|---|
| 2 tsps. toasted sesame oil | 1 garlic clove, minced |
| 3 tsps. vegetable oil, divided | 1 tbsp. soy sauce |
| | ½ tsp. finely chopped fresh thyme leaves |
| 7 ounces (198 g) maitake (hen of the woods) mushrooms | ½ tsp. sesame seeds |
| | ½ tsp. flaky sea salt |

1. Preheat the air fryer oven to 300ºF (149ºC).
2. In a small bowl, whisk together the soy sauce, sesame oil, 1 tsp. of vegetable oil, and garlic.
3. Spread the mushrooms in the air fryer basket in a single layer. Drizzle the soy sauce mixture over the mushrooms. Then place the air fryer basket onto the baking pan, and slide the baking pan into Rack Position 2, select Air Fry and set time to 10 minutes.
4. Flip the mushrooms and scatter the sea salt, sesame seeds, and thyme leaves on top. Drizzle the remaining 2 tsps. of vegetable oil all over. Broil for another 5 minutes.
5. Remove the mushrooms from the oven to a plate and serve hot.

## Simple Broccoli Gratin

Prep time: 5 minutes | Cook time: 12 minutes | Serves 2

| | |
|---|---|
| Olive oil spray | 1 tbsp. all-purpose or gluten-free flour |
| ½ tbsp. olive oil | 1 tbsp. grated Parmesan cheese |
| 2 cups roughly chopped broccoli florets | ½ tsp. ground sage |
| ⅓ cup fat-free milk | ¼ tsp. kosher salt |
| 6 tbsps. shredded Cheddar cheese | ⅛ tsp. freshly ground black pepper |
| 2 tbsps. panko bread crumbs | |

1. Preheat the air fryer oven to 330ºF (166ºC). Spray a baking pan lightly with olive oil spray.
2. In a medium bowl, mix the milk, flour, olive oil, sage, salt, and pepper and whisk to combine. Stir in the broccoli florets, bread crumbs, Cheddar cheese, and Parmesan cheese and toss to coat well.
3. Place the broccoli mixture into the prepared baking pan.
4. Slide the baking pan into Rack Position 1, select Convection Bake and set time to 12 minutes, until the top is golden brown and the broccoli is soft.
5. Serve hot.

## Simple Macaroni Balls

Prep time: 10 minutes | Cook time: 10 minutes | Serves 2

2 cups leftover macaroni
3 large eggs
1 cup shredded Cheddar cheese
1 cup bread crumbs
1 cup milk
½ cup flour
½ tsp. salt
¼ tsp. black pepper

1. Preheat the air fryer oven to 365ºF (185ºC).
2. Combine the leftover macaroni and shredded cheese in a bowl.
3. Pour the flour in a separate bowl. Place the bread crumbs in a third bowl. Finally, mix the eggs and milk with a whisk in a fourth bowl.
4. With an ice-cream scoop, create balls from the macaroni mixture. Coat them in the flour, then in the egg mixture, and lastly in the bread crumbs.
5. Place the balls in the air fryer basket. Then place the air fryer basket onto the baking pan, and slide the baking pan into Rack Position 2, select Air Fry and set time to 10 minutes, giving them an good stir. Ensure they crisp up nicely.
6. Serve warm.

## Healthy Tahini Kale

Prep time: 5 minutes | Cook time: 15 minutes | Serves 2 to 4

**Dressing:**
2 tbsps. olive oil
¼ cup tahini
¼ cup fresh lemon juice
1 tsp. sesame seeds
½ tsp. garlic powder
¼ tsp. cayenne pepper
**Kale:**
4 cups packed torn kale leaves (stems and ribs removed and leaves torn into palm-size pieces)
Kosher salt and freshly ground black pepper, to taste

1. Preheat the air fryer oven to 350ºF (177ºC).
2. Make the dressing: In a large bowl, whisk together the tahini, lemon juice, olive oil, sesame seeds, garlic powder, and cayenne pepper until well mixed.
3. Place the kale and massage the dressing thoroughly all over the leaves. Season with the salt and pepper to taste.
4. Arrange the kale in the air fryer basket. Then place the air fryer basket onto the baking pan, and slide the baking pan into Rack Position 2, select Air Fry and set time to 15 minutes, until the leaves are slightly wilted and crispy.
5. Transfer the kale from the oven and serve on a plate.

## Garlic Broccoli

Prep time: 5 minutes | Cook time: 10 minutes | Serves 2

2 tbsps. Asian hot chili oil
12 ounces (340 g) broccoli florets
1 tsp. ground Sichuan peppercorns (or black pepper)
2 garlic cloves, finely
chopped
1 (2-inch) piece fresh ginger, peeled and finely chopped
Kosher salt and freshly ground black pepper

1. Preheat the air fryer oven to 375ºF (191ºC).
2. In a mixing bowl, toss the broccoli florets with the chili oil, Sichuan peppercorns, ginger, garlic, salt, and pepper until well coated.
3. Take the broccoli florets to the air fryer basket. Then place the air fryer basket onto the baking pan, and slide the baking pan into Rack Position 2, select Convection Broil and set time to 10 minutes, flipping halfway through.
4. Transfer the broccoli from the oven and serve on a plate.

## Honey Eggplant with Yogurt

Prep time: 5 minutes | Cook time: 15 minutes | Serves 2

2 tbsps. vegetable oil
1 medium eggplant, quartered and cut crosswise into ½-inch-thick slices
½ cup plain yogurt (not Greek)
1 garlic clove, grated
2 tbsps. harissa paste
2 tsps. honey
Kosher salt and freshly ground black pepper, to taste

1. Preheat the air fryer oven to 400ºF (204ºC).
2. In a large bowl, toss the eggplant slices with the vegetable oil, salt, and pepper until well coated.
3. Place the eggplant slices in the air fryer basket. Then place the air fryer basket onto the baking pan, and slide the baking pan into Rack Position 2, select Air Fry and set time to 15 minutes, until golden brown. Flip the eggplant two to three times during the cooking time.
4. Meanwhile, make the yogurt sauce: in a small bowl, whisk together the yogurt, harissa paste, and garlic.
5. Spread the yogurt sauce on a platter, and arrange the eggplant slices over the top. Drizzle the honey and serve.

## Basic Asparagus

Prep time: 5 minutes | Cook time: 5 minutes | Serves 4

| | |
|---|---|
| 1 tbsp. olive oil | trimmed |
| 1 pound (454 g) fresh asparagus spears, | Salt and ground black pepper, to taste |

1. Preheat the air fryer oven to 375ºF (191ºC).
2. Mix all the ingredients and transfer them to the air fryer basket.
3. Then place the air fryer basket onto the baking pan, and slide the baking pan into Rack Position 2, select Air Fry and set time to 5 minutes, until tender.
4. Serve immediately.

## Air Fried Green Beans with Shallot

Prep time: 10 minutes | Cook time: 10 minutes | Serves 4

| | |
|---|---|
| 2 tbsps. olive oil | peeled and cut into |
| 1½ pounds (680 g) French green beans, stems removed and blanched | quarters |
| | 1 tbsp. salt |
| | ½ tsp. ground white pepper |
| ½ pound (227 g) shallots, | |

1. Preheat the air fryer oven to 400ºF (204ºC).
2. In a bowl, coat the green beans and shallots with the remaining ingredients.
3. Transfer to the air fryer basket. Then place the air fryer basket onto the baking pan, and slide the baking pan into Rack Position 2, select Air Fry and set time to 10 minutes, making sure the green beans appear a light brown color.
4. Serve warm.

## Buttered Broccoli with Shallot

Prep time: 5 minutes | Cook time: 4 minutes | Serves 4

| | |
|---|---|
| 2 tbsps. olive oil | 1 medium shallot, minced |
| 1 pound (454 g) broccoli florets | 2 tbsps. unsalted butter, melted |
| ¼ cup grated Parmesan cheese | 2 tsps. minced garlic |

1. Preheat the air fryer oven to 360ºF (182ºC).
2. In a medium bowl, combine the broccoli florets with the shallot, olive oil, butter, garlic, and Parmesan cheese and toss until the broccoli florets are well coated.
3. Place the broccoli florets in the air fryer basket in a single layer. Then place the air fryer basket onto the baking pan, and slide the baking pan into Rack Position 2, select Convection Broil and set time to 4 minutes.
4. Serve hot.

## Nutmeg-Spiced Acorn Squash

Prep time: 5 minutes | Cook time: 15 minutes | Serves 2

| | |
|---|---|
| 1 tsp. coconut oil | Few dashes of ground nutmeg |
| 1 medium acorn squash, halved crosswise and deseeded | Few dashes of ground cinnamon |
| 1 tsp. light brown sugar | |

1. Preheat the air fryer oven to 325ºF (163ºC).
2. Rub the cut sides of the acorn squash with coconut oil on a clean work surface. Sprinkle with the brown sugar, cinnamon, and nutmeg.
3. Arrange the squash halves in the air fryer basket, cut-side up. Then place the air fryer basket onto the baking pan, and slide the baking pan into Rack Position 2, select Air Fry and set time to 15 minutes, until just soft when pierced in the center with a paring knife.
4. Let cool for 5 to 10 minutes and serve warm.

## Sriracha Breaded Cauliflower

Prep time: 5 minutes | Cook time: 17 minutes | Serves 4

| | |
|---|---|
| 4 cups cauliflower florets | melted |
| 1 cup bread crumbs | ¼ cup sriracha sauce |
| ¼ cup vegan butter, | 1 tsp. salt |

1. Preheat the air fryer oven to 375ºF (191ºC).
2. In a bowl, mix the sriracha and vegan butter and pour this mixture over the cauliflower, taking care to coat each floret well.
3. Combine the bread crumbs and salt in a separate bowl.
4. Dip the cauliflower florets in the bread crumbs, coating each one well. Put the cauliflower in the air fryer basket. Then place the air fryer basket onto the baking pan, and slide the baking pan into Rack Position 2, select Air Fry and set time to 17 minutes.
5. Serve warm.

## Marinara Mushroom Pepperoni Pizza

Prep time: 5 minutes | Cook time: 18 minutes | Serves 4

| | |
|---|---|
| 4 tsps. olive oil | 10 slices sugar-free |
| 4 large portobello | pepperoni |
| mushrooms, stems | 1 cup shredded |
| removed | Mozzarella cheese |
| 1 cup marinara sauce | |

1. Preheat the air fryer oven to 375ºF (191ºC).
2. Coat each mushroom cap with the olive oil, one tsp. for each cap.
3. Arrange the mushrooms on a baking pan, stem-side down. Slide the baking pan into Rack Position 1, select Convection Bake and set time to 8 minutes.
4. Remove from the air fryer oven and distribute the marinara sauce, Mozzarella cheese and pepperoni evenly among the caps.
5. Bake for an additional 10 minutes until browned.
6. Serve warm.

## Breaded Brussels Sprouts with Sage

Prep time: 5 minutes | Cook time: 15 minutes | Serves 4

| | |
|---|---|
| 2 tbsps. canola oil | 2 tbsps. grated Grana |
| 1 pound (454 g) Brussels | Padano cheese |
| sprouts, halved | 1 tbsp. chopped sage |
| 1 cup bread crumbs | 1 tbsp. paprika |

1. Preheat the air fryer oven to 400ºF (204ºC). Line the baking pan with parchment paper.
2. Thoroughly mix the bread crumbs, cheese, and paprika in a small bowl. Place the Brussels sprouts in a large bowl, and drizzle the canola oil over the top. Scatter with the bread crumb mixture and toss to coat well.
3. Arrange the Brussels sprouts in the air fryer basket. Then place the air fryer basket onto the baking pan, and slide the baking pan into Rack Position 2, select Air Fry and set time to 15 minutes. Flip a few times during the cooking time to ensure even cooking.
4. Take the Brussels sprouts to a plate and scatter the sage on top before serving.

## Air Fryer Butternut Squash and Parsnip

Prep time: 5 minutes | Cook time: 16 minutes | Serves 2

| | |
|---|---|
| 2 tsps. olive oil | into wedges |
| 1 parsnip, sliced | 1 tbsp. chopped fresh |
| 1 cup sliced butternut | thyme |
| squash | Salt and black pepper, to |
| ½ chopped celery stalk | taste |
| 1 small red onion, cut | |

1. Preheat the air fryer oven to 380ºF (193ºC).
2. In a large bowl, toss all the ingredients until the vegetables are well coated.
3. Take the vegetables to the air fryer basket. Then place the air fryer basket onto the baking pan, and slide the baking pan into Rack Position 2, select Air Fry and set time to 16 minutes, stirring the vegetables halfway through, or until the vegetables are golden brown and soft.
4. Transfer the vegetables from the oven and serve hot.

## Baked Potatoes with Chives

Prep time: 5 minutes | Cook time: 35 minutes | Serves 4

| | |
|---|---|
| Olive oil spray | chives |
| 4 (7-ounce / 198-g) | ½ tsp. kosher salt, |
| russet potatoes, rinsed | divided |
| ½ cup 2% plain Greek | Freshly ground black |
| yogurt | pepper, to taste |
| ¼ cup minced fresh | |

1. Preheat the air fryer oven to 400ºF (204ºC).
2. Pat the potatoes dry with a paper towel and pierce them all over by using a fork. Spray the potatoes lightly with olive oil spray. Season with ¼ tsp. of the salt.
3. Place the potatoes in the baking pan. Slide the baking pan into Rack Position 1, select Convection Bake and set time to 35 minutes, until a knife can be inserted into the center of the potatoes easily.
4. Transfer from the oven and split open the potatoes. Place the yogurt, chives, the remaining ¼ tsp. of salt, and black pepper on top. Serve immediately.

## Spicy Corn Pakodas

Prep time: 10 minutes | Cook time: 8 minutes |
Serves 5

Cooking spray
10 cobs baby corn,
blanched
1 cup flour
¼ cup water

½ tsp. curry powder
½ tsp. red chili powder
¼ tsp. turmeric powder
¼ tsp. baking soda
¼ tsp. salt

1. Preheat the air fryer oven to 425ºF (218ºC).
2. Cover the air fryer baske with aluminum foil and
   spray lightly with the cooking spray.
3. In a large bowl, mix all the ingredients, save for the
   corn. Stir with a whisk until combined well.
4. Coat the corn in the batter and place inside the air
   fryer basket.
5. Then place the air fryer basket onto the baking pan,
   and slide the baking pan into Rack Position 2, select
   Air Fry and set time to 8 minutes, until a golden
   brown color is achieved.
6. Serve warm.

## Broiled Potatoes with Rosemary

Prep time: 5 minutes | Cook time: 20 minutes |
Serves 4

2 tbsps. olive oil
1½ pounds (680 g) small
red potatoes, cut into
1-inch cubes
2 tbsps. minced fresh
rosemary

1 tbsp. minced garlic
1 tsp. salt, plus additional
as needed
½ tsp. freshly ground
black pepper, plus
additional as needed

1. Preheat the air fryer oven to 400ºF (204ºC).
2. In a large bowl, toss the potato cubes with the olive
   oil, rosemary, garlic, salt, and pepper until well
   coated.
3. Put the potato cubes in the air fryer basket in a single
   layer. Then place the air fryer basket onto the baking
   pan, and slide the baking pan into Rack Position 2,
   select Convection Broil and set time to 20 minutes.
4. Transfer the potatoes from the oven to a plate.
   Taste and season with additional salt and pepper as
   needed. Serve warm.

## Cauliflower and Chickpea Flatbread with Avocado Mash

Prep time: 10 minutes | Cook time: 25 minutes |
Serves 4

1 tbsp. extra-virgin olive
oil
1 medium head
cauliflower, cut into
florets
1 can chickpeas, drained

and rinsed
4 flatbreads, toasted
2 ripe avocados, mashed
2 tbsps. lemon juice
Salt and ground black
pepper, to taste

1. Preheat the air fryer oven to 425ºF (218ºC).
2. Mix the chickpeas, cauliflower, lemon juice and olive
   oil in a bowl. Season with salt and pepper as desired.
3. Place inside the air fryer basket. Then place the
   air fryer basket onto the baking pan, and slide the
   baking pan into Rack Position 2, select Air Fry and set
   time to 25 minutes.
4. Spread on top of the flatbread along with the
   mashed avocado. Scatter with more pepper and salt
   and serve warm.

## Broiled Squash with Goat Cheese

Prep time: 5 minutes | Cook time: 20 minutes |
Serves 2

2 tbsps. olive oil
1 pound (454 g) butternut
squash, cut into wedges
1 cup crumbled goat

cheese
1 tbsp. maple syrup
1 tbsp. dried rosemary
Salt, to salt

1. Preheat the air fryer oven to 350ºF (177ºC).
2. In a large bowl, toss the squash wedges with the
   olive oil, rosemary, and salt until well coated.
3. Take the squash wedges to the air fryer basket,
   spreading them out in as even a layer as possible.
4. Then place the air fryer basket onto the baking pan,
   and slide the baking pan into Rack Position 2, select
   Convection Broil and set time to 10 minutes. Flip the
   squash and cook for an additional 10 minutes until
   golden brown.
5. Scatter the goat cheese on top and drizzle with the
   maple syrup. Serve warm.

## Homemade Cabbage

Prep time: 5 minutes | Cook time: 7 minutes | Serves 4

| | |
|---|---|
| 1 tbsp. olive oil | 1 tsp. garlic powder |
| 1 head cabbage, sliced into 1-inch-thick ribbons | 1 tsp. salt |
| 1 tsp. red pepper flakes | 1 tsp. freshly ground black pepper |

1. Preheat the air fryer oven to 350ºF (177ºC).
2. In a large mixing bowl, toss the cabbage with the olive oil, garlic powder, red pepper flakes, salt, and pepper until well coated.
3. Place the cabbage in the air fryer basket. Then place the air fryer basket onto the baking pan, and slide the baking pan into Rack Position 2, select Convection Broil and set time to 7 minutes. Gently flip the cabbage with tongs halfway through the cooking time.
4. Transfer the cabbage from the oven to a plate and serve hot.

## Creamy Potatoes with Olives

Prep time: 15 minutes | Cook time: 40 minutes | Serves 1

| | |
|---|---|
| 1 tsp. olive oil | Dollop of cream cheese |
| 1 medium russet potatoes, scrubbed and peeled | 1 tbsp. Kalamata olives |
| Dollop of butter | 1 tbsp. chopped chives |
| | ¼ tsp. onion powder |
| | ⅛ tsp. salt |

1. Preheat the air fryer oven to 400ºF (204ºC).
2. Coat the potatoes with the onion powder, salt, olive oil, and butter in a bowl.
3. Take to the air fryer basket. Then place the air fryer basket onto the baking pan, and slide the baking pan into Rack Position 2, select Air Fry and set time to 40 minutes. turning the potatoes over at the halfway point.
4. Transfer the potatoes from the air fryer oven and top with the cream cheese, Kalamata olives and chives. Serve warm.

## Broiled Broccoli

Prep time: 5 minutes | Cook time: 15 minutes | Serves 6

| | |
|---|---|
| 2 tsps. extra-virgin olive oil, plus more for coating | 1 clove garlic, minced |
| 2 heads broccoli, cut into florets | ½ tsp. lemon juice |
| | 1 tsp. salt |
| | ½ tsp. black pepper |

1. Cover the baking pan with aluminum foil and coat with a light brushing of oil.
2. Preheat the air fryer oven to 375ºF (191ºC).
3. Combine all the ingredients, except the lemon juice in a bowl, and transfer to the air fryer basket. Then place the air fryer basket onto the baking pan, and slide the baking pan into Rack Position 2, select Convection Broil and set time to 15 minutes.
4. Serve warm with the lemon juice.

## Pesto Gnocchi with Onion

Prep time: 10 minutes | Cook time: 15 minutes | Serves 4

| | |
|---|---|
| 1 tbsp. extra-virgin olive oil | 1 medium onion, chopped |
| 1 (1-pound / 454-g) package gnocchi | ⅓ cup grated Parmesan cheese |
| 1 (8-ounce / 227-g) jar pesto | 3 cloves garlic, minced |

1. Preheat the air fryer oven to 340ºF (171ºC).
2. Combine the onion, garlic, and gnocchi in a large bowl, and drizzle with the olive oil. Mix thoroughly.
3. Take the mixture to the air fryer basket. Then place the air fryer basket onto the baking pan, and slide the baking pan into Rack Position 2, select Air Fry and set time to 15 minutes, stirring sometimes, making sure the gnocchi become light brown and crispy.
4. Toss in the pesto and Parmesan cheese.
5. Serve hot.

## Brazilian Chicken

Prep time: 5 minutes | Cook time: 20 minutes | Serves 4

| | |
|---|---|
| 2 tbsps. olive oil | 1 tsp. dried parsley |
| 1½ pounds (680 g) chicken drumsticks | 1 tsp. ground turmeric |
| ¼ cup fresh lime juice | ½ tsp. coriander seeds |
| 1 tsp. cumin seeds | ½ tsp. cayenne pepper |
| 1 tsp. dried oregano | 1 tsp. kosher salt |
| | ½ tsp. black peppercorns |

1. Combine the cumin, oregano, parsley, turmeric, coriander seeds, salt, peppercorns, and cayenne in a clean coffee grinder or spice mill. Process until finely ground.
2. Combine the ground spices with the lime juice and oil in a small bowl. Put the chicken in a resealable plastic bag. Add the marinade, seal, and massage until the chicken is well coated. Marinate at room temperature for about 30 minutes or in the refrigerator for up to 24 hours.
3. Preheat the air fryer oven to 400ºF (204ºC).
4. Arrange the drumsticks skin-side up in the air fryer basket. Then place the air fryer basket onto the baking pan, and slide the baking pan into Rack Position 2, select Air Fry and set time to 20 minutes, flipping the drumsticks halfway through the cooking time. Use a meat thermometer to ensure that the chicken has reached an internal temperature of 165ºF (74ºC). Serve hot.

## Parmesan Breaded Chicken

Prep time: 10 minutes | Cook time: 20 minutes | Serves 4

| | |
|---|---|
| Olive oil spray | cheese |
| 4 boneless, skinless chicken breasts, thin cut | 2 tbsps. lemon juice |
| 1 egg | 2 tsps. minced garlic |
| ½ cup whole-wheat bread crumbs | ½ tsp. salt |
| ¼ cup grated Parmesan | ½ tsp. freshly ground black pepper |

1. In a medium bowl, whisk together the egg, lemon juice, garlic, salt, and pepper. Add the chicken breasts, cover, and refrigerate for up to 1 hour.
2. Combine the bread crumbs and Parmesan cheese in a shallow bowl.
3. Preheat the air fryer oven to 360ºF (182ºC). Spray the baking pan lightly with olive oil spray.
4. Transfer the chicken breasts from the egg mixture, then dredge them in the bread crumb mixture, and arrange in the baking pan in a single layer. Spritz the chicken breasts lightly with olive oil spray. You may need to cook the chicken in batches.
5. Slide the baking pan into Rack Position 1, select Convection Bake and set time to 8 minutes. Flip the chicken over, lightly spritz with olive oil spray, and bake for an additional 7 to 12 minutes, until the chicken reaches an internal temperature of 165ºF (74ºC).
6. Serve hot.

## Curried Chicken Satay with Peanut Sauce

Prep time: 12 minutes | Cook time: 8 minutes | Serves 4

| | |
|---|---|
| 2 tbsps. olive oil | 2 cloves garlic, minced |
| 1 pound (454 g) chicken tenders | 3 tbsps. low-sodium soy sauce |
| ½ cup crunchy peanut butter | 2 tbsps. lemon juice |
| ⅓ cup chicken broth | 1 tsp. curry powder |

1. Preheat the air fryer oven to 390ºF (199ºC).
2. Combine the peanut butter, chicken broth, soy sauce, lemon juice, garlic, olive oil, and curry powder in a medium bowl, and mix well with a wire whisk until smooth. Take 2 tbsps. of this mixture to a small bowl. Place remaining sauce into a serving bowl and set aside.
3. Put the chicken tenders to the bowl with the 2 tbsps. sauce and stir to coat well. Let rest for a few minutes to marinate, then run a bamboo skewer through each chicken tender lengthwise.
4. Arrange the chicken the air fryer basket. Then place the air fryer basket onto the baking pan, and slide the baking pan into Rack Position 2, select Air Fry and set time to 8 minutes, until the chicken reaches 165ºF (74ºC) on a meat thermometer. Repeat with the remaining chicken. Serve the chicken with the reserved sauce.

## Italian Chicken Strips

Prep time: 15 minutes | Cook time: 10 minutes | Serves 4

Cooking spray
2 whole boneless, skinless chicken breasts, halved lengthwise
3 cups finely crushed potato chips
1 cup Italian dressing
1 large egg, beaten
1 tbsp. dried dill weed
1 tbsp. garlic powder

1. Combine the chicken and Italian dressing in a large resealable bag. Seal the bag and refrigerate to marinate at least 1 hour.
2. Stir together the potato chips, dill, and garlic powder in a shallow dish. Put the beaten egg in a second shallow dish.
3. Transfer the chicken from the marinade. Roll the chicken pieces in the egg and the potato chip mixture, coating well.
4. Preheat the air fryer oven to 325ºF (163ºC). Line the baking pan with parchment paper.
5. Arrange the coated chicken on the parchment and spray lightly with cooking spray.
6. Slide the baking pan into Rack Position 1, select Convection Bake and set time to 5 minutes. Flip the chicken, spray it with cooking spray, and bake for another 5 minutes until the outsides are crispy and the insides are no longer pink. Serve hot.

## Cheese Crusted Chicken with Potato

Prep time: 15 minutes | Cook time: 22 to 25 minutes | Serves 4

Cooking spray
2 whole boneless, skinless chicken breasts (about 1 pound / 454 g each), halved
1 large egg, beaten
1 cup instant potato flakes
¼ cup buttermilk
¼ cup grated Parmesan cheese
1 tsp. salt
½ tsp. freshly ground black pepper

1. Preheat the air fryer oven to 325ºF (163ºC). Line the baking pan with parchment paper.
2. Whisk the buttermilk and egg until blended in a shallow bowl. Stir together the potato flakes, cheese, salt, and pepper in another shallow bowl.
3. One at a time, dip the chicken pieces in the buttermilk mixture and the potato flake mixture, coating well.
4. Arrange the coated chicken on the parchment and spray lightly with cooking spray.
5. Slide the baking pan into Rack Position 1, select Convection Bake and set time to 15 minutes. Flip the chicken, spray lightly with cooking spray, and bake for another 7 to 10 minutes until the outside is crispy and the inside is no longer pink. Serve hot.

## Healthy Pomegranate-Glazed Chicken with Couscous Salad

Prep time: 25 minutes | Cook time: 20 minutes | Serves 4

Cooking spray
1 tbsp. extra-virgin olive oil
2 (12-ounce / 340-g) bone-in split chicken breasts, trimmed
¼ cup chicken broth
½ cup couscous
¼ cup water
2 ounces (57 g) cherry tomatoes, quartered
1 ounce (28 g) feta cheese, crumbled
1 scallion, white part minced, green part sliced thin on bias
3 tbsps. plus 2 tsps. pomegranate molasses
1 tbsp. minced fresh parsley
1 tsp. minced fresh thyme
½ tsp. ground cinnamon
Salt and ground black pepper, to taste

1. Preheat the air fryer oven to 350ºF (177ºC). Spray the air fryer basket lightly with cooking spray.
2. In a small bowl, combine 3 tbsps. of pomegranate molasses, cinnamon, thyme, and ⅛ tsp. of salt. Stir to mix well. Set it aside.
3. Arrange the chicken breasts in the air fryer basket, skin side down, and spray lightly with cooking spray. Season with salt and ground black pepper.
4. Place the air fryer basket onto the baking pan, and slide the baking pan into Rack Position 2, select Air Fry and set time to 10 minutes, then coat the chicken with half of pomegranate molasses mixture and flip. Air fry for another 5 minutes.
5. Coat the chicken with remaining pomegranate molasses mixture and flip. Air fry for 5 minutes more or until the internal temperature of the chicken breasts reaches at least 165ºF (74ºC).
6. At the same time, pour the broth and water in a pot and bring to a boil over medium-high heat. Place the couscous and season with salt. Cover and simmer for about 7 minutes or until the liquid is almost absorbed.
7. Mix the remaining ingredients, save for the cheese, with cooked couscous in a large bowl. Toss to combine well. Sprinkle with the feta cheese.
8. When the air frying is complete, transfer the chicken from the air fryer oven and let cool for 10 minutes. Serve with vegetable and couscous salad.

## Hoisin Turkey Meatballs

Prep time: 15 minutes | Cook time: 15 minutes | Serves 6

| | |
|---|---|
| Olive oil spray | sauce, divided |
| 1 pound (454 g) lean ground turkey | 1 tbsp. soy sauce |
| ½ cup whole-wheat panko bread crumbs | 2 tsps. minced garlic |
| | 1 tsp. sriracha |
| 1 egg, beaten | ⅛ tsp. salt |
| ¼ cup plus 1 tbsp. hoisin | ⅛ tsp. freshly ground black pepper |

1. Preheat the air fryer oven to 350ºF (177ºC). Spritz the air fryer basket with olive oil spray.
2. Mix together the turkey, panko bread crumbs, egg, soy sauce, 1 tbsp. of hoisin sauce, garlic, salt, and black pepper in a large bowl.
3. With a tablespoon, shape the mixture into 24 meatballs.
4. Combine the remaining ¼ cup of hoisin sauce and sriracha in a small bowl to make a glaze and set aside.
5. Arrange the meatballs in the air fryer basket in a single layer. You may need to cook them in batches.
6. Place the air fryer basket onto the baking pan, and slide the baking pan into Rack Position 2, select Air Fry and set time to 8 minutes. Brush the meatballs generously with the glaze and air fry for an additional 4 to 7 minutes, until cooked through. Serve hot.

## Korean Chicken Wings with Sesame Seeds

Prep time: 10 minutes | Cook time: 25 minutes | Serves 4

| | |
|---|---|
| **Wings:** | 2 tbsps. gochujang |
| 2 pounds (907 g) chicken wings | 1 tbsp. mayonnaise |
| | 1 tbsp. minced ginger |
| 1 tsp. salt | 1 tbsp. minced garlic |
| 1 tsp. ground black pepper | 1 tsp. agave nectar |
| | **For Garnish:** |
| **Sauce:** | ¼ cup chopped green onions |
| 1 tbsp. sesame oil | |
| 2 packets Splenda | 2 tsps. sesame seeds |

1. Preheat the air fryer oven to 400ºF (204ºC). Line a baking pan with aluminum foil, then place the rack on the pan.
2. Rub the chicken wings with salt and ground black pepper on a clean work surface, then arrange the seasoned wings on the rack.
3. Air fry for about 20 minutes or until the wings are well browned. Turn the wings halfway through. You may need to work in batches to avoid overcrowding.
4. At the same time, combine the ingredients for the sauce in a small bowl. Stir to combine well. Reserve half of the sauce in a separate bowl until ready to serve.
5. Transfer the air fried chicken wings from the air fryer oven and toss with remaining half of the sauce to coat well.
6. Put the wings back to the air fryer oven and air fry for another 5 minutes or until the internal temperature of the wings reaches at least 165ºF (74ºC).
7. Take the wings from the air fryer oven and place on a large plate. Scatter with sesame seeds and green onions. Serve hot with reserved sauce.

## Simple Chicken Skewers with Satay Sauce

Prep time: 5 minutes | Cook time: 10 minutes | Serves 4

| | |
|---|---|
| Cooking spray | fresh ginger |
| 4 (6-ounce / 170-g) boneless, skinless chicken breasts, sliced into strips | 1 tsp. sugar |
| | ½ tsp. hot sauce |
| | **For Serving:** |
| 1 tsp. sea salt | ¼ cup chopped cilantro leaves |
| 1 tsp. paprika | |
| **Satay Sauce:** | Red pepper flakes, to taste |
| ¼ cup creamy almond butter | Thinly sliced red, orange, or/and yellow bell peppers |
| 1 clove garlic, minced | |
| 2 tbsps. chicken broth | **Special Equipment:** |
| 1½ tbsps. coconut vinegar | 16 wooden or bamboo skewers, soaked in water for 15 minutes |
| 1 tsp. peeled and minced | |

1. Preheat the air fryer oven to 400ºF (204ºC). Spray the baking pan lightly with cooking spray.
2. Run the bamboo skewers through the chicken strips, then place the chicken skewers in the air fryer oven and season with salt and paprika.
3. Slide the baking pan into Rack Position 2, select Roast and set time to 10 minutes, until lightly browned on all sides. Turn the chicken skewers halfway during the cooking time.
4. At the same time, combine the ingredients for the sauce in a small bowl. Stir to mix well.
5. Take the cooked chicken skewers on a large plate, then place cilantro, sliced bell peppers, red pepper flakes on top. Serve hot with the sauce or just baste the sauce over before serving.

# Mirin Yakitori

Prep time: 10 minutes | Cook time: 15 minutes | Serves 4

Cooking spray
1½ pounds (680 g) boneless, skinless chicken thighs, cut into 1½-inch pieces, fat trimmed
½ cup soy sauce
½ cup mirin
¼ cup dry white wine

4 medium scallions, trimmed, cut into 1½-inch pieces
1 tbsp. light brown sugar
**Special Equipment:**
4 (4-inch) bamboo skewers, soaked in water for at least 30 minutes

1. In a saucepan, combine the mirin, dry white wine, soy sauce, and brown sugar. Bring to a boil over medium heat. Keep stirring.
2. Boil for 2 minutes more or until it has a thick consistency. Remove from the heat.
3. Preheat the air fryer oven to 400ºF (204ºC). Spray the baking pan lightly with cooking spray.
4. Run the bamboo skewers through the chicken pieces and scallions alternatively.
5. Place the skewers in the baking pan, then coat with mirin mixture on both sides. Spray lightly with cooking spray.
6. Slide the baking pan into Rack Position 2, select Roast and set time to 10 minutes, until the chicken and scallions are glossy. Flip the skewers halfway through.
7. Serve hot.

# Maple Turkey Breast

Prep time: 2 hours 20 minutes | Cook time: 30 minutes | Serves 6

¼ cup olive oil
2½ pounds (1.1 kg) turkey breast
¼ cup pure maple syrup
2 minced garlic cloves
1 tbsp. stone-ground brown mustard

1 tbsp. melted vegan butter
½ tsp. dried rosemary
2 tsps. salt
1 tsp. ground black pepper

1. In a large bowl, combine the rosemary, garlic, salt, ground black pepper, and olive oil. Stir to mix well.
2. Dip the turkey breast in the mixture and wrap the bowl in plastic. Refrigerate for about 2 hours to marinate.
3. Take the bowl from the refrigerator and allow to sit for half an hour before cooking.
4. Preheat the air fryer oven to 400ºF (204ºC). Spray the baking pan lightly with cooking spray.

5. Remove the turkey from the marinade and arrange in the baking pan. Slide the baking pan into Rack Position 2, select Roast and set time to 20 minutes, until well browned. Turn the breast halfway through.
6. At the same time, combine the remaining ingredients in a small bowl. Stir to mix well.
7. Add half of the butter mixture over the turkey breast in the air fryer oven and roast for another 10 minutes. Turn the breast and pour the remaining half of butter mixture over halfway through.
8. Take the turkey on a plate and slice to serve.

# Lettuce-Wrapped Turkey Meatballs

Prep time: 10 minutes | Cook time: 15 minutes | Serves 6

**Sauce:**
Cooking spray
2 tbsps. toasted sesame oil
½ cup chicken broth
⅓ cup sugar
1 clove garlic, smashed to a paste
2 tbsps. tamari
2 tbsps. tomato sauce
1 tbsp. lime juice
¼ tsp. peeled and grated fresh ginger
**Meatballs:**
2 tsps. toasted sesame oil
2 pounds (907 g) ground turkey

¾ cup finely chopped button mushrooms
2 large eggs, beaten
¼ cup finely chopped green onions, plus more for garnish
1 clove garlic, smashed
2 tbsps. sugar
2 tsps. peeled and grated fresh ginger
1½ tsps. tamari
**For Serving:**
Lettuce leaves, for serving
Sliced red chiles, for garnish (optional)
Toasted sesame seeds, for garnish (optional)

1. Preheat the air fryer oven to 350ºF (177ºC). Spray a baking pan lightly with cooking spray.
2. In a small bowl, combine the ingredients for the sauce. Stir to mix well. Set it aside.
3. In a large bowl, combine the ingredients for the meatballs. Stir to mix well, then shape the mixture into twelve 1½-inch meatballs.
4. Place the meatballs in a single layer on the baking pan, then baste with the sauce. You may need to work in batches to avoid overcrowding.
5. Slide the baking pan into Rack Position 1, select Convection Bake and set time to 15 minutes, until the meatballs are golden brown. Turn the balls halfway through the cooking time.
6. Unfold the lettuce leaves on a large serving plate, then take the cooked meatballs on the leaves. Sprinkle the red chiles and sesame seeds over the balls, then serve hot.

## Chinese Turkey Thighs

Prep time: 10 minutes | Cook time: 25 minutes | Serves 6

Cooking spray
2 pounds (907 g) turkey thighs
2 tbsps. soy sauce
1 tbsp. Chinese rice vinegar
1 tbsp. mustard

1 tbsp. chili sauce
1 tsp. Chinese five-spice powder
1 tsp. pink Himalayan salt
¼ tsp. Sichuan pepper

1. Preheat the air fryer oven to 360ºF (182ºC). Spray the air fryer basket lightly with cooking spray.
2. Season the turkey thighs with five-spice powder, Sichuan pepper, and salt on a clean work surface.
3. Arrange the turkey thighs in the air fryer basket and spray lightly with cooking spray. You may need to work in batches to avoid overcrowding.
4. Place the air fryer basket onto the baking pan, and slide the baking pan into Rack Position 2, select Air Fry and set time to 22 minutes, until well browned. Turn the thighs at least three times during the cooking time.
5. At the same time, heat the remaining ingredients over medium-high heat in a saucepan. Cook for about 3 minutes or until the sauce is thickened and reduces to two thirds.
6. Take the thighs onto a plate and baste with sauce before serving.

## Crispy Breaded Chicken Strips

Prep time: 15 minutes | Cook time: 20 minutes | Serves 4

Cooking spray
1 tbsp. olive oil
1 pound (454 g) boneless, skinless chicken tenderloins
½ cup whole-wheat seasoned bread crumbs

½ tsp. paprika
½ tsp. garlic powder
1 tsp. dried parsley
1 tsp. salt
½ tsp. freshly ground black pepper

1. Preheat the air fryer oven to 370ºF (188ºC). Spritz the air fryer basket with cooking spray.
2. Toss the chicken with the salt, pepper, paprika, and garlic powder in a medium bowl, until evenly coated.
3. Pour in the olive oil and toss to coat the chicken well.
4. Mix together the bread crumbs and parsley in a separate, shallow bowl.
5. Coat each piece of chicken evenly in the bread crumb mixture.

6. Arrange the chicken in the air fryer basket in a single layer and spritz it with cooking spray. You may need to cook them in batches.
7. Place the air fryer basket onto the baking pan, and slide the baking pan into Rack Position 2, select Air Fry and set time to 10 minutes. Flip the chicken over, lightly spritz it with cooking spray, and air fry for another 8 to 10 minutes, until golden brown. Serve hot.

## Honey Glazed Duck with Apple

Prep time: 5 minutes | Cook time: 15 minutes | Serves 2 to 3

1 pound (454 g) duck breasts (2 to 3 breasts)
2 firm tart apples, such as Fuji
¼ cup honey
Juice and zest of 1

orange
2 sprigs thyme, plus more for garnish
Kosher salt and pepper, to taste

1. Preheat the air fryer oven to 400ºF (204ºC).
2. Pat the duck breasts dry and make 3 to 4 shallow, diagonal slashes in the skin with a sharp knife. Turn the breasts and score the skin on the diagonal in the opposite direction to create a cross-hatch pattern. Sprinkle with salt and pepper.
3. Arrange the duck breasts skin-side up in the air fryer basket. Then place the air fryer basket onto the baking pan, and slide the baking pan into Rack Position 2, select Convection Broil and set time to 8 minutes. Flip and cook for 4 more minutes on the second side.
4. When the duck is cooking, prepare the sauce. In a small saucepan, combine the orange juice and zest, honey, and thyme. Bring to a boil, stirring to dissolve the honey, then lower the heat and simmer until thickened. Core the apples and cut into quarters. Slice each quarter into 3 or 4 slices depending on the size.
5. After the duck has cooked on both sides, turn it and coat the skin with the orange-honey glaze. Broil for another 1 minute. Transfer the duck breasts to a cutting board and let rest.
6. In a medium bowl, toss the apple slices with the remaining orange-honey sauce. Spread the apples in a single layer in the basket. Air fry for about 10 minutes while the duck breast rests. Slice the duck breasts on the bias and distribute them and the apples evenly among 2 or 3 plates.
7. Garnish with additional thyme and serve hot.

## Seasoned Chicken Breasts

Prep time: 10 minutes | Cook time: 20 minutes | Serves 4

Cooking spray
2 whole boneless, skinless chicken breasts (about 1 pound / 454 g
each), halved
1 large egg, beaten
¾ cup Blackened seasoning

1. Preheat the air fryer oven to 360ºF (182ºC). Line the air fryer basket with parchment paper.
2. Add the beaten egg in one shallow bowl and the Blackened seasoning in another shallow bowl.
3. One at a time, dip the chicken pieces in the beaten egg, then the Blackened seasoning, coating thoroughly.
4. Arrange the chicken pieces on the parchment and spray lightly with cooking spray.
5. Place the air fryer basket onto the baking pan, and slide the baking pan into Rack Position 2, select Air Fry and set time to10 minutes. Flip the chicken, spray it with cooking spray, and air fry for about 10 minutes more, or until the internal temperature reaches 165ºF (74ºC) and the chicken is no longer pink inside. Allow to sit for about 5 minutes before serving.

## Traditional Israeli Chicken Schnitzel

Prep time: 5 minutes | Cook time: 10 minutes | Serves 4

Vegetable oil spray
2 large boneless, skinless chicken breasts, each weighing about 1 pound (454 g)
1 cup all-purpose flour
2 eggs beaten with 2 tbsps. water
2 cups panko bread crumbs
2 tsps. garlic powder
1 tsp. paprika
Lemon juice, for serving
2 tsps. kosher salt
1 tsp. black pepper

1. Preheat the air fryer oven to 375ºF (191ºC).
2. Put 1 chicken breast between 2 pieces of plastic wrap. Pound the chicken with a mallet or a rolling pin until it is ¼ inch thick. Set it aside. Repeat with the second breast. On a large plate, whisk together the flour, garlic powder, salt, pepper, and paprika. Add the panko in a separate shallow bowl or pie plate.
3. Dredge 1 chicken breast in the flour, shaking off any excess, then dip it in the egg mixture. Dredge the chicken breast in the panko, making sure to coat it entirely. Shake off any excess panko. Arrange the battered chicken breast on a plate. Repeat with the second chicken breast.

4. Spritz the air fryer basket lightly with oil spray. Put 1 of the battered chicken breasts in the air fryer basket and spray the top lightly with oil spray. Place the air fryer basket onto the baking pan, and slide the baking pan into Rack Position 2, select Air Fry and set time to 5 minutes, until the top is browned. Flip the chicken and spritz the second side with oil spray. Air fry until the second side is browned and crispy and the internal temperature reaches 165ºF (74ºC). Transfer the first chicken breast from the air fryer oven and repeat with the second chicken breast.
5. Serve warm with lemon juice.

## Piri-Piri Chicken

Prep time: 5 minutes | Cook time: 25 minutes | Serves 4

1 tbsp. extra-virgin olive oil
4 bone-in, skin-on chicken thighs, each weighing approximately 7 to 8 ounces (198 to 227 g)
¼ cup piri-piri sauce
2 cloves garlic, minced
2 tbsps. brown sugar, divided
1 tbsp. freshly squeezed lemon juice
½ tsp. cornstarch

1. To make the marinade: in a small bowl, whisk together the piri-piri sauce, lemon juice, 1 tbsp. of brown sugar, and the garlic. While whisking, slowly pour in the oil in a steady stream and continue to whisk until emulsified. With a skewer, poke holes in the chicken thighs and arrange them in a small glass dish. Pour the marinade over the chicken and turn the thighs to coat them with the sauce. Cover the dish and refrigerate for at least 15 minutes and up to 1 hour.
2. Preheat the air fryer oven to 375ºF (191ºC). Transfer the chicken thighs from the dish, reserving the marinade, and put them skin-side down in the baking pan. Slide the baking pan into Rack Position 2, select Roast and set time to 20 minutes, until the internal temperature reaches 165ºF (74ºC).
3. At the same time, whisk the remaining brown sugar and the cornstarch into the marinade and microwave it on high power for about 1 minute until it is bubbling and thickened to a glaze.
4. Once the chicken is cooked, turn the thighs over and coat them with the glaze. Roast for a few additional minutes until the glaze browns and begins to char in spots.
5. Transfer the chicken to a platter and serve with additional piri-piri sauce, if desired.

## Sweet and Sour Drumsticks

Prep time: 5 minutes | Cook time: 24 minutes | Serves 4

| | |
|---|---|
| 1 tbsp. peanut oil | divided |
| 6 chicken drumsticks | 3 tbsps. low-sodium soy |
| ¼ cup pineapple juice | sauce, divided |
| 3 tbsps. brown sugar | 3 tbsps. honey |
| 3 tbsps. lemon juice, | 2 tbsps. ketchup |

1. Preheat the air fryer oven to 350ºF (177ºC).
2. Season the drumsticks with 1 tbsp. of lemon juice and 1 tbsp. of soy sauce. Arrange in the baking pan and drizzle with the peanut oil. Toss to coat well. Bake for 18 minutes or until the chicken is almost done.
3. At the same time, combine the remaining 2 tbsps. of lemon juice, the remaining 2 tbsps. of soy sauce, honey, brown sugar, ketchup, and pineapple juice in a metal bowl.
4. Place the cooked chicken to the bowl and stir to coat the chicken well with the sauce.
5. Arrange the metal bowl in the oven. Slide the bowl into Rack Position 1, select Convection Bake and set time to 6 minutes, until the chicken is glazed and registers 165ºF (74ºC) on a meat thermometer. Serve hot.

## Chicken Tenders with Potato and Carrot

Prep time: 10 minutes | Cook time: 18 minutes | Serves 4

| | |
|---|---|
| 1 tbsp. olive oil | crumbs |
| 1 pound (454 g) chicken | ½ tsp. dried thyme |
| tenders | 1 tbsp. honey |
| 12 small red potatoes | Pinch salt |
| 2 carrots, sliced | Freshly ground black |
| ½ cup soft fresh bread | pepper, to taste |

1. Preheat the air fryer oven to 380ºF (193ºC).
2. Toss the chicken tenders with the honey, salt, and pepper in a medium bowl.
3. Combine the bread crumbs, thyme, and olive oil in a shallow bowl, and mix well.
4. Coat the tenders in the bread crumbs, pressing firmly onto the meat.
5. Arrange the carrots and potatoes in the air fryer basket and top with the chicken tenders.
6. Place the air fryer basket onto the baking pan, and slide the baking pan into Rack Position 2, select

Convection Broil and set time to 18 minutes, until the chicken is cooked to 165ºF (74ºC) and the vegetables are soft, flipping halfway during the cooking time.
7. Serve hot.

## Spicy Chicken Thighs with Lemony Snow Peas

Prep time: 30 minutes | Cook time: 34 minutes | Serves 4

| | |
|---|---|
| 4 (5-ounce / 142-g) | 1 tbsp. mirin |
| bone-in chicken thighs, | ½ tsp. grated fresh ginger |
| trimmed | ½ tsp. lemon juice |
| 6 ounces (170 g) snow | ½ tsp. cornstarch |
| peas, strings removed | ⅛ tsp. red pepper flakes |
| ¼ cup chicken broth | ⅛ tsp. lemon zest |
| 1 garlic clove, minced | ¼ tsp. salt |
| 1½ tbsps. soy sauce | Ground black pepper, to |
| 1 tbsp. sugar | taste |

1. In a large bowl, combine the broth, ginger, pepper flakes, and soy sauce. Stir to mix well.
2. Pierce 10 to 15 holes into the chicken skin. Place the chicken in the broth mixture and toss to coat well. Allow to rest for 10 minutes to marinate.
3. Preheat the air fryer oven to 400ºF (205ºC).
4. Take the marinated chicken on a plate and pat dry with paper towels.
5. Spoon 2 tbsps. of marinade in a microwave-safe bowl and combine with mirin, cornstarch and sugar. Stir to mix well. Microwave for about 1 minute or until frothy and has a thick consistency. Set aside.
6. Put the chicken in the air fryer basket, skin side up. Place the air fryer basket onto the baking pan, and slide the baking pan into Rack Position 2, select Air Fry and set time to 25 minutes, until the internal temperature of the chicken reaches at least 165ºF (74ºC). Carefully flip the chicken over halfway through.
7. When the frying is complete, coat the chicken skin with marinade mixture. Air fryer the chicken for another 5 minutes or until glazed.
8. Transfer the chicken from the air fryer oven and reserve ½ tsp. of chicken fat remains in the air fryer oven. Let the chicken cool for 10 minutes.
9. At the same time, combine the reserved chicken fat, snow peas, lemon zest, garlic, salt, and ground black pepper in a small bowl. Toss to coat well.
10. Take the snow peas in the air fryer oven and air fry for about 3 minutes or until soft. Transfer the peas from the air fryer oven and toss with lemon juice.
11. Serve the chicken with lemony snow peas.

## Honey Glazed Chicken

Prep time: 10 minutes | Cook time: 20 minutes | Serves 4

Cooking spray
2 tbsps. olive oil
2 whole boneless, skinless chicken breasts (about 1 pound / 454 g each), halved
¼ cup balsamic vinegar
¼ cup honey
1 tbsp. dried rosemary leaves
1 tsp. salt
½ tsp. freshly ground black pepper

1.  Combine the vinegar, honey, olive oil, rosemary, salt, and pepper in a large resealable bag. Place the chicken pieces, seal the bag, and refrigerate to marinate for at least 2 hours.
2.  Preheat the air fryer oven to 325ºF (163ºC). Line the baking pan with parchment paper.
3.  Transfer the chicken from the marinade and put it on the parchment. Spray lightly with cooking spray.
4.  Slide the baking pan into Rack Position 1, select Convection Bake and set time to 10 minutes. Flip the chicken, spray it with cooking spray, and bake for another 10 minutes until the internal temperature reaches 165ºF (74ºC) and the chicken is no longer pink inside. Allow to rest for 5 minutes before serving.

## Ginger Chicken Thighs with Cilantro

Prep time: 10 minutes | Cook time: 10 minutes | Serves 4

Vegetable oil spray
2 tbsps. vegetable oil
1 pound (454 g) boneless, skinless chicken thighs, cut crosswise into thirds
¼ cup julienned peeled fresh ginger
¼ cup chopped fresh
cilantro, for garnish
1 tbsp. honey
1 tbsp. soy sauce
1 tbsp. ketchup
1 tsp. garam masala
1 tsp. ground turmeric
¼ tsp. kosher salt
½ tsp. cayenne pepper

1.  Combine the ginger, oil, honey, soy sauce, ketchup, garam masala, turmeric, salt, and cayenne in a small bowl. Whisk until combined well. Put the chicken in a resealable plastic bag and pour the marinade over. Seal the bag and massage to cover all of the chicken with the marinade. Marinate at room temperature for about 30 minutes or in the refrigerator for up to 24 hours.
2.  Preheat the air fryer oven to 350ºF (177ºC).
3.  Spritz the baking pan lightly with vegetable oil spray and place the chicken and as much of the marinade and julienned ginger as possible. Slide the baking pan into Rack Position 1, select Convection Bake and set time to 10 minutes. Use a meat thermometer to ensure the chicken has reached an internal temperature of 165ºF (74ºC).
4.  Garnish with cilantro and serve hot.

## Glazed Whole Duck with Cherry Sauce

Prep time: 20 minutes | Cook time: 32 minutes | Serves 12

1 tsp. olive oil
1 whole duck (about 5 pounds / 2.3 kg in total), split in half, back and rib bones removed, fat trimmed
Salt and freshly ground black pepper, to taste
**Cherry Sauce:**
1 cup chicken stock
¾ cup cherry preserves
½ cup sherry
1 shallot, minced
1 tbsp. butter
1 tsp. white wine vinegar
1 tsp. fresh thyme leaves
Salt and freshly ground black pepper, to taste

1.  Preheat the air fryer oven to 400ºF (204ºC).
2.  On a clean work surface, brush the duck with olive oil, then season with salt and ground black pepper to taste.
3.  Put the duck in the air fryer basket, breast side up. Place the air fryer basket onto the baking pan, and slide the baking pan into Rack Position 2, select Air Fry and set time to 25 minutes, until well browned. Turn the duck during the last 10 minutes.
4.  At the same time, make the cherry sauce: in a nonstick skillet over medium-high heat, heat the butter or until melted.
5.  Place the shallot and sauté for 5 minutes or until lightly browned.
6.  Add the sherry and simmer for about 6 minutes or until it reduces in half.
7.  Pour in the chicken stock, white wine vinegar, and cherry preserves. Stir to mix well. Simmer for another 6 minutes or until thickened.
8.  Fold in the thyme leaves and season with salt and ground black pepper. Stir to combine well.
9.  When the air frying of the duck is complete, glaze the duck with a quarter of the cherry sauce, then air fry for 4 minutes more.
10. Flip the duck and glaze with another quarter of the cherry sauce. Air fry for another 3 minutes.
11. Take the duck on a large plate and serve hot with remaining cherry sauce.

## Paprika Turkey Tenderloin

Prep time: 20 minutes | Cook time: 30 minutes | Serves 4

Olive oil spray
1½ pounds (680 g) turkey breast tenderloin
½ tsp. paprika
½ tsp. garlic powder
½ tsp. salt
½ tsp. freshly ground black pepper
Pinch cayenne pepper

1. Preheat the air fryer oven to 370ºF (188ºC). Spritz the baking pan with olive oil spray.
2. Combine the paprika, garlic powder, salt, black pepper, and cayenne pepper in a small bowl. Rub the mixture all over the turkey.
3. Arrange the turkey in the baking pan and lightly spritz with olive oil spray.
4. Slide the baking pan into Rack Position 2, select Roast and set time to 15 minutes. Turn the turkey over and spritz lightly with olive oil spray. Roast for an additional 10 to 15 minutes, until the internal temperature reaches at least 170ºF (77ºC).
5. Allow the turkey to cool for 10 minutes before slicing and serving.

## Chicken and Celery

Prep time: 10 minutes | Cook time: 15 minutes | Serves 4

Olive oil spray
8 boneless, skinless chicken tenderloins
1 cup chopped celery
1 medium red bell pepper, diced
½ cup soy sauce
2 tbsps. hoisin sauce
4 tsps. minced garlic
1 tsp. freshly ground black pepper

1. Preheat the air fryer oven to 375ºF (191ºC). Spritz the baking pan with olive oil spray.
2. Make a marinade: in a large bowl, mix together the soy sauce, hoisin sauce, garlic, and black pepper. Place the chicken, celery, and bell pepper in the bowl of marinade and toss to coat well.
3. Shake the excess marinade off the chicken, arrange it and the vegetables in the baking pan, and lightly spritz with olive oil spray. You may need to cook them in batches. Reserve the remaining marinade.
4. Slide the baking pan into Rack Position 2, select Roast and set time to 8 minutes. Turn the chicken over and coat with some of the remaining marinade. Roast for another 5 to 7 minutes, or until the chicken reaches an internal temperature of at least 165ºF (74ºC). Serve hot.

## Thai Game Hens and Cucumber Salad

Prep time: 25 minutes | Cook time: 25 minutes | Serves 6

Cooking spray
2 tsps. vegetable oil
2 (1¼-pound / 567-g) Cornish game hens, giblets discarded
1 English cucumber, halved lengthwise and sliced thin
1 Thai chile, stemmed, deseeded, and minced
1 small shallot, sliced thinly
2 garlic cloves, minced
6 tbsps. chopped fresh cilantro
2 tbsps. chopped dry-roasted peanuts
2 tbsps. packed light brown sugar
1 tbsp. lime juice
1 tbsp. fish sauce
2 tsps. lime zest
1 tsp. ground coriander
Salt and ground black pepper, to taste
Lime wedges, for serving

1. Place a game hen on a clean work surface, remove the backbone with kitchen shears, then pound the hen breast to flat. Cut the breast in half. Repeat this work with the remaining game hen.
2. Loose the breast and thigh skin with your fingers, then pat the game hens dry and pierce about 10 holes into the fat deposits of the hens. Tuck the wings under the hens.
3. In a small bowl, combine 2 tsps. of fish sauce, ¼ cup of cilantro, lime zest, coriander, garlic, 4 tsps. of sugar, 1 tsp. of vegetable oil, ½ tsp. of salt, and ⅛ tsp. of ground black pepper. Stir to combine well.
4. Rub the fish sauce mixture under the breast and thigh skin of the game hens, then allow to sit for 10 minutes to marinate.
5. Preheat the air fryer oven to 400ºF (204ºC). Spray the air fryer basket lightly with cooking spray.
6. Place the marinated game hens in the air fryer basket, skin side down.
7. Put the air fryer basket onto the baking pan, and slide the baking pan into Rack Position 2, select Air Fry and set time to 15 minutes. Gently turn the game hens over and air fry for 10 more minutes or until the skin is golden brown and the internal temperature of the hens reads at least 165ºF (74ºC).
8. At the same time, in a large bowl, combine all the remaining ingredients, except for the lime wedges, and season with salt and black pepper. Toss to combine well.
9. Take the fried hens on a large plate, then sit the salad aside and squeeze the lime wedges over before serving.

Crispy Breaded Chicken Strips, page 45

Seasoned Chicken Breasts, page 46

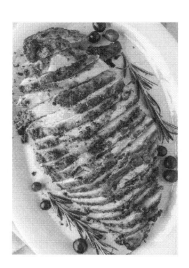

Mustard Turkey Breast, page 54

Sweet and Sour Drumsticks, page 47

## Authentic Goulash

Prep time: 5 minutes | Cook time: 17 minutes |
Serves 2

Cooking spray
1 pound (454 g) ground
chicken
2 red bell peppers,
chopped

2 medium tomatoes,
diced
½ cup chicken broth
Salt and ground black
pepper, to taste

1. Preheat the air fryer oven to 365ºF (185ºC). Spray
   the air fryer basket lightly with cooking spray.
2. Place the bell pepper in the air fryer basket. Then put
   the air fryer basket onto the baking pan, and slide the
   baking pan into Rack Position 2, select Convection
   Broil and set time to 5 minutes, until the bell pepper
   is tender, flipping halfway through.
3. Put the ground chicken and diced tomatoes in the
   baking pan and stir to combine well. Broil for another
   6 minutes or until the chicken is lightly browned.
4. Add the chicken broth over and season with salt
   and ground black pepper. Stir to mix well. Broil for 6
   minutes more.
5. Serve hot.

## Golden Chicken Nuggets

Prep time: 10 minutes | Cook time: 20 minutes |
Serves 4

Cooking spray
1 pound (454 g)
boneless, skinless
chicken breasts, cut into
1-inch pieces
2 eggs
6 tbsps. breadcrumbs

2 tbsps. panko
breadcrumbs
Chicken seasoning or
rub, to taste
Salt and ground black
pepper, to taste

1. Preheat the air fryer oven to 400ºF (204ºC). Spray
   the air fryer basket lightly with cooking spray.
2. In a large bowl, combine the breadcrumbs, chicken
   seasoning, salt, and black pepper. Stir to mix well.
   Whisk the eggs in a separate bowl.
3. Dip the chicken pieces in the egg mixture, then in the
   breadcrumb mixture. Shake the excess off.
4. Spread the well-coated chicken pieces in the air fryer
   basket and spray lightly with cooking spray. Place the
   air fryer basket onto the baking pan, and slide the
   baking pan into Rack Position 2, select Air Fry and
   set time to 8 minutes, until crispy and golden brown,
   flipping halfway through. You may need to work in
   batches to avoid overcrowding.
5. Serve hot.

## Crispy Buffalo Chicken Taquitos

Prep time: 15 minutes | Cook time: 7 minutes |
Serves 6

Olive oil spray
8 ounces (227 g) fat-free
cream cheese, softened
2 cups shredded cooked

chicken
12 (7-inch) low-carb flour
tortillas
⅛ cup Buffalo sauce

1. Preheat the air fryer oven to 360ºF (182ºC). Spritz
   the air fryer basket with olive oil spray.
2. Mix together the cream cheese and Buffalo sauce
   until well combined in a large bowl. Place the chicken
   and stir until combined well.
3. Arrange the tortillas on a clean workspace. Scoop 2
   to 3 tbsps. of the chicken mixture in a thin line down
   the center of each tortilla. Roll up the tortillas.
4. Put the tortillas in the air fryer basket, seam-side
   down. Spritz each tortilla with olive oil spray. You may
   need to cook the taquitos in batches.
5. Place the air fryer basket onto the baking pan, and
   slide the baking pan into Rack Position 2, select Air
   Fry and set time to 7 minutes, until golden brown.
   Serve warm.

## Crisp Chicken Drumsticks

Prep time: 5 minutes | Cook time: 22 minutes |
Serves 2

1 tsp. vegetable oil
4 (5-ounce / 142-g)
chicken drumsticks,
trimmed
2 tsps. paprika
1 scallion, green part
only, sliced thin on bias

1 tsp. packed brown
sugar
1 tsp. garlic powder
½ tsp. dry mustard
½ tsp. salt
Pinch pepper

1. Preheat the air fryer oven to 400ºF (204ºC).
2. In a bowl, combine paprika, sugar, garlic powder,
   mustard, salt, and pepper. Pat drumsticks dry with
   paper towels. Poke 10 to 15 holes in skin of each
   drumstick with metal skewer. Rub with oil and season
   evenly with spice mixture.
3. Place drumsticks in the air fryer basket, spaced
   evenly apart, alternating ends. Put the air fryer
   basket onto the baking pan, and slide the baking pan
   into Rack Position 2, select Air Fry and set time to
   22 minutes, until chicken is crisp and registers 195ºF
   (91ºC), flipping chicken halfway through cooking.
4. Take chicken to serving platter, tent loosely with
   aluminum foil, and allow to lest for 5 minutes. Scatter
   with scallion and serve warm.

## Spicy Fajita Chicken Strips

Prep time: 10 minutes | Cook time: 15 minutes | Serves 4

Cooking spray
1 tbsp. olive oil
1 pound (454 g) boneless, skinless chicken tenderloins, cut into strips

3 bell peppers, any color, cut into chunks
1 onion, cut into chunks
1 tbsp. fajita seasoning mix

1. Preheat the air fryer oven to 370ºF (188ºC).
2. Mix together the chicken, bell peppers, onion, olive oil, and fajita seasoning mix in a large bowl, until completely coated.
3. Spritz the baking pan with cooking spray.
4. Arrange the chicken and vegetables in the baking pan and lightly spritz with cooking spray.
5. Slide the baking pan into Rack Position 2, select Roast and set time to 7 minutes. Flip and roast for another 5 to 8 minutes, until the chicken is cooked through and the veggies are starting to char.
6. Serve hot.

## Air Fried Chicken with Cilantro

Prep time: 35 minutes | Cook time: 20 minutes | Serves 4

Cooking spray
4 (4-ounce / 113-g) boneless, skinless chicken breasts
½ cup chopped fresh cilantro

Juice of 1 lime
Chicken seasoning or rub, to taste
Salt and ground black pepper, to taste

1. In a large bowl, add the chicken breasts, cilantro, lime juice, chicken seasoning, salt, and black pepper. Toss to coat well.
2. Wrap the bowl in plastic and refrigerate to marinate for at least 30 minutes.
3. Preheat the air fryer oven to 400ºF (204ºC). Spray the air fryer basket lightly with cooking spray.
4. Transfer the marinated chicken breasts from the bowl and put in the air fryer basket. Spray lightly with cooking spray. You may need to work in batches to avoid overcrowding.
5. Place the air fryer basket onto the baking pan, and slide the baking pan into Rack Position 2, select Air Fry and set time to 10 minutes, until the internal temperature of the chicken reaches at least 165ºF (74ºC). Flip the breasts halfway through.
6. Serve hot.

## Mayonnaise Chicken

Prep time: 10 minutes | Cook time: 15 minutes | Serves 4

1 pound (454 g) chicken tenders
6 tbsps. mayonnaise
2 tbsps. coarse-ground mustard

2 tsps. honey (optional)
2 tsps. curry powder
1 tsp. kosher salt
1 tsp. cayenne pepper

1. Preheat the air fryer oven to 350ºF (177ºC).
2. In a large bowl, whisk together the mayonnaise, mustard, honey (if using), curry powder, salt, and cayenne. Take half of the mixture to a serving bowl to serve as a dipping sauce. Put the chicken tenders to the large bowl and toss until coated well.
3. Place the tenders in the baking pan. Slide the baking pan into Rack Position 1, select Convection Bake and set time to 15 minutes. Use a meat thermometer to ensure the chicken has reached an internal temperature of 165ºF (74ºC).
4. Place the dipping sauce on top and serve hot.

## Turkey Breast with Dijon Sauce

Prep time: 5 minutes | Cook time: 30 minutes | Serves 4

Cooking spray
1 (2-pound / 907-g) turkey breast
3 tbsps. Dijon mustard
3 tbsps. butter, melted
1 tsp. chopped fresh sage
1 tsp. chopped fresh

thyme leaves
1 tsp. chopped fresh tarragon
1 tsp. chopped fresh rosemary leaves
1½ tsps. sea salt
1 tsp. ground black pepper

1. Preheat the air fryer oven to 390ºF (199ºC). Spray the baking pan lightly with cooking spray.
2. In a small bowl, combine the herbs, salt, and black pepper. Stir to mix well. Set it aside.
3. In a separate bowl, combine the Dijon mustard and butter. Stir to mix well.
4. Coat the turkey with the herb mixture on a clean work surface, then coat the turkey with Dijon mixture.
5. Place the turkey in the baking pan. Slide the baking pan into Rack Position 2, select Roast and set time to 30 minutes, until an instant-read thermometer inserted in the thickest part of the turkey breast reaches at least 165ºF (74ºC).
6. Take the cooked turkey breast on a large plate and slice to serve.

## Chicken Tenders and Pecans

Prep time: 5 minutes | Cook time: 12 minutes | Serves 4

1 pound (454 g) chicken tenders
1 cup finely crushed pecans
¼ cup coarse mustard
2 tbsps. honey
½ tsp. smoked paprika
1 tsp. kosher salt
1 tsp. black pepper

1. Preheat the air fryer oven to 350ºF (177ºC).
2. In a large bowl, add the chicken. Season with the salt, pepper, and paprika. Toss until the chicken is well coated with the spices. Place the mustard and honey and toss until the chicken is coated.
3. Put the pecans on a plate. Working with one piece of chicken at a time, roll the chicken in the pecans until both sides are coated. Brush off any loose pecans. Arrange the chicken in the baking pan.
4. Slide the baking pan into Rack Position 1, select Convection Bake and set time to 12 minutes, until the chicken is cooked through and the pecans are golden brown.
5. Serve hot.

## Turkey Tenderloin with Apricot Preserves

Prep time: 20 minutes | Cook time: 30 minutes | Serves 4

Olive oil spray
1½ pounds (680 g) turkey breast tenderloin
¼ cup sugar-free apricot preserves
½ tbsp. spicy brown mustard
Salt and freshly ground black pepper, to taste

1. Preheat the air fryer oven to 370ºF (188ºC). Spritz the baking pan with olive oil spray.
2. Combine the apricot preserves and mustard in a small bowl to make a paste.
3. Sprinkle the turkey with salt and pepper. Coat the apricot paste all over the turkey.
4. Arrange the turkey in the baking pan and spritz with olive oil spray.
5. Slide the baking pan into Rack Position 2, select Roast and set time to 15 minutes. Flip the turkey over and lightly spray with olive oil spray. Roast for an additional 10 to 15 minutes, until the internal temperature reaches at least 170ºF (77ºC).
6. Allow the turkey to rest for 10 minutes before slicing and serving.

## Glazed Turkey with Strawberries

Prep time: 15 minutes | Cook time: 37 minutes | Serves 2

1 tbsp. olive oil
2 pounds (907 g) turkey breast
1 cup fresh strawberries
Salt and ground black pepper, to taste

1. Preheat the air fryer oven to 375ºF (191ºC).
2. Brush the turkey bread with olive oil on a clean work surface, then season with salt and ground black pepper.
3. Put the turkey in the air fryer basket. Then place the air fryer basket onto the baking pan, and slide the baking pan into Rack Position 2, select Air Fry and set time to 30 minutes, until the internal temperature of the turkey reaches at least 165ºF (74ºC). Turn the turkey breast halfway through.
4. At the same time, place the strawberries in a food processor and pulse until smooth.
5. When the frying of the turkey is complete, lay the puréed strawberries over the turkey and fry for another 7 minutes.
6. Serve hot.

## Hoisin Turkey Burgers

Prep time: 10 minutes | Cook time: 20 minutes | Serves 4

Olive oil spray
1 pound (454 g) lean ground turkey
4 whole-wheat buns
¼ cup whole-wheat bread crumbs
¼ cup hoisin sauce
2 tbsps. soy sauce

1. Mix together the turkey, bread crumbs, hoisin sauce, and soy sauce in a large bowl.
2. Shape the mixture into 4 equal patties. Cover with plastic wrap and refrigerate the patties for about 30 minutes.
3. Preheat the air fryer oven to 370ºF (188ºC). Spritz the air fryer basket with olive oil spray.
4. Put the patties in the air fryer basket in a single layer. Spritz the patties with olive oil spray.
5. Place the air fryer basket onto the baking pan, and slide the baking pan into Rack Position 2, select Air Fry and set time to 10 minutes. Turn the patties over, lightly spritz with olive oil spray, and air fry for another 5 to 10 minutes, until golden brown.
6. Arrange the patties on buns and top with your choice of low-calorie burger toppings like sliced tomatoes, onions, and cabbage slaw. Serve warm.

## Simple Baked Whole Chicken

Prep time: 10 minutes | Cook time: 1 hour | Serves 2 to 4

| | |
|---|---|
| 1 (1-pound / 454-g) whole chicken | Salt, to taste |
| ½ cup melted butter | 1 tsp. ground black pepper |
| 3 tbsps. garlic, minced | |

1. Preheat the air fryer oven to 350ºF (177ºC).
2. In a small bowl, combine the butter with garlic, salt, and ground black pepper.
3. Coat the butter mixture over the whole chicken, then arrange the chicken in the baking pan, skin side down.
4. Slide the baking pan into Rack Position 1, select Convection Bake and set time to 1 hour, until an instant-read thermometer inserted in the thickest part of the chicken registers at least 165ºF (74ºC). Turn the chicken halfway through.
5. Transfer the chicken from the air fryer oven and let cool for 15 minutes before serving.

## Mustard Turkey Breast

Prep time: 20 minutes | Cook time: 45 minutes | Serves 6

| | |
|---|---|
| Cooking spray | 1½ tsps. rosemary |
| 1 tbsp. olive oil | 1½ tsps. sage |
| 3 pounds (1.4 kg) turkey breast, thawed if frozen | 1½ tsps. thyme |
| 2 garlic cloves, minced | 1 tsp. salt |
| 2 tsps. Dijon mustard | ½ tsp. freshly ground black pepper |

1. Preheat the air fryer oven to 370ºF (188ºC). Spritz the baking pan with cooking spray.
2. Mix together the garlic, olive oil, Dijon mustard, rosemary, sage, thyme, salt, and pepper in a small bowl to make a paste. Smear the paste all over the turkey breast.
3. Arrange the turkey breast in the baking pan. Slide the baking pan into Rack Position 2, select Roast and set time to 20 minutes. Flip turkey breast over and brush it with any drippings that have collected in the bottom drawer of the air fryer oven. Roast for 20 more minutes, until the internal temperature of the meat reaches at least 170ºF (77ºC).
4. If desired, raise the temperature to 400ºF (204ºC), flip the turkey breast over one last time, and roast for about 5 minutes to get a crispy exterior.
5. Allow the turkey to rest for 10 minutes before slicing and serving.

## Garlic Duck Leg Quarters

Prep time: 5 minutes | Cook time: 45 minutes | Serves 4

| | |
|---|---|
| 4 (½-pound / 227-g) skin-on duck leg quarters | ½ tsp. salt |
| 2 medium garlic cloves, minced | ½ tsp. ground black pepper |

1. Preheat the air fryer oven to 300ºF (149ºC). Spray a baking pan lightly with cooking spray.
2. Rub the duck leg quarters with garlic, salt, and black pepper on a clean work surface.
3. Place the leg quarters in the baking pan and spritz lightly with cooking spray.
4. Slide the baking pan into Rack Position 2, select Roast and set time to 30 minutes, then flip the leg quarters and raise the temperature to 375ºF (191ºC). Roast for another 15 minutes or until well browned and crispy.
5. Transfer the duck leg quarters from the air fryer oven and let cool for 10 minutes before serving.

## Crispy Tandoori Chicken Drumsticks

Prep time: 70 minutes | Cook time: 14 minutes | Serves 4

| | |
|---|---|
| 8 (4- to 5-ounce / 113- to 142-g) skinless bone-in chicken drumsticks | 2 tsps. ground coriander |
| ½ cup plain full-fat or low-fat yogurt | 2 tsps. mild paprika |
| ¼ cup buttermilk | 2 tsps. minced fresh ginger |
| 2 tsps. minced garlic | 1 tsp. Tabasco hot red pepper sauce |
| 2 tsps. ground cinnamon | 1 tsp. salt |

1. Preheat the air fryer oven to 375ºF (191ºC).
2. Stir together all the ingredients except for chicken drumsticks in a large bowl until well combined. Place the chicken drumsticks to the bowl and toss until well coated. Cover in plastic and set in the refrigerator to marinate for 1 hour, tossing once.
3. Put the marinated drumsticks in a single layer in the air fryer basket, leaving enough space between them. Place the air fryer basket onto the baking pan, and slide the baking pan into Rack Position 2, select Air Fry and set time to 14 minutes, until the internal temperature of the chicken drumsticks reaches 160ºF (71ºC) on a meat thermometer. Turn the drumsticks once halfway through to ensure even cooking.
4. Take the drumsticks to plates. Let cool for 5 minutes before serving.

## Easy Air Fried Chicken Wings

Prep time: 10 minutes | Cook time: 15 minutes | Serves 4

1 tbsp. olive oil
8 whole chicken wings
Chicken seasoning or rub, to taste
1 tsp. garlic powder
Freshly ground black pepper, to taste

1. Preheat the air fryer oven to 400ºF (204ºC). Grease the air fryer basket lightly with olive oil.
2. Rub the chicken wings with chicken seasoning and rub, garlic powder, and ground black pepper on a clean work surface.
3. Place the well-coated chicken wings in the air fryer basket. Then put the air fryer basket onto the baking pan, and slide the baking pan into Rack Position 2, select Air Fry and set time to 15 minutes, until the internal temperature of the chicken wings reaches at least 165ºF (74ºC). Turn the chicken wings halfway through.
4. Take the chicken wings from the air fryer oven. Serve hot.

## Cheesy Turkey and Cranberry Quesadillas

Prep time: 7 minutes | Cook time: 4 to 8 minutes | Serves 4

Olive oil spray, for spraying the tortillas
6 low-sodium whole-wheat tortillas
¾ cup shredded cooked low-sodium turkey breast
⅓ cup shredded low-sodium low-fat Swiss cheese
2 tbsps. cranberry sauce
2 tbsps. dried cranberries
½ tsp. dried basil

1. Preheat the air fryer oven to 400ºF (204ºC).
2. Arrange 3 tortillas on a work surface.
3. Evenly distribute the Swiss cheese, turkey, cranberry sauce, and dried cranberries among the tortillas. Scatter with the basil and top with the remaining tortillas.
4. Spritz the outsides of the tortillas lightly with olive oil spray.
5. One at a time, put the quesadilla in the air fryer basket. Then place the air fryer basket onto the baking pan, and slide the baking pan into Rack Position 2, select Air Fry and set time to 6 minutes until crisp and the cheese is melted. Repeat with the remaining quesadillas.
6. Cut into quarters and serve hot.

## Broiled Cajun Turkey with Carrot

Prep time: 10 minutes | Cook time: 30 minutes | Serves 4

Nonstick cooking spray
2 pounds (907 g) turkey thighs, skinless and boneless
1 carrot, sliced
2 bell peppers, sliced
1 habanero pepper,
minced
2 cups chicken broth
1 red onion, sliced
1 tbsp. Cajun seasoning mix
1 tbsp. fish sauce

1. Preheat the air fryer oven to 360ºF (182ºC).
2. Spray the bottom and sides of the air fryer basket lightly with nonstick cooking spray.
3. Arrange the turkey thighs in the air fryer basket. Put the onion, peppers, and carrot. Season with Cajun seasoning. Add the fish sauce and chicken broth.
4. Place the air fryer basket onto the baking pan, and slide the baking pan into Rack Position 2, select Convection Broil and set time to 30 minutes, until cooked through. Serve hot.

## Turkey Burgers

Prep time: 10 minutes | Cook time: 15 minutes | Serves 4

1 tbsp. olive oil
1 pound (454 g) ground turkey
⅓ cup finely crushed corn tortilla chips
1 egg, beaten
¼ cup salsa
⅓ cup shredded pepper Jack cheese
1 tsp. paprika
Pinch salt
Freshly ground black pepper, to taste

1. Preheat the air fryer oven to 330ºF (166ºC).
2. Combine the tortilla chips, egg, salsa, cheese, salt, and pepper in a medium bowl and mix well.
3. Place the turkey and mix gently but thoroughly with clean hands.
4. Shape the meat mixture into patties about ½ inch thick. Make an indentation in the center of each patty with your thumb so the burgers don't puff up while cooking.
5. Coat the patties on both sides with the olive oil and season with paprika.
6. Arrange in the air fryer basket. Then place the air fryer basket onto the baking pan, and slide the baking pan into Rack Position 2, select Air Fry and set time to 15 minutes, until the meat registers at least 165ºF (74ºC).
7. Allow to cool for 5 minutes before serving.

## Mini Turkey and Carrot Meatloaves

Prep time: 6 minutes | Cook time: 20 minutes | Serves 4

2 tsps. olive oil
¾ pound (340 g) ground turkey breast
⅓ cup minced onion
¼ cup grated carrot
1 egg white
2 garlic cloves, minced
2 tbsps. ground almonds
1 tsp. dried marjoram

1. Preheat the air fryer oven to 400ºF (204ºC).
2. Stir together the onion, carrot, garlic, almonds, olive oil, marjoram, and egg white in a medium bowl.
3. Place the ground turkey. With your hands, gently but thoroughly mix until combined.
4. Double 16 foil muffin cup liners to make 8 cups. Distribute the turkey mixture evenly among the liners.
5. Put the cups in the air fryer basket. Then place the air fryer basket onto the baking pan, and slide the baking pan into Rack Position 2, select Air Fry and set time to 20 minutes, until the meatloaves reach an internal temperature of 165ºF (74ºC) on a meat thermometer. Serve hot.

## Rosemary Turkey Scotch Eggs

Prep time: 15 minutes | Cook time: 12 minutes | Serves 4

Cooking spray
1 pound (454 g) ground turkey
4 hard-boiled eggs, peeled
1 cup panko
breadcrumbs
1 egg
½ tsp. rosemary
Salt and ground black pepper, to taste

1. Preheat the air fryer oven to 400ºF (204ºC). Spray the baking pan lightly with cooking spray.
2. In a bowl, whisk the egg with salt. Combine the breadcrumbs with rosemary in a shallow dish.
3. In a separate large bowl, stir the ground turkey with salt and ground black pepper, then divide the ground turkey into four portions.
4. Wrap each hard-boiled egg with a portion of ground turkey. Dredge in the whisked egg, then roll over the breadcrumb mixture.
5. Arrange the wrapped eggs in the baking pan and spray with cooking spray. Slide the baking pan into Rack Position 1, select Convection Bake and set time to 12 minutes, until golden brown and crunchy. Turn the eggs halfway through.
6. Serve hot.

## Air Fryer Seasoned Chicken Tenders

Prep time: 5 minutes | Cook time: 7 minutes | Serves 4

**Seasoning:**
1 tsp. kosher salt
½ tsp. chili powder
½ tsp. garlic powder
½ tsp. onion powder
¼ tsp. sweet paprika
¼ tsp. freshly ground black pepper
**Chicken:**
8 (1 pound / 454 g total) chicken breast tenders
2 tbsps. mayonnaise

1. Preheat the air fryer oven to 375ºF (191ºC).
2. For the seasoning: Combine the salt, garlic powder, onion powder, chili powder, paprika, and pepper in a small bowl.
3. For the chicken: In a medium bowl, add the chicken and mayonnaise. Mix well to coat all over, then scatter with the seasoning mix.
4. Working in batches, place a single layer of the chicken in the air fryer basket. Then put the air fryer basket onto the baking pan, and slide the baking pan into Rack Position 2, select Air Fry and set time to 7 minutes, flipping halfway, until cooked through in the center. Serve hot.

## Marmalade Balsamic Glazed Duck Breasts

Prep time: 5 minutes | Cook time: 13 minutes | Serves 4

4 (6-ounce / 170-g) skin-on duck breasts
1 tsp. salt
¼ cup orange marmalade
1 tbsp. white balsamic vinegar
¾ tsp. ground black pepper

1. Preheat the air fryer oven to 400ºF (204ºC).
2. Cut 10 slits into the skin of the duck breasts, then season with salt on both sides.
3. Arrange the breasts in the air fryer basket, skin side up. Then place the air fryer basket onto the baking pan, and slide the baking pan into Rack Position 2, select Air Fry and set time to 10 minutes.
4. At the same time, in a small bowl, combine the remaining ingredients. Stir to mix well.
5. When the frying is complete, coat the duck skin with the marmalade mixture. Turn the breast and air fry for another 3 minutes or until the skin is crispy and the breast is well browned.
6. Serve hot.

## Turkey and Black Bean Stuffed Bell Peppers

Prep time: 20 minutes | Cook time: 12 minutes | Serves 4

Olive oil spray
1 (15-ounce / 425-g) can black beans, drained and rinsed
½ pound (227 g) lean ground turkey
4 medium bell peppers
1 cup shredded reduced-fat Cheddar cheese
1 cup cooked long-grain brown rice
1 cup mild salsa
1¼ tsps. chili powder
½ tsp. ground cumin
Chopped fresh cilantro, for garnish
1 tsp. salt
½ tsp. freshly ground black pepper

1. Preheat the air fryer oven to 360ºF (182ºC).
2. In a large skillet, cook the turkey over medium-high heat, breaking it up with a spoon, until browned, for about 5 minutes. Drain off any excess fat.
3. Cut about ½ inch off the tops of the peppers and then cut in half lengthwise. Remove and discard the seeds and set the peppers aside.
4. Combine the browned turkey, black beans, Cheddar cheese, rice, salsa, chili powder, salt, cumin, and black pepper in a large bowl. Scoop the mixture into the bell peppers.
5. Spray the air fryer basket lightly with olive oil spray.
6. Arrange the stuffed peppers in the air fryer basket. Then place the air fryer basket onto the baking pan, and slide the baking pan into Rack Position 2, select Air Fry and set time to 12 minutes. until heated through. Garnish with cilantro and serve hot.

## Chicken and Onion Tacos with Peanut Sauce

Prep time: 10 minutes | Cook time: 6 minutes | Serves 4

Cooking spray
1 pound (454 g) ground chicken
¼ cup diced onions
2 cloves garlic, minced
¼ tsp. sea salt
**Peanut Sauce:**
¼ cup creamy peanut butter, at room temperature
2 tbsps. tamari
2 tbsps. grated fresh ginger
2 tbsps. lime juice
2 tbsps. chicken broth
2 tsps. sugar
1½ tsps. hot sauce
**For Serving:**
2 small heads butter lettuce, leaves separated
Lime slices (optional)

1. Preheat the air fryer oven to 350ºF (177ºC). Spray a baking pan lightly with cooking spray.
2. Mix the ground chicken, garlic, and onions in the baking pan, then season with salt. Break the ground chicken with a fork and combine them well.
3. Slide the baking pan into Rack Position 1, select Convection Bake and set time to 5 minutes, until the chicken is lightly browned. Stir them halfway through the cooking time.
4. At the same time, in a small bowl, combine the ingredients for the sauce. Stir to mix well.
5. Add the sauce in the pan of chicken, then cook for 1 more minute or until heated through.
6. Unfold the lettuce leaves on a large serving plate, then distribute the chicken mixture on the lettuce leaves. Drizzle with lime juice and serve hot.

## Asian Turkey and Water Chestnuts Meatballs

Prep time: 10 minutes | Cook time: 11 to 12 minutes | Serves 4

2 tbsps. peanut oil, divided
1 pound (454 g) ground turkey
1 egg, beaten
1 small onion, minced
¼ cup water chestnuts, finely chopped
¼ cup panko bread crumbs
2 tbsps. low-sodium soy sauce
½ tsp. ground ginger

1. Preheat the air fryer oven to 400ºF (204ºC).
2. Combine 1 tbsp. of peanut oil and onion in the air fryer basket. Place the air fryer basket onto the baking pan, and slide the baking pan into Rack Position 2, select Air Fry and set time to 1 or 2 minutes, until crisp and tender. Take the onion to a medium bowl.
3. Place the water chestnuts, ground ginger, soy sauce, and bread crumbs to the onion and mix well. Add egg and stir well. Mix in the ground turkey until well combined.
4. Shape the mixture into 1-inch meatballs. Drizzle the remaining 1 tbsp. of oil over the meatballs. Arrange in the basket and cook in batches.
5. Slide the baking pan into Rack Position 1, select Convection Bake and set time to 10 minutes. until they are 165ºF (74ºC) on a meat thermometer. Let cool for 5 minutes before serving.

## Simple Sweet-and-Sour Chicken Nuggets

Prep time: 15 minutes | Cook time: 15 minutes | Serves 4

| | |
|---|---|
| Cooking spray | 1-inch pieces |
| 1 cup cornstarch | 2 eggs |
| 1½ cups sweet-and-sour sauce | Chicken seasoning or rub, to taste |
| 2 (4-ounce/ 113-g) boneless, skinless chicken breasts, cut into | Salt and ground black pepper, to taste |

1. Preheat the air fryer oven to 360ºF (182ºC). Spray the air fryer basket with cooking spray.
2. In a large bowl, combine the cornstarch, chicken seasoning, salt, and pepper. Stir to mix well. Whisk the eggs in a separate bowl.
3. Dredge the chicken pieces in the bowl of cornstarch mixture first, then in the bowl of whisked eggs, and then in the cornstarch mixture again.
4. Place the well-coated chicken pieces in the air fryer basket. Spray lightly with cooking spray.
5. Put the air fryer basket onto the baking pan, and slide the baking pan into Rack Position 2, select Air Fry and set time to 15 minutes, until golden brown and crispy. Flip halfway through the cooking time.
6. Take the chicken pieces on a large serving plate, then baste with sweet-and-sour sauce before serving.

## Spicy Chicken and Sweet Pepper Baguette

Prep time: 10 minutes | Cook time: 20 minutes | Serves 2

| | |
|---|---|
| Cooking spray | ¼ cup light mayonnaise |
| 2 tsps. olive oil | ½ clove garlic, crushed |
| 1¼ pounds (567 g) assorted small chicken parts, breasts cut into halves | ¼ tsp. smoked paprika |
| | ¼ tsp. salt |
| | ¼ tsp. ground black pepper |
| ½ pound (227 g) mini sweet peppers | Baguette, for serving |

1. Preheat air fryer oven to 375ºF (191ºC). Spray the air fryer basket lightly with cooking spray.
2. In a large bowl, toss the chicken with salt, ground black pepper, and olive oil.
3. Place the sweet peppers and chicken in the air fryer basket. Put the air fryer basket onto the baking pan, and slide the baking pan into Rack Position 2, select

Air Fry and set time to 10 minutes, then transfer the peppers on a plate.
4. Flip the chicken and air fry for another 10 minutes or until well browned.
5. At the same time, combine the mayo, paprika, and garlic in a small bowl. Stir to mix well.
6. Assemble the baguette with chicken and sweet pepper, then spread with mayo mixture and serve hot.

## Turkey Cutlets with Pecan

Prep time: 10 minutes | Cook time: 12 minutes | Serves 4

| | |
|---|---|
| Cooking spray | ¼ cup cornstarch |
| ¾ cup panko bread crumbs | ¼ tsp. salt |
| | ¼ tsp. pepper |
| 1 pound (454 g) turkey cutlets, ½-inch thick | ¼ tsp. dry mustard |
| | ¼ tsp. poultry seasoning |
| 1 egg, beaten | Salt and pepper, to taste |
| ½ cup pecans | |

1. Preheat the air fryer oven to 360ºF (182ºC).
2. In a food processor, place the panko crumbs, salt, pepper, mustard, and poultry seasoning. Process until crumbs are finely crushed. Place pecans and process just until nuts are finely chopped.
3. Put cornstarch in a shallow dish and beaten egg in another. Take coating mixture from food processor into a third shallow dish.
4. Season turkey cutlets with salt and pepper to taste.
5. Dip cutlets in cornstarch and shake off excess, then dip in beaten egg and finally roll in crumbs, pressing to coat well. Spritz both sides lightly with cooking spray.
6. Arrange 2 cutlets in the air fryer basket in a single layer. Place the air fryer basket onto the baking pan, and slide the baking pan into Rack Position 2, select Air Fry and set time to 12 minutes. Repeat with the remaining cutlets.
7. Serve hot.

## Cheesy Turkey and Hummus Wraps

Prep time: 10 minutes | Cook time: 8 minutes | Serves 4

1 cup fresh baby spinach, or more to taste
16 thin slices deli turkey
8 slices provolone cheese

4 large whole wheat wraps
½ cup hummus

1.  Preheat the air fryer oven to 360ºF (182ºC).
2.  To assemble, put 2 tbsps. of hummus on each wrap and spread to within about a half inch from edges. Place 4 slices of turkey and 2 slices of provolone on top. Finish with ¼ cup of baby spinach, or pile on as much as you like.
3.  Roll up each wrap. You don't need to fold or seal the ends.
4.  Arrange 2 wraps in the air fryer basket, seam-side down.
5.  Place the air fryer basket onto the baking pan, and slide the baking pan into Rack Position 2, select Air Fry and set time to 4 minutes. warm filling and melt cheese. Repeat step 4 to air fry the remaining wraps. Serve hot.

## Healthy Turkey and Cauliflower Meatloaf

Prep time: 15 minutes | Cook time: 50 minutes | Serves 6

Cooking spray
2 pounds (907 g) lean ground turkey
1⅓ cups riced cauliflower
2 large eggs, lightly beaten
⅔ cup chopped yellow or white onion
¼ cup almond flour

1 tsp. ground dried turmeric
1 tsp. ground coriander
1 tsp. ground cumin
1 tbsp. minced garlic
1 tsp. salt
1 tsp. ground black pepper

1.  Preheat the air fryer oven to 350ºF (177ºC). Spray a loaf pan lightly with cooking spray.
2.  In a large bowl, combine all the ingredients. Stir to mix well. Pour half of the mixture in the prepared loaf pan and press by using a spatula to coat the bottom evenly. Spray the mixture lightly with cooking spray.
3.  Slide the loaf pan into Rack Position 1, select Convection Bake and set time to 25 minutes, until the meat is well browned and the internal temperature reaches at least 165ºF (74ºC). Repeat this with remaining mixture.
4.  Transfer the loaf pan from the air fryer oven and serve hot.

# Chapter 5 Fish and Seafood

## Spicy Catfish Strips

Prep time: 5 minutes | Cook time: 16 to 18 minutes | Serves 4

Cooking spray
5 catfish fillets, cut into 1½-inch strips
1 cup cornmeal

1 cup buttermilk
1 tbsp. Creole, Cajun, or Old Bay seasoning

1. In a shallow baking dish, pour the buttermilk. Then place the catfish in the dish and refrigerate for at least 1 hour to help remove any fishy taste.
2. Preheat the air fryer oven to 400ºF (204ºC). Spritz the baking pan with cooking spray.
3. Combine cornmeal and Creole seasoning in a shallow bowl.
4. Shake any excess buttermilk off the catfish. Arrange each strip in the cornmeal mixture and coat well. Press the cornmeal into the catfish gently to help it stick.
5. Put the strips in the baking pan in a single layer. Spritz the catfish lightly with cooking spray. You may need to cook them in more than one batch.
6. Slide the baking pan into Rack Position 1, select Convection Bake and set time to 8 minutes. Flip the catfish strips and spritz with cooking spray. Bake for 8 to 10 more minutes, until golden brown and crispy.
7. Serve hot.

## Parmesan Hake with Garlic Sauce

Prep time: 5 minutes | Cook time: 10 minutes | Serves 3

**Fish:**
Nonstick cooking spray
3 hake fillets, patted dry
1 cup grated Parmesan cheese
6 tbsps. mayonnaise
1 tbsp. fresh lime juice
1 tsp. Dijon mustard
Salt, to taste

¼ tsp. ground black pepper, or more to taste
**Garlic Sauce:**
2 tbsps. olive oil
¼ cup plain Greek yogurt
2 cloves garlic, minced
½ tsp. minced tarragon leaves

1. Preheat the air fryer oven to 395ºF (202ºC).
2. In a shallow bowl, mix the mayo, lime juice, and mustard and whisk to combine well. Stir together the grated Parmesan cheese, salt, and pepper in another

shallow bowl.
3. Dredge each fillet in the mayo mixture, then roll them in the cheese mixture until they are well coated on both sides.
4. Spritz the air fryer basket lightly with nonstick cooking spray. Place the fillets in the air fryer basket. Then put the air fryer basket onto the baking pan, and slide the baking pan into Rack Position 2, select Air Fry and set time to 10 minutes, until the fish flakes easily with a fork. Flip the fillets halfway through the cooking time.
5. At the same time, whisk all the ingredients for the sauce in a small bowl, until well incorporated.
6. Serve the fish hot with the sauce.

## Rice Wine Glazed Salmon

Prep time: 5 minutes | Cook time: 12 to 16 minutes | Serves 4

Cooking spray
1 tbsp. toasted sesame oil
4 (6-ounce / 170-g) salmon fillets, skin-on
3 tbsps. soy sauce

1 tbsp. rice wine or dry sherry
1 tbsp. brown sugar
1 tsp. minced garlic
¼ tsp. minced ginger
½ tbsp. sesame seeds

1. Mix the soy sauce, rice wine, brown sugar, toasted sesame oil, garlic, and ginger in a small bowl.
2. In a shallow baking dish, place the salmon and pour the marinade over the fillets. Cover and refrigerate for at least 1 hour, turning the fillets occasionally to coat in the marinade.
3. Preheat the air fryer oven to 370ºF (188ºC). Spritz the air fryer basket with cooking spray.
4. Shake off as much marinade as possible and put the fillets, skin-side down, in the air fryer basket in a single layer. Reserve the marinade. You may need to cook the fillets in batches.
5. Place the air fryer basket onto the baking pan, and slide the baking pan into Rack Position 2, select Air Fry and set time to 10 minutes. Coat the tops of the salmon fillets with the reserved marinade and scatter with sesame seeds.
6. Raise the temperature to 400ºF (204ºC) and air fry for another 2 to 5 minutes for medium, 1 to 3 minutes for medium rare, or 4 to 6 minutes for well done.
7. Serve hot.

# Easy Salmon Fillets

Prep time: 10 minutes | Cook time: 15 minutes | Serves 4

Cooking spray
1 tbsp. olive oil
4 (6-ounce / 170-g) salmon fillets, skin-on
¼ cup soy sauce
¼ cup rice wine vinegar

1 tbsp. brown sugar
1 tsp. mustard powder
½ tsp. minced garlic
1 tsp. ground ginger
½ tsp. freshly ground black pepper

1. Combine the soy sauce, rice wine vinegar, brown sugar, olive oil, mustard powder, ginger, black pepper, and garlic in a small bowl to make a marinade.
2. In a shallow baking dish, place the fillets and pour the marinade over them. Cover the baking dish and marinate for at least 1 hour in the refrigerator, turning the fillets occasionally to keep them coated in the marinade.
3. Preheat the air fryer oven to 370ºF (188ºC). Spritz the air fryer basket with cooking spray.
4. Shake off as much marinade as possible from the fillets and arrange them, skin-side down, in the air fryer basket in a single layer. You may need to cook the fillets in batches.
5. Place the air fryer basket onto the baking pan, and slide the baking pan into Rack Position 2, select Air Fry and set time to 15 minutes. The minimum internal temperature should be 145ºF (63ºC) at the thickest part of the fillets.
6. Serve warm.

## Coconut Shrimp with Sweet Chili Mayo

Prep time: 15 minutes | Cook time: 8 minutes | Serves 4

**Sweet Chili Mayo:**
3 tbsps. Thai sweet chili sauce
3 tbsps. mayonnaise
1 tbsp. Sriracha sauce
**Shrimp:**
Cooking spray
24 extra-jumbo shrimp (about 1 pound / 454 g),

peeled and deveined
2 large eggs
⅔ cup sweetened shredded coconut
⅔ cup panko bread crumbs
2 tbsps. all-purpose or gluten-free flour
Kosher salt, to taste

1. Combine the mayonnaise, Thai sweet chili sauce, and Sriracha in a medium bowl, and mix well.
2. Combine the coconut, panko, and ¼ tsp. Salt in another medium bowl. Put the flour in a shallow bowl. Whisk the eggs in another shallow bowl.
3. Sprinkle the shrimp with ⅛ tsp. salt. Dip the shrimp in the flour, shaking off any excess, then into the egg. Coat in the coconut-panko mixture, gently pressing to adhere, then take to a large plate. Spritz both sides of the shrimp lightly with oil.
4. Preheat the air fryer oven to 360ºF (182ºC).
5. Working in batches, put a single layer of the shrimp in the air fryer basket. Then place the air fryer basket onto the baking pan, and slide the baking pan into Rack Position 2, select Air Fry and set time to 8 minutes, flipping halfway, until the crust is golden brown and the shrimp are cooked through.
6. Serve hot with the sweet chili mayo for dipping.

## Traditional Shrimp Empanadas

Prep time: 10 minutes | Cook time: 8 minutes | Serves 5

Cooking spray
½ pound (227g) raw shrimp, peeled, deveined and chopped
10 frozen Goya Empanada Discos, thawed
1 large egg, beaten
¼ cup chopped red onion
2 garlic cloves, minced

1 scallion, chopped
2 tbsps. chopped fresh cilantro
2 tbsps. minced red bell pepper
½ tbsp. fresh lime juice
¼ tsp. sweet paprika
⅛ tsp. kosher salt
⅛ tsp. crushed red pepper flakes (optional)

1. Combine the shrimp, red onion, scallion, garlic, bell pepper, cilantro, lime juice, paprika, salt, and pepper flakes (if using) in a medium bowl.
2. Beat the egg with 1 tsp. water in a small bowl until smooth.
3. Put an empanada disc on a work surface and place 2 tbsps. of the shrimp mixture in the center. Brush the outer edges of the disc with the egg wash. Fold the disc over and carefully press the edges to seal. With a fork, press around the edges to crimp and seal completely. Then brush the tops of the empanadas with the egg wash.
4. Preheat the air fryer oven to 380ºF (193ºC).
5. Spritz the bottom of the air fryer basket lightly with cooking spray to prevent sticking. Working in batches, spread a single layer of the empanadas in the air fryer basket. Place the air fryer basket onto the baking pan, and slide the baking pan into Rack Position 2, select Air Fry and set time to 8 minutes, flipping halfway, until golden brown and crispy.
6. Serve warm.

## Herbed Shrimp and Zucchini

Prep time: 15 minutes | Cook time: 7 minutes | Serves 4

1½ tbsps. olive oil
1¼ pounds (567 g) extra-large raw shrimp, peeled and deveined
2 medium zucchinis (about 8 ounces / 227 g each), halved lengthwise and cut into ½-inch-thick slices

Juice of ½ lemon
1 tbsp. chopped fresh mint
1 tbsp. chopped fresh dill
½ tsp. garlic salt
1½ tsps. dried oregano
⅛ tsp. crushed red pepper flakes (optional)

1. Preheat the air fryer oven to 350ºF (177ºC).
2. Combine the shrimp, zucchini, oil, garlic salt, oregano, and pepper flakes (if using) in a large bowl, and toss to coat well.
3. Working in batches, place a single layer of the shrimp and zucchini in the air fryer basket. Then put the air fryer basket onto the baking pan, and slide the baking pan into Rack Position 2, select Air Fry and set time to 7 minutes, flipping halfway, until the zucchini is golden and the shrimp are cooked through.
4. Take to a serving dish and tent with foil while you air fry the remaining shrimp and zucchini.
5. Squeeze fresh lime juice over top and garnish with mint, and dill. Serve hot.

## Blackened Salmon with Cucumber-Avocado Salsa

Prep time: 10 minutes | Cook time: 6 minutes | Serves 4

**Salmon:**
Cooking spray
4 (6 ounces / 170 g each) wild salmon fillets
1 tbsp. sweet paprika
1 tsp. garlic powder
1 tsp. dried oregano
1 tsp. dried thyme
½ tsp. cayenne pepper
¾ tsp. kosher salt
⅛ tsp. freshly ground black pepper
**Cucumber-Avocado Salsa:**

1 tsp. extra-virgin olive oil
4 Persian cucumbers, diced
6 ounces (170 g) Hass avocado, diced
2 tbsps. chopped red onion
1½ tbsps. fresh lemon juice
¼ tsp. plus ⅛ tsp. kosher salt
Freshly ground black pepper, to taste

1. For the salmon: Combine the paprika, cayenne, garlic powder, oregano, thyme, salt, and black pepper in a small bowl. Spritz both sides of the fish lightly with oil and rub all over. Coat the fish all over with the spices.
2. For the cucumber-avocado salsa: Combine the red onion, lemon juice, olive oil, salt, and pepper in a medium bowl. Let rest for 5 minutes, then place the cucumbers and avocado.
3. Preheat the air fryer oven to 400ºF (204ºC).
4. Working in batches, put the salmon fillets skin side down in the baking pan. Slide the baking pan into Rack Position 2, select Roast and set time to 6 minutes, until the fish flakes easily with a fork, depending on the thickness of the fish.
5. Top with the salsa and serve warm.

## Tortilla Shrimp Tacos with Spicy Mayo

Prep time: 10 minutes | Cook time: 6 minutes | Serves 4

**Spicy Mayo:**
3 tbsps. mayonnaise
1 tbsp. Louisiana-style hot pepper sauce
**Cilantro-Lime Slaw:**
2 cups shredded green cabbage
1 small jalapeño, thinly sliced
½ small red onion, thinly sliced
Juice of 1 lime
2 tbsps. chopped fresh

cilantro
¼ tsp. kosher salt
**Shrimp:**
Cooking spray
8 corn tortillas, for serving
24 jumbo shrimp (about 1 pound / 454 g), peeled and deveined
1 large egg, beaten
1 cup crushed tortilla chips
⅛ tsp. kosher salt

1. For the spicy mayo: Mix the mayonnaise and hot pepper sauce in a small bowl.
2. For the cilantro-lime slaw: Toss together the cabbage, onion, jalapeño, cilantro, lime juice, and salt to combine in a large bowl. Cover and refrigerate to chill.
3. For the shrimp: Put the egg in a shallow bowl and the crushed tortilla chips in another. Sprinkle the shrimp with the salt. Dip the shrimp in the egg, then in the crumbs, pressing gently to adhere. Arrange on a work surface and spray both sides lightly with oil.
4. Preheat the air fryer oven to 360ºF (182ºC).
5. Working in batches, lay a single layer of the shrimp in the baking pan. Slide the baking pan into Rack Position 2, select Roast and set time to 6 minutes, flipping halfway, until golden and cooked through in the center.
6. To serve, put 2 tortillas on each plate and top each with 3 shrimps and ¼ cup slaw, then drizzle with spicy mayo. Serve hot.

## Chili Shrimp and Black Beans Bowl

Prep time: 10 minutes | Cook time: 10 to 15 minutes | Serves 4

Cooking spray
1 tsp. olive oil
12 ounces (340 g) medium shrimp, peeled and deveined
1 (15-ounce / 425-g) can seasoned black beans, warmed
2 cups cooked brown rice
1 cup sliced cherry tomatoes
1 large avocado, chopped
2 tsps. lime juice
1 tsp. honey
1 tsp. minced garlic
1 tsp. chili powder
Salt, to taste

1. Preheat the air fryer oven to 400ºF (204ºC). Spritz the air fryer basket with cooking spray.
2. Mix together the lime juice, olive oil, honey, garlic, chili powder, and salt in a medium bowl to make a marinade.
3. Place the shrimp and toss to coat well in the marinade.
4. Arrange the shrimp in the air fryer basket. Then place the air fryer basket onto the baking pan, and slide the baking pan into Rack Position 2, select Air Fry and set time to 5 minutes. Flip and air fry for an additional 5 to 10 minutes, until the shrimp are cooked through and starting to brown.
5. To assemble the bowls, scoop ¼ of the rice, avocado, black beans, and cherry tomatoes into each of four bowls. Place the shrimp on top and serve warm.

## Breaded Fish Sticks

Prep time: 15 minutes | Cook time: 11 to 13 minutes | Serves 4

Cooking spray
4 fish fillets
2 eggs
1½ cups whole-wheat panko bread crumbs
½ cup whole-wheat flour
½ tbsp. dried parsley flakes
1 tsp. seasoned salt

1. Preheat the air fryer oven to 400ºF (204ºC). Spritz the baking pan with cooking spray.
2. Cut the fish fillets lengthwise into "sticks."
3. Mix the whole-wheat flour and seasoned salt in a shallow bowl.
4. Whisk the eggs with 1 tsp. of water in a small bowl.
5. Mix the panko bread crumbs and parsley flakes in another shallow bowl.
6. Coat each fish stick in the seasoned flour, then in the egg mixture, and dredge them in the panko bread crumbs.

7. Arrange the fish sticks in the baking pan in a single layer and spritz lightly the fish sticks with cooking spray. You may need to cook them in batches.
8. Slide the baking pan into Rack Position 1, select Convection Bake and set time to 6 minutes. Flip the fish sticks over and lightly spritz with the cooking spray. Bake for 5 to 7 more minutes, until golden brown and crispy.
9. Serve hot.

## Cod Croquettes with Lemon-Dill Aioli

Prep time: 15 minutes | Cook time: 10 minutes | Serves 4

**Croquettes:**
Cooking spray
2 tsps. olive oil
3 large eggs, divided
12 ounces (340 g) raw cod fillet, flaked apart with two forks
¾ cup plus 2 tbsps. bread crumbs, divided
½ cup boxed instant mashed potatoes
⅓ cup chopped fresh dill
¼ cup 1% milk
1 shallot, minced
1 large garlic clove, minced
1 tsp. fresh lemon juice
½ tsp. dried thyme
1 tsp. kosher salt
¼ tsp. freshly ground black pepper
**Lemon-Dill Aioli:**
5 tbsps. mayonnaise
Juice of ½ lemon
1 tbsp. chopped fresh dill

1. For the croquettes: Lightly beat 2 of the eggs in a medium bowl. Then add the fish, milk, instant mashed potatoes, olive oil, shallot, dill, garlic, 2 tbsps. of the bread crumbs, lemon juice, salt, thyme, and pepper. Mix to combine well. Put in the refrigerator for 30 minutes.
2. For the lemon-dill aioli: Combine the mayonnaise, lemon juice, and dill in a small bowl. Set it aside.
3. Measure out about 3½ tbsps. of the fish mixture and gently roll in your hands to form a log about 3 inches long. Repeat this to make a total of 12 logs.
4. In a small bowl, beat the remaining egg. Put the remaining ¾ cup bread crumbs in a separate bowl. Dip the croquettes in the egg, then coat in the bread crumbs, carefully pressing to adhere. Arrange on a work surface and spritz both sides lightly with cooking spray.
5. Preheat the air fryer oven to 350ºF (177ºC).
6. Working in batches, lay a single layer of the croquettes in the air fryer basket. Then place the air fryer basket onto the baking pan, and slide the baking pan into Rack Position 2, select Air Fry and set time to 10 minutes, flipping halfway, until golden.
7. Serve hot with the aioli for dipping.

## Spicy Orange Glazed Shrimp

Prep time: 20 minutes | Cook time: 10 to 15 minutes | Serves 4

Cooking spray
⅓ cup orange juice
1 pound (454 g) medium shrimp, peeled and deveined, with tails off

3 tsps. minced garlic
1 tsp. Old Bay seasoning
¼ to ½ tsp. cayenne pepper

1. Combine the orange juice, garlic, Old Bay seasoning, and cayenne pepper in a medium bowl.
2. Pat the shrimp with paper towels to remove excess water.
3. Place the shrimp to the marinade and stir to coat well. Cover with plastic wrap and put in the refrigerator for 30 minutes so the shrimp can soak up the marinade.
4. Preheat the air fryer oven to 400ºF (204ºC). Spritz the air fryer basket with cooking spray.
5. Place the shrimp into the air fryer basket. Put the air fryer basket onto the baking pan, and slide the baking pan into Rack Position 2, select Air Fry and set time to 5 minutes. Flip and spritz with olive oil. Air fry for 5 to 10 more minutes until the shrimp are opaque and crisp.
6. Serve hot.

## Simple Roasted Fish with Almond-Lemon Crumbs

Prep time: 10 minutes | Cook time: 7 minutes | Serves 4

Cooking spray
½ tbsp. extra-virgin olive oil
4 (6 ounces / 170 g each) skinless fish fillets
½ cup raw whole almonds
1 scallion, finely chopped

Grated zest and juice of 1 lemon
1 tsp. Dijon mustard
¾ tsp. kosher salt, divided
Freshly ground black pepper, to taste

1. Pulse the almonds to coarsely chop in a food processor. Transfer to a small bowl and place the scallion, lemon zest, and olive oil. Sprinkle with ¼ tsp. of the salt and pepper to taste and mix to combine well.
2. Spritz the top of the fish lightly with oil and squeeze the lemon juice over the fish. Sprinkle with the remaining ½ tsp. salt and pepper to taste. Lay the mustard on top of the fish. Dividing evenly, press the almond mixture onto the top of the fillets to adhere.
3. Preheat the air fryer oven to 375ºF (191ºC).
4. Working in batches, arrange the fillets in the baking pan in a single layer. Slide the baking pan into Rack Position 2, select Roast and set time to 7 minutes, until the crumbs start to brown and the fish is cooked through.
5. Serve hot.

## Salmon Burgers with Lemon-Caper Rémoulade

Prep time: 15 minutes | Cook time: 12 minutes | Serves 5

**Lemon-Caper Rémoulade:**
½ cup mayonnaise
2 tbsps. chopped fresh parsley
2 tbsps. minced drained capers
2 tsps. fresh lemon juice
**Salmon Patties:**
1 pound (454 g) wild salmon fillet, skinned and pin bones removed
1 large egg, lightly beaten
¼ cup minced red onion

plus ¼ cup slivered for serving
6 tbsps. panko bread crumbs
1 garlic clove, minced
1 tbsp. chopped fresh parsley
1 tbsp. Dijon mustard
1 tsp. fresh lemon juice
½ tsp. kosher salt
**For Serving:**
5 whole wheat potato buns or gluten-free buns
10 butter lettuce leaves

1. For the lemon-caper rémoulade: Combine the mayonnaise, capers, parsley, and lemon juice in a small bowl and mix well.
2. For the salmon patties: Cut off a 4-ounce / 113-g piece of the salmon and take to a food processor. Pulse until it becomes pasty. Using a sharp knife, cut the remaining salmon into small cubes.
3. Combine the chopped and processed salmon with the panko, minced red onion, garlic, egg, mustard, lemon juice, parsley, and salt in a medium bowl. Toss to combine well. Shape the mixture into 5 patties about ¾ inch thick. Refrigerate for at least 30 minutes.
4. Preheat the air fryer oven to 400ºF (204ºC).
5. Working in batches, arrange the patties in the baking pan. Slide the baking pan into Rack Position 2, select Roast and set time to 12 minutes, gently flipping halfway, until golden and cooked through.
6. To serve, take each patty to a bun. Then place 2 lettuce leaves, 2 tbsps. of the rémoulade, and the slivered red onions on each patty. Serve hot.

## Lemony Shrimp with Parsley

Prep time: 10 minutes | Cook time: 5 minutes | Serves 4

2 tbsps. extra-virgin olive oil
18 shrimp, shelled and deveined
½ cup fresh parsley, coarsely chopped
2 garlic cloves, peeled and minced

2 tbsps. freshly squeezed lemon juice
1 tsp. lemon-pepper seasoning
1 tsp. onion powder
½ tsp. hot paprika
½ tsp. salt
¼ tsp. cumin powder

1. In a mixing bowl, toss all the ingredients until the shrimp are well coated.
2. Cover and let marinate in the refrigerator for about 30 minutes.
3. Preheat the air fryer oven to 400ºF (204ºC).
4. Place the shrimp in the baking pan. Slide the baking pan into Rack Position 2, select Roast and set time to 5 minutes, until the shrimp are pink on the outside and opaque in the center.
5. Transfer the shrimp from the oven to a plate and serve hot.

## Remoulade Golden Crab Cakes

Prep time: 15 minutes | Cook time: 10 minutes | Serves 4

**Remoulade:**
¾ cup mayonnaise
2 tsps. Dijon mustard
1½ tsps. yellow mustard
1 tsp. vinegar
1 tsp. tiny capers, drained and chopped
¼ tsp. hot sauce
¼ tsp. salt
⅛ tsp. ground black pepper
**Crab Cakes:**
Cooking spray

6 ounces (170 g) crab meat
1 cup bread crumbs, divided
1 scallion, finely chopped
2 tbsps. mayonnaise
2 tbsps. pasteurized egg product (liquid eggs in a carton)
2 tsps. lemon juice
½ tsp. red pepper flakes
½ tsp. Old Bay seasoning

1. Preheat the air fryer oven to 400ºF (204ºC).
2. Whisk to combine the mayonnaise, Dijon mustard, yellow mustard, vinegar, hot sauce, capers, salt, and pepper in a small bowl.
3. Refrigerate for at least 1 hour before serving.
4. Put a parchment liner in the baking pan.
5. Mix to combine ½ cup of bread crumbs with the mayonnaise and scallion in a large bowl. Set the other ½ cup of bread crumbs aside in a small bowl.

6. Place the crab meat, egg product, red pepper flakes, lemon juice, and Old Bay seasoning to the large bowl, and stir to combine well.
7. Distribute the crab mixture evenly into 4 portions, and form into patties.
8. Dredge each patty in the remaining bread crumbs to coat well.
9. Arrange the prepared patties on the liner in the baking pan in a single layer.
10. Spritz with cooking spray. Slide the baking pan into Rack Position 1, select Convection Bake and set time to 6 minutes. Flip the crab cakes over, bake for an additional 5 minutes, until golden, and serve hot.

## Panko Crab and Fish Cakes

Prep time: 20 minutes | Cook time: 10 minutes | Serves 4

Cooking spray
8 ounces (227 g) imitation crab meat
¾ cup crushed saltine cracker crumbs
4 ounces (113 g) leftover cooked fish (such as cod, pollock, or haddock)
½ cup panko bread crumbs
2 tbsps. light mayonnaise
2 tbsps. minced celery

2 tbsps. minced green onion
1 tbsp. plus 2 tsps. Worcestershire sauce
2 tsps. dried parsley flakes
1 tsp. prepared yellow mustard
½ tsp. garlic powder
½ tsp. dried dill weed, crushed
½ tsp. Old Bay seasoning

1. Preheat the air fryer oven to 390ºF (199ºC).
2. In a food processor, pulse the crab meat and fish until finely chopped.
3. Take the meat mixture to a large bowl, along with the celery, green onion, mayo, Worcestershire sauce, cracker crumbs, mustard, parsley flakes, garlic powder, dill weed, and Old Bay seasoning. Stir to combine well.
4. Spoon out the meat mixture and shape into 8 equal-sized patties with your hands.
5. Put the panko bread crumbs on a plate. Roll the patties in the bread crumbs until they are evenly coated on both sides. Spray the patties lightly with cooking spray.
6. Arrange the patties in the baking pan. Slide the baking pan into Rack Position 1, select Convection Bake and set time to 10 minutes, flipping them halfway through, or until they are golden brown and cooked through.
7. Distribute the patties among four plates and serve warm.

## Cod Cakes with Basil

Prep time: 15 minutes | Cook time: 12 minutes | Serves 4

Cooking spray
1 pound (454 g) cod fillets, cut into chunks
1 large egg, beaten
1 cup panko bread crumbs
⅓ cup packed fresh basil leaves
3 cloves garlic, crushed
½ tsp. smoked paprika
¼ tsp. salt
¼ tsp. pepper
Salad greens, for serving

1. Pulse cod, basil, garlic, smoked paprika, salt, and pepper in a food processor until cod is finely chopped, stirring occasionally. Shape into 8 patties, about 2 inches in diameter. Dip each first into the egg, then into the panko, patting to adhere. Spritz lightly with oil on one side.
2. Preheat the air fryer oven to 400ºF (204ºC).
3. Working in batches, arrange half the cakes in the baking pan, oil-side down; spray lightly with oil. Slide the baking pan into Rack Position 1, select Convection Bake and set time to 12 minutes, until golden brown and cooked through.
4. Serve hot with salad greens.

## Lemony Shrimp

Prep time: 10 minutes | Cook time: 10 to 15 minutes | Serves 4

Cooking spray
2 tsps. olive oil
12 ounces (340 g) medium shrimp, deveined, with tails on
2 tsps. minced garlic
2 tsps. lemon juice
½ to 1 tsp. crushed red pepper

1. Mix together the garlic, lemon juice, olive oil, and crushed red pepper in a medium bowl to make a marinade.
2. Place the shrimp and toss to coat well in the marinade. Cover with plastic wrap and put the bowl in the refrigerator for 30 minutes.
3. Preheat the air fryer oven to 400ºF (204ºC). Spritz the air fryer basket with cooking spray.
4. Arrange the shrimp in the air fryer basket. Place the air fryer basket onto the baking pan, and slide the baking pan into Rack Position 2, select Air Fry and set time to 5 minutes. Flip and air fry for an additional 5 to 10 minutes, until the shrimp are cooked through and nicely browned. Let cool for 5 minutes before serving.

## Easy Shrimp and Artichoke Paella

Prep time: 5 minutes | Cook time: 14 to 17 minutes | Serves 4

1 (10-ounce / 284-g) package frozen cooked rice, thawed
1 (6-ounce / 170-g) jar artichoke hearts, drained and chopped
1 cup frozen cooked small shrimp
1 tomato, diced
½ cup frozen baby peas
¼ cup vegetable broth
½ tsp. dried thyme
½ tsp. turmeric

1. Preheat the air fryer oven to 340ºF (171ºC).
2. Mix together the chopped artichoke hearts, cooked rice, vegetable broth, thyme, and turmeric in a baking pan and stir to combine well.
3. Slide the baking pan into Rack Position 1, select Convection Bake and set time to 9 minutes, until the rice is heated through.
4. Transfer the pan from the air fryer oven and gently fold in the shrimp, baby peas, and diced tomato and mix well.
5. Return to the air fryer oven and continue cooking for about 5 to 8 minutes, or until the shrimp are done and the paella is bubbling.
6. Let rest for 5 minutes before serving.

## Country Shrimp and Sausage

Prep time: 10 minutes | Cook time: 18 minutes | Serves 4

Cooking spray
2 tbsps. olive oil
1 pound (454 g) large shrimp, deveined, with tails on
1 pound (454 g) smoked turkey sausage, cut into thick slices
1 zucchini, cut into bite-sized pieces
2 corn cobs, quartered
1 red bell pepper, cut into chunks
1 tbsp. Old Bay seasoning

1. Preheat the air fryer oven to 400ºF (204ºC). Spritz the air fryer basket with cooking spray.
2. Mix the shrimp, turkey sausage, corn, zucchini, bell pepper, and Old Bay seasoning in a large bowl, and toss to coat with the spices. Pour in the olive oil and toss again until evenly coated.
3. Arrange the mixture in the air fryer basket in a single layer. You will need to cook in batches.
4. Place the air fryer basket onto the baking pan, and slide the baking pan into Rack Position 2, select Air Fry and set time to 18 minutes, or until cooked through, flipping every 5 minutes for even cooking.
5. Serve warm.

# Cheesy Fish Fillets

Prep time: 8 minutes | Cook time: 17 minutes | Serves 4

4 (4-ounce / 113-g) fish fillets, halved
2 eggs, beaten
⅓ cup grated Parmesan cheese
½ tsp. fennel seed
½ tsp. tarragon
⅓ tsp. mixed peppercorns
2 tbsps. dry white wine
1 tsp. seasoned salt

1. Preheat the air fryer oven to 345ºF (174ºC).
2. In a food processor, place the grated Parmesan cheese, fennel seed, tarragon, and mixed peppercorns and pulse for about 20 seconds until well combined. Take the cheese mixture to a shallow dish.
3. In another shallow dish, place the beaten eggs.
4. Drizzle the dry white wine over the top of fish fillets. Dredge each fillet in the beaten eggs on both sides, shaking off any excess, then roll them in the cheese mixture until fully coated. Sprinkle with the salt to taste.
5. Place the fillets in the air fryer basket. Then put the air fryer basket onto the baking pan, and slide the baking pan into Rack Position 2, select Air Fry and set time to 17 minutes, until the fish is cooked through and no longer translucent. Flip the fillets once halfway through the cooking time.
6. Let rest for 5 minutes before serving.

# Quick Shrimp and Cherry Tomato Kebabs

Prep time: 15 minutes | Cook time: 5 minutes | Serves 4

1½ pounds (680 g) jumbo shrimp, cleaned, shelled and deveined
1 pound (454 g) cherry tomatoes
2 tbsps. butter, melted
1 tbsps. Sriracha sauce
1 tsp. dried parsley flakes
½ tsp. dried oregano
½ tsp. mustard seeds
½ tsp. dried basil
½ tsp. marjoram
Sea salt and ground black pepper, to taste
**Special Equipment:**
4 to 6 wooden skewers, soaked in water for 30 minutes

1. Preheat the air fryer oven to 400ºF (204ºC).
2. In a large bowl, place all the ingredients and toss to coat well.
3. Make the kebabs: Thread, alternating jumbo shrimp and cherry tomatoes, onto the wooden skewers that

fit into the air fryer oven.

4. Place the kebabs in the baking pan. You may need to work in batches depending on the size of your air fryer oven.
5. Slide the baking pan into Rack Position 2, select Roast and set time to 5 minutes, until the shrimp are pink and the cherry tomatoes are soft. Repeat with the remaining kebabs.
6. Allow the shrimp and cherry tomato kebabs to rest for 5 minutes and serve warm.

# Appetizing Spring Rolls

Prep time: 10 minutes | Cook time: 17 to 22 minutes | Serves 4

Cooking spray
16 square spring roll wrappers
2 (4-ounce / 113-g) cans tiny shrimp, drained
2 cups finely sliced cabbage
1 cup matchstick cut carrots
4 tsps. soy sauce
2 tsps. minced garlic
Salt and freshly ground black pepper, to taste

1. Preheat the air fryer oven to 370ºF (188ºC).
2. Spritz the air fryer basket with cooking spray. Spray a medium sauté pan lightly with cooking spray.
3. Place the garlic to the sauté pan and cook over medium heat until fragrant, about 30 to 45 seconds. Put the cabbage and carrots and sauté until the vegetables are slightly soft, about 5 minutes.
4. Add the shrimp and soy sauce and sprinkle with salt and pepper to taste, then stir to combine well. Sauté until the moisture has evaporated, 2 more minutes. Set it aside to cool.
5. Arrange a spring roll wrapper on a work surface so it looks like a diamond. Spread 1 tbsp. of the shrimp mixture on the lower end of the wrapper.
6. Roll the wrapper away from you halfway, then fold in the right and left sides, like an envelope. Continue to roll to the very end and use a little water to seal the edge. Repeat this with the remaining wrappers and filling.
7. Put the spring rolls in the air fryer basket in a single layer, leaving room between each roll. Spritz lightly with cooking spray. You may need to cook them in batches.
8. Place the air fryer basket onto the baking pan, and slide the baking pan into Rack Position 2, select Air Fry and set time to 5 minutes. Turn the rolls over, lightly spritz with cooking spray, and air fry for 5 to 10 more minutes until heated through and the rolls start to brown. Let cool for 5 minutes before serving.

Italian Scallops, page 73

Lemony Shrimp, page 67

Breaded Fish Sticks, page 64

Crispy Salmon Patty Bites, page 77

## Lemony Tilapia

Prep time: 5 minutes | Cook time: 12 minutes |
Serves 4

| | |
|---|---|
| 1 tbsp. olive oil | 1 tbsp. lemon juice |
| 4 (6-ounce / 170-g) tilapia | 1 tsp. minced garlic |
| fillets | ½ tsp. chili powder |

1. Preheat the air fryer oven to 380ºF (193ºC). Line the air fryer basket with parchment paper.
2. Mix together the lemon juice, olive oil, garlic, and chili powder in a large, shallow bowl to make a marinade. Put the tilapia fillets in the bowl and coat well.
3. Arrange the fillets in the air fryer basket in a single layer, leaving space between each fillet. You may need to work in more than one batch.
4. Place the air fryer basket onto the baking pan, and slide the baking pan into Rack Position 2, select Convection Broil and set time to 12 minutes, until the fish is cooked and flakes easily with a fork.
5. Serve warm.

## Air-Fried Scallops with Shallot

Prep time: 10 minutes | Cook time: 12 minutes |
Serves 2

| | |
|---|---|
| Cooking spray | aminos |
| 1½ tbsps. olive oil | 1 tbsp. Mediterranean |
| 1 pound (454 g) scallops, | seasoning mix |
| cleaned | ½ tbsp. balsamic vinegar |
| ⅓ cup shallots, chopped | ½ tsp. ginger, grated |
| 1 clove garlic, chopped | Belgian endive, for |
| 1½ tbsps. coconut | garnish |

1. In a small skillet over medium heat, place all the ingredients except the scallops and Belgian endive and stir to combine well. Allow this mixture to simmer for 2 minutes.
2. Transfer the mixture from the skillet to a large bowl and keep aside to cool.
3. Put the scallops, coating them all over, then transfer to the refrigerator to marinate for at least 2 hours.
4. Preheat the air fryer oven to 345ºF (174ºC).
5. Spread the scallops in the air fryer basket in a single layer and spritz lightly with cooking spray.
6. Place the air fryer basket onto the baking pan, and slide the baking pan into Rack Position 2, select Air Fry and set time to 10 minutes, flipping the scallops halfway through, or until the scallops are tender and opaque.
7. Garnish with the Belgian endive and serve warm.

## Simple Bacon-Wrapped Scallops

Prep time: 5 minutes | Cook time: 10 minutes |
Serves 4

| | |
|---|---|
| Cooking spray | black pepper, to taste |
| 16 sea scallops, patted | 16 toothpicks, soaked |
| dry | in water for at least 30 |
| 8 slices bacon, cut in half | minutes |
| Salt and freshly ground | |

1. Preheat the air fryer oven to 370ºF (188ºC).
2. Wrap half of a slice of bacon around each scallop and secure with a toothpick on a clean work surface.
3. Arrange the bacon-wrapped scallops in the air fryer basket in a single layer. You may need to cook in batches to avoid overcrowding.
4. Spray the scallops lightly with cooking spray and season the salt and pepper to taste.
5. Place the air fryer basket onto the baking pan, and slide the baking pan into Rack Position 2, select Air Fry and set time to 10 minutes, flipping the scallops halfway through, until the bacon is cooked through and the scallops are firm.
6. Transfer the scallops from the oven to a plate and repeat this with the remaining scallops. Serve hot.

## Simple Breaded Scallops

Prep time: 5 minutes | Cook time: 7 minutes | Serves 4

| | |
|---|---|
| 2 tbsps. olive oil | 1 cup bread crumbs |
| 1 pound (454 g) fresh | 3 tbsps. flour |
| scallops | Salt and black pepper, to |
| 1 egg | taste |

1. Preheat the air fryer oven to 360ºF (182ºC).
2. Lightly beat the egg in a bowl. Add the flour and bread crumbs into separate shallow dishes.
3. Dredge the scallops in the flour and shake off any excess. Dip the flour-coated scallops in the beaten egg and roll in the bread crumbs.
4. Coat the scallops generously with olive oil and sprinkle with salt and pepper, to taste.
5. Spread the scallops in the air fryer basket. Then place the air fryer basket onto the baking pan, and slide the baking pan into Rack Position 2, select Air Fry and set time to 7 minutes, until the scallops are firm and reach an internal temperature of just 145ºF (63ºC) on a meat thermometer. Flip halfway through the cooking time.
6. Allow the scallops to rest for 5 minutes and serve warm.

## Fried Shrimp with Mayo Sauce

Prep time: 5 minutes | Cook time: 7 minutes | Serves 4

**Shrimp:**
12 jumbo shrimp
½ tsp. garlic salt
¼ tsp. freshly cracked mixed peppercorns
**Sauce:**

4 tbsps. mayonnaise
1 tsp. chipotle powder
1 tsp. Dijon mustard
1 tsp. grated lemon rind
½ tsp. cumin powder

1. Preheat the air fryer oven to 395ºF (202ºC).
2. Season the shrimp with garlic salt and cracked mixed peppercorns in a medium bowl.
3. Arrange the shrimp in the air fryer basket. Place the air fryer basket onto the baking pan, and slide the baking pan into Rack Position 2, select Air Fry and set time to 5 minutes. Turn the shrimp over and cook for an additional 2 minutes until they are pink and no longer opaque.
4. At the same time, stir together all the ingredients for the sauce in a small bowl until well combined.
5. Transfer the shrimp from the oven and serve hot alongside the sauce.

## Red Cabbage and Fish Tacos

Prep time: 10 minutes | Cook time: 10 minutes | Serves 4

2 tsps. olive oil
1 pound (454 g) white fish fillets
4 soft low-sodium whole-wheat tortillas
1 large carrot, grated
1½ cups chopped red

cabbage
½ cup low-sodium salsa
⅓ cup low-fat Greek yogurt
3 tbsps. freshly squeezed lemon juice, divided

1. Preheat the air fryer oven to 400ºF (204ºC).
2. Coat the fish with the olive oil and scatter with 1 tbsp. of lemon juice. Put the fish in the air fryer basket. Then place the air fryer basket onto the baking pan, and slide the baking pan into Rack Position 2, select Air Fry and set time to 10 minutes, until the fish just flakes when tested with a fork.
3. At the same time, stir together the remaining 2 tbsps. of lemon juice, the red cabbage, carrot, salsa, and yogurt in a medium bowl.
4. When the fish is cooked, transfer it from the oven and break it up into large pieces.
5. Provide the fish, tortillas, and the cabbage mixture, and let each person assemble a taco.
6. Serve hot.

## Balsamic Shrimp with Goat Cheese

Prep time: 15 minutes | Cook time: 7 minutes | Serves 2

1½ tbsps. olive oil
1 pound (454 g) shrimp, deveined
1 cup shredded goat cheese
1½ tbsps. balsamic vinegar
1 tbsp. coconut aminos
½ tbsp. fresh parsley,

roughly chopped
1 tsp. Dijon mustard
½ tsp. smoked cayenne pepper
½ tsp. garlic powder
Sea salt flakes, to taste
Salt and ground black peppercorns, to taste

1. Preheat the air fryer oven to 385ºF (196ºC).
2. In a large bowl, stir together all the ingredients, except for the cheese, until the shrimp are evenly coated.
3. Place the shrimp in the air fryer basket. Then put the air fryer basket onto the baking pan, and slide the baking pan into Rack Position 2, select Air Fry and set time to 7 minutes, flipping halfway through, or until the shrimp are pink and cooked through.
4. Sprinkle with the shredded goat cheese and serve warm.

## Breaded Flounder Fillets

Prep time: 8 minutes | Cook time: 12 minutes | Serves 2

Cooking spray
2 flounder fillets, patted dry
1 egg
¼ cup almond flour
¼ cup coconut flour

½ tsp. Worcestershire sauce
¼ tsp. chili powder
½ tsp. coarse sea salt
½ tsp. lemon pepper

1. Preheat the air fryer oven to 390ºF (199ºC). Spray the baking pan lightly with cooking spray.
2. Beat together the egg with Worcestershire sauce in a shallow bowl until well incorporated.
3. Thoroughly combine the almond flour, coconut flour, sea salt, lemon pepper, and chili powder in another bowl.
4. Dredge the fillets in the egg mixture, shaking off any excess, then roll in the flour mixture to coat well.
5. Arrange the fillets in the baking pan. Slide the baking pan into Rack Position 1, select Convection Bake and set time to 7 minutes. Turn the fillets over and spritz lightly with cooking spray. Continue cooking for about 5 minutes, or until the fish is flaky.
6. Serve hot.

## Garlic Shrimp

Prep time: 10 minutes | Cook time: 8 minutes | Serves 4

4 tbsps. olive oil
1 pound (454 g) shrimp, deveined
2 cloves garlic, finely minced
1½ tbsps. lemon juice

1½ tbsps. fresh parsley, roughly chopped
1 tsp. crushed red pepper flakes, or more to taste
Garlic pepper, to taste
Sea salt flakes, to taste

1. Preheat the air fryer oven to 385ºF (196ºC).
2. In a large bowl, toss all the ingredients until the shrimp are coated on all sides.
3. Place the shrimp in the baking pan. Slide the baking pan into Rack Position 2, select Roast and set time to 8 minutes, until the shrimp are pink and cooked through.
4. Serve hot.

## Old Bay Breaded Shrimp

Prep time: 15 minutes | Cook time: 10 minutes | Serves 4

Cooking spray
1 pound (454 g) large shrimp, deveined, with tails on
2 large eggs
½ cup whole-wheat

panko bread crumbs
2 tsps. Old Bay seasoning, divided
½ tsp. garlic powder
½ tsp. onion powder

1. Preheat the air fryer oven to 380ºF (193ºC).
2. Spritz the air fryer basket with cooking spray.
3. Mix together 1 tsp. of Old Bay seasoning, garlic powder, and onion powder in a medium bowl. Place the shrimp and toss with the seasoning mix to lightly coat.
4. Whisk the eggs with 1 tsp. Water in a separate small bowl.
5. Mix together the remaining 1 tsp. Old Bay seasoning and the panko bread crumbs in a shallow bowl.
6. Dip each shrimp in the egg mixture and dredge in the bread crumb mixture to evenly coat.
7. Arrange the shrimp in the air fryer basket, in a single layer. Spritz the shrimp lightly with cooking spray. You many need to work the shrimp in batches.
8. Place the air fryer basket onto the baking pan, and slide the baking pan into Rack Position 2, select Convection Broil and set time to 10 minutes, or until the shrimp is cooked through and crispy, flipping at 5-minute intervals to redistribute and evenly cook.
9. Serve hot.

## Honey Cod with Sesame Seeds

Prep time: 5 minutes | Cook time: 8 minutes | Makes 1 fillet

Cooking spray
6 ounces (170 g) fresh cod fillet
1 tbsp. reduced-sodium

soy sauce
2 tsps. honey
1 tsp. sesame seeds

1. Preheat the air fryer oven to 360ºF (182ºC).
2. Combine the soy sauce and honey in a small bowl.
3. Spritz the air fryer basket lightly with cooking spray, then arrange the cod in the air fryer basket, brush with the soy mixture, and scatter sesame seeds on top. Place the air fryer basket onto the baking pan, and slide the baking pan into Rack Position 2, select Convection Broil and set time to 8 minutes, until opaque.
4. Remove the fish and let cool on a wire rack for about 5 minutes before serving.

## Browned Shrimp and Bell Pepper Patties

Prep time: 15 minutes | Cook time: 10 minutes | Serves 4

Cooking spray
½ pound (227 g) raw shrimp, shelled, deveined, and chopped finely
2 cups cooked sushi rice
½ cup plain bread crumbs
¼ cup chopped red bell

pepper
¼ cup chopped green onion
¼ cup chopped celery
2 tsps. Worcestershire sauce
½ tsp. garlic powder
½ tsp. Old Bay seasoning
½ tsp. salt

1. Preheat the air fryer oven to 390ºF (199ºC).
2. In a large bowl, add all the ingredients except the bread crumbs and oil and stir to incorporate well.
3. Scoop out the shrimp mixture and form into 8 equal-sized patties with your hands, no more than ½-inch thick. Roll the patties in the bread crumbs on a plate and spritz both sides lightly with cooking spray.
4. Arrange the patties in the baking pan. You may need to cook in batches to avoid overcrowding.
5. Slide the baking pan into Rack Position 1, select Convection Bake and set time to 10 minutes, flipping the patties halfway through, until the outside is crispy brown.
6. Distribute the patties among four plates and serve hot.

## Italian Scallops

Prep time: 10 minutes | Cook time: 10 to 15 minutes | Serves 4

Cooking spray
2 tsps. olive oil
16 ounces (454 g) small scallops, patted dry

1 packet dry zesty Italian dressing mix
1 tsp. minced garlic

1. Preheat the air fryer oven to 400ºF (204ºC).
2. Spritz the air fryer basket with cooking spray.
3. Combine the olive oil, Italian dressing mix, and garlic in a large zip-top plastic bag.
4. Place the scallops, seal the zip-top bag, and coat the scallops in the seasoning mixture.
5. Arrange the scallops in the air fryer basket and spritz lightly with cooking spray.
6. Place the air fryer basket onto the baking pan, and slide the baking pan into Rack Position 2, select Air Fry and set time to 5 minutes. Flip over, and air fry for another 5 to 10 minutes, or until the scallops reach an internal temperature of 120ºF (49ºC).
7. Serve hot.

## Cajun Salmon Burgers

Prep time: 10 minutes | Cook time: 11 to 14 minutes | Serves 4

Cooking spray
4 (5-ounce / 142-g) cans pink salmon in water, any skin and bones removed, drained
2 eggs, beaten

4 whole-wheat buns
1 cup whole-wheat bread crumbs
4 tbsps. light mayonnaise
2 tsps. Cajun seasoning
2 tsps. dry mustard

1. Mix the salmon, egg, bread crumbs, mayonnaise, Cajun seasoning, and dry mustard in a medium bowl. Cover with plastic wrap and refrigerate for 30 minutes.
2. Preheat the air fryer oven to 360ºF (182ºC). Spritz the baking pan with cooking spray.
3. Form the mixture into four ½-inch-thick patties about the same size as the buns.
4. Arrange the salmon patties in the baking pan in a single layer and spritz lightly the tops with cooking spray. You may need to cook them in batches.
5. Slide the baking pan into Rack Position 2, select Roast and set time to 7 minutes. Flip the patties over and lightly spray with cooking spray. Roast for 4 to 7 more minutes until crispy on the outside.
6. Serve hot on whole-wheat buns.

## Cayenne Prawns

Prep time: 10 minutes | Cook time: 8 minutes | Serves 2

Cooking spray
8 prawns, cleaned
½ tsp. ground cayenne pepper
½ tsp. red chili flakes

½ tsp. garlic powder
½ tsp. ground cumin
Salt and black pepper, to taste

1. Preheat the air fryer oven to 340ºF (171ºC). Spray the air fryer basket lightly with cooking spray.
2. In a large bowl, toss the remaining ingredients until the prawns are well coated.
3. Arrange the coated prawns evenly in the air fryer basket and spray them lightly with cooking spray.
4. Place the air fryer basket onto the baking pan, and slide the baking pan into Rack Position 2, select Air Fry and set time to 8 minutes, flipping the prawns halfway through, or until the prawns are pink.
5. Transfer the prawns from the oven to a plate. Serve hot.

## Air Fried Scallops with Thyme

Prep time: 5 minutes | Cook time: 4 minutes | Serves 2

Avocado oil spray
12 medium sea scallops, rinsed and patted dry
Fresh thyme leaves, for garnish (optional)

1 tsp. fine sea salt
¾ tsp. ground black pepper, plus more for garnish

1. Preheat the air fryer oven to 390ºF (199ºC). Spray the air fryer basket lightly with avocado oil spray.
2. In a medium bowl, place the scallops and spritz lightly with avocado oil spray. Season the salt and pepper to taste.
3. Take the seasoned scallops to the air fryer basket, spacing them apart. You may need to cook in batches to avoid overcrowding.
4. Place the air fryer basket onto the baking pan, and slide the baking pan into Rack Position 2, select Air Fry and set time to 4 minutes, flipping the scallops halfway through, until the scallops are firm and reach an internal temperature of just 145ºF (63ºC) on a meat thermometer.
5. Transfer them from the oven and repeat with the remaining scallops.
6. Garnish with the pepper and thyme leaves, if desired. Serve hot.

## Lemony Breaded Calamari

Prep time: 5 minutes | Cook time: 12 minutes | Serves 4

| | |
|---|---|
| Cooking spray | 1 cup bread crumbs |
| 1 pound (454 g) calamari rings | ½ cup cornstarch |
| 2 large eggs | 2 garlic cloves, minced |
| | 1 lemon, sliced |

1. Whisk the eggs with minced garlic in a small bowl. Put the cornstarch and bread crumbs into separate shallow dishes.
2. Dredge the calamari rings in the cornstarch, then dip in the egg mixture, shaking off any excess, finally roll them in the bread crumbs to coat evenly. Allow the calamari rings to stand for 10 minutes in the refrigerator.
3. Preheat the air fryer oven to 390ºF (199ºC). Spray the air fryer basket lightly with cooking spray.
4. Arrange the calamari rings in the air fryer basket. Place the air fryer basket onto the baking pan, and slide the baking pan into Rack Position 2, select Air Fry and set time to 12 minutes, until cooked through. Flip halfway through the cooking time.
5. Garnish with the lemon slices and serve hot.

## Green Curry Shrimp with Basil

Prep time: 15 minutes | Cook time: 5 minutes | Serves 4

| | |
|---|---|
| 2 tbsps. coconut oil, melted | 1 clove garlic, minced |
| 1 pound (454 g) jumbo raw shrimp, peeled and deveined | 1 to 2 tbsps. Thai green curry paste |
| ¼ cup chopped fresh Thai basil or sweet basil | 1 tbsp. half-and-half or coconut milk |
| ¼ cup chopped fresh cilantro | 1 tsp. fish sauce |
| | 1 tsp. soy sauce |
| | 1 tsp. minced fresh ginger |

1. Combine the curry paste, coconut oil, half-and-half, fish sauce, soy sauce, ginger, and garlic in a baking pan. Whisk until well combined.
2. Place the shrimp and toss until well coated. Marinate at room temperature for about 15 to 30 minutes.
3. Preheat the air fryer oven to 400ºF (204ºC).
4. Slide the baking pan into Rack Position 2, select Roast and set time to 5 minutes, stirring halfway through the cooking time.
5. Take the shrimp to a serving bowl or platter. Sprinkle with the basil and cilantro. Serve hot.

## Cajun Tilapia Tacos

Prep time: 5 minutes | Cook time: 12 minutes | Serves 6

| | |
|---|---|
| 2 tsps. avocado oil | package coleslaw mix |
| 4 tilapia fillets | 2 limes, cut into wedges |
| 12 corn tortillas | 1 tbsp. Cajun seasoning |
| 1 (14-ounce / 397-g) | |

1. Preheat the air fryer oven to 380ºF (193ºC). Line the baking pan with parchment paper.
2. Mix the avocado oil and the Cajun seasoning in a medium, shallow bowl to make a marinade. Place the tilapia fillets and coat evenly.
3. Arrange the fillets in the baking pan in a single layer, leaving room between each fillet. You may need to work in batches.
4. Slide the baking pan into Rack Position 2, select Roast and set time to 12 minutes, until the fish is cooked and easily flakes with a fork.
5. Assemble the tacos by adding some of the coleslaw mix in each tortilla. Place ⅓ of a tilapia fillet to each tortilla. Squeeze some lime juice over the top of each taco and serve hot.

## Parmesan Tuna Patty Sliders

Prep time: 15 minutes | Cook time: 11 to 14 minutes | Serves 4

| | |
|---|---|
| Cooking spray | panko bread crumbs |
| 3 (5-ounce / 142-g) cans tuna, packed in water | ⅓ cup shredded Parmesan cheese |
| 10 whole-wheat slider buns | 1 tbsp. sriracha |
| ⅔ cup whole-wheat | ¾ tsp. black pepper |

1. Preheat the air fryer oven to 350ºF (177ºC).
2. Spritz the air fryer basket with cooking spray.
3. Combine the tuna, bread crumbs, Parmesan cheese, sriracha, and black pepper in a medium bowl and stir to combine well.
4. Shape the mixture into 10 patties.
5. Arrange the patties in the air fryer basket in a single layer. Spritz the patties with cooking spray. You may need to cook the patties in batches.
6. Place the air fryer basket onto the baking pan, and slide the baking pan into Rack Position 2, select Air Fry and set time to 7 minutes. Turn the patties over and spritz lightly with cooking spray. Air fry for another 4 to 7 minutes, until golden brown and crisp. Serve hot with buns.

## Simple Piri-Piri King Prawn

Prep time: 10 minutes | Cook time: 8 minutes | Serves 2

1 tbsp. coconut oil
12 king prawns, rinsed
1 tsp. curry powder
1 tsp. onion powder
1 tsp. garlic paste
½ tsp. piri piri powder
½ tsp. cumin powder
Salt and ground black pepper, to taste

1. Preheat the air fryer oven to 360ºF (182ºC).
2. In a large bowl, combine all the ingredients and toss until the prawns are well coated.
3. Arrange the prawns in the air fryer basket. Then place the air fryer basket onto the baking pan, and slide the baking pan into Rack Position 2, select Air Fry and set time to 8 minutes, flipping halfway through, or until the prawns turn pink.
4. Serve warm.

## Crispy Crab Sticks with Mayo Sauce

Prep time: 5 minutes | Cook time: 12 minutes | Serves 4

**Crab Sticks:**
Cooking spray
1 pound (454 g) crab sticks
2 eggs
1 cup flour
⅓ cup panko bread
crumbs
1 tbsp. old bay seasoning
**Mayo Sauce:**
½ cup mayonnaise
1 lime, juiced
2 garlic cloves, minced

1. Preheat air fryer oven to 390ºF (199ºC).
2. Beat the eggs in a bowl. In a shallow bowl, put the flour. In another shallow bowl, thoroughly mix the panko bread crumbs and old bay seasoning.
3. Dredge the crab sticks in the flour, shaking off any excess, then in the beaten eggs, finally press them in the bread crumb mixture to coat evenly.
4. Place the crab sticks in the air fryer basket and spritz lightly with cooking spray.
5. Put the air fryer basket onto the baking pan, and slide the baking pan into Rack Position 2, select Air Fry and set time to 12 minutes, until golden brown. Flip the crab sticks halfway through the cooking time.
6. At the same time, make the sauce: in a small bowl, whisk together the mayo, lime juice, and garlic.
7. Place the mayo sauce on the side of crab sticks and serve warm.

## Quick Paprika Shrimp

Prep time: 5 minutes | Cook time: 10 minutes | Serves 4

2 tbsps. olive oil
1 pound (454 g) tiger shrimp
½ tbsp. old bay
seasoning
¼ tbsp. smoked paprika
¼ tsp. cayenne pepper
A pinch of sea salt

1. Preheat air fryer oven to 380ºF (193ºC).
2. In a large bowl, toss all the ingredients until the shrimp are evenly coated.
3. Put the shrimp in the air fryer basket. Then place the air fryer basket onto the baking pan, and slide the baking pan into Rack Position 2, select Air Fry and set time to 10 minutes, flipping halfway through, until the shrimp are pink and cooked through.
4. Serve warm.

## Garlic Basil Shrimp Scampi

Prep time: 5 minutes | Cook time: 8 minutes | Serves 4

**Sauce:**
¼ cup unsalted butter
2 cloves garlic, minced
2 tbsps. fish stock or chicken broth
2 tbsps. chopped fresh basil leaves
1 tbsp. lemon juice
1 tbsp. chopped fresh
parsley, plus more for garnish
1 tsp. red pepper flakes
**Shrimp:**
1 pound (454 g) large shrimp, peeled and deveined, tails removed
Fresh basil sprigs, for garnish

1. Preheat the air fryer oven to 350ºF (177ºC).
2. Mix all the ingredients for the sauce in the air fryer basket and stir to incorporate well.
3. Place the air fryer basket onto the baking pan, and slide the baking pan into Rack Position 2, select Air Fry and set time to 3 minutes, until the sauce is heated through.
4. Once done, put the shrimp to the air fryer basket, flipping to coat in the sauce.
5. Take the air fryer basket back to the air fryer oven and cook for an additional 5 minutes, or until the shrimp are pink and opaque. Stir the shrimp twice during the cooking.
6. Garnish with the parsley and basil sprigs. Serve warm.

## Mayo Crab Cakes with Bell Peppers

Prep time: 5 minutes | Cook time: 10 minutes | Serves 4

Cooking spray
8 ounces (227 g) jumbo lump crab meat
1 egg, beaten
⅓ cup bread crumbs
¼ cup diced green bell pepper
¼ cup diced red bell pepper
¼ cup mayonnaise
Juice of ½ lemon
1 tbsp. Old Bay seasoning
1 tsp. flour

1. Preheat the air fryer oven to 375ºF (190ºC).
2. Make the crab cakes: In a large bowl, place all the ingredients except the flour and oil and stir until well incorporated.
3. Distribute the crab mixture evenly into four equal portions and form each portion into a patty with your hands. Top each patty with a sprinkle of ¼ tsp. of flour.
4. Spread the crab cakes in the baking pan and spray them lightly with cooking spray.
5. Slide the baking pan into Rack Position 1, select Convection Bake and set time to 10 minutes, flipping the crab cakes halfway through, until they are cooked through.
6. Divide the crab cakes among four plates and serve hot.

## Coconut Chili Curried Fish

Prep time: 10 minutes | Cook time: 20 to 22 minutes | Serves 4

2 tbsps. sunflower oil, divided
1 pound (454 g) fish, chopped
1 ripe tomato, pureéd
1 cup coconut milk
2 red chilies, chopped
1 shallot, minced
1 garlic clove, minced
1 tbsp. coriander powder
1 tsp. red curry paste
½ tsp. fenugreek seeds
Salt and white pepper, to taste

1. Preheat the air fryer oven to 380ºF (193ºC). Brush the air fryer basket with 1 tbsp. of sunflower oil.
2. Arrange the fish in the air fryer basket. Place the air fryer basket onto the baking pan, and slide the baking pan into Rack Position 2, select Air Fry and set time to 10 minutes. Flip the fish halfway through the cooking time.
3. When done, grease the air fryer basket with the remaining 1 tbsp. of sunflower oil and put the fish. Stir in the remaining ingredients and take back to the air fryer oven.

4. Lower the temperature to 350ºF (177ºC) and air fry for an additional 10 to 12 minutes until heated through.
5. Cool for about 5 to 8 minutes before serving.

## Herbed Scallops with Peas and Green Beans

Prep time: 15 minutes | Cook time: 8 to 11 minutes | Serves 4

2 tsps. olive oil
12 ounces (340 g) sea scallops, rinsed and patted dry
1 cup frozen peas
1 cup green beans
1 cup frozen chopped broccoli
½ tsp. dried oregano
½ tsp. dried basil

1. Preheat the air fryer oven to 400ºF (204ºC).
2. In a large bowl, put the peas, green beans, and broccoli. Drizzle with the olive oil and toss to coat well. Take the vegetables to the air fryer basket. Then place the air fryer basket onto the baking pan, and slide the baking pan into Rack Position 2, select Air Fry and set time to 5 minutes, until they are fork-tender.
3. Transfer the vegetables from the oven to a serving bowl. Sprinkle with the oregano and basil and keep aside.
4. Arrange the scallops in the air fryer basket and air fry for about 4 to 5 minutes, or until the scallops are firm and just opaque in the center.
5. Take the cooked scallops to the bowl of vegetables and toss well. Serve hot.

## Crispy Salmon Patty Bites

Prep time: 15 minutes | Cook time: 12 minutes |
Serves 4

Cooking spray
4 (5-ounce / 142-g) cans
pink salmon, skinless,
boneless in water,
drained
2 eggs, beaten
1 cup whole-wheat panko

bread crumbs
4 tbsps. finely minced red
bell pepper
2 tbsps. parsley flakes
2 tsps. Old Bay
seasoning

1. Preheat the air fryer oven to 360ºF (182ºC).
2. Spritz the air fryer basket with cooking spray.
3. Mix the salmon, eggs, panko bread crumbs, red bell
   pepper, parsley flakes, and Old Bay seasoning in a
   medium bowl.
4. With a small cookie scoop, shape the mixture into 20
   balls.
5. Arrange the salmon bites in the air fryer basket in a
   single layer and spritz lightly with cooking spray. You
   may need to cook them in batches.
6. Place the air fryer basket onto the baking pan, and
   slide the baking pan into Rack Position 2, select Air
   Fry and set time to 12 minutes, flipping a couple of
   times for even cooking.
7. Serve hot.

## Blackened Shrimp Tacos with Lime

Prep time: 10 minutes | Cook time: 10 to 15 minutes
| Serves 4

Cooking spray
1 tsp. olive oil
12 ounces (340 g)
medium shrimp,
deveined, with tails off
8 corn tortillas, warmed

1 (14-ounce / 397-g) bag
coleslaw mix
2 limes, cut in half
1 to 2 tsps. Blackened
seasoning

1. Preheat the air fryer oven to 400ºF (204ºC).
2. Spritz the air fryer basket with cooking spray.
3. Pat the shrimp with a paper towel to remove excess
   water.
4. Toss the shrimp with olive oil and Blackened
   seasoning in a medium bowl.
5. Arrange the shrimp in the air fryer basket. Then place
   the air fryer basket onto the baking pan, and slide the
   baking pan into Rack Position 2, select Air Fry and set
   time to 5 minutes. Flip the shrimp, lightly spritz with
   cooking spray, and cook for 5 to 10 more minutes,
   until the shrimp are cooked through and starting to
   brown.

6. Fill each tortilla with the coleslaw mix and place the
   blackened shrimp on top. Squeeze fresh lime juice
   over top and serve hot.

## Crab Ratatouille with Tomatoes and Eggplant

Prep time: 15 minutes | Cook time: 11 to 14 minutes
| Serves 4

1 tbsp. olive oil
1½ cups cooked crab
meat
2 large tomatoes,
chopped
1½ cups peeled and
cubed eggplant
1 red bell pepper,

chopped
1 onion, chopped
½ tsp. dried basil
½ tsp. dried thyme
Pinch salt
Freshly ground black
pepper, to taste

1. Preheat the air fryer oven to 400ºF (204ºC).
2. Stir together the eggplant, tomatoes, bell pepper,
   onion, olive oil, basil and thyme in a metal bowl.
   Sprinkle with salt and pepper to taste.
3. Put the bowl in the air fryer basket. Then place the
   air fryer basket onto the baking pan, and slide the
   baking pan into Rack Position 2, select Convection
   Broil and set time to 9 minutes.
4. Transfer the bowl from the air fryer oven. Place the
   crab meat and stir well and broil for another 2 to
   5 minutes, or until the vegetables are soft and the
   ratatouille is bubbling.
5. Serve hot.

# Chapter 6 Meats

## Lemony Pork Loin Chop Schnitzel

Prep time: 15 minutes | Cook time: 15 minutes | Serves 4

Cooking spray
4 thin boneless pork loin chops
2 eggs
1 cup panko breadcrumbs
½ cup flour
2 tbsps. lemon juice
Lemon wedges, for serving
¼ tsp. marjoram
1 tsp. salt

1. Preheat the air fryer oven to 390ºF (199ºC) and spray the air fryer basket lightly with cooking spray.
2. On a clean work surface, coat the pork chops with lemon juice on both sides.
3. On a shallow plate, combine the flour with marjoram and salt. On a separate shallow dish, pour the breadcrumbs. Beat the eggs in a large bowl.
4. Dredge the pork chops in the flour, then dip in the beaten eggs to coat well. Shake the excess off and roll over the breadcrumbs.
5. Place the chops in the air fryer basket and spray lightly with cooking spray. Place the air fryer basket onto the baking pan, and slide the baking pan into Rack Position 2, select Air Fry and set time to 15 minutes, until the chops are golden and crispy. Flip the chops halfway through.
6. Squeeze the lemon wedges over the fried chops and serve hot.

## Beef, Broccoli and Mushroom Cubes

Prep time: 15 minutes | Cook time: 17 minutes | Serves 4

2 tbsps. olive oil
1 pound (454 g) top round steak, cut into cubes
4 ounces (113 g) broccoli, cut into florets
4 ounces (113 g) mushrooms, sliced
1 tbsp. apple cider vinegar
1 tsp. shallot powder
1 tsp. dried basil
1 tsp. celery seeds
¾ tsp. smoked cayenne pepper
½ tsp. garlic powder
¼ tsp. ground cumin
1 tsp. fine sea salt
½ tsp. ground black pepper

1. Massage the olive oil, vinegar, salt, black pepper, garlic powder, shallot powder, cayenne pepper, and cumin into the cubed steak, ensuring to coat each piece well.
2. Let marinate for at least 3 hours.
3. Preheat the air fryer oven to 365ºF (185ºC).
4. Place the beef cubes in the baking pan. Slide the baking pan into Rack Position 2, select Roast and set time to 12 minutes.
5. When the steak is cooked through, put it in a bowl.
6. Wipe the grease from the baking pan and pour in the vegetables. Sprinkle them with basil and celery seeds.
7. Raise the temperature of the air fryer oven to 400ºF (204ºC) and roast for about 5 to 6 minutes. When the vegetables are hot, serve them with the steak.

## Mustard Lamb Rack with Pistachio

Prep time: 10 minutes | Cook time: 20 minutes | Serves 2

1 tbsp. olive oil
1 lamb rack, bones fat trimmed and frenched
½ cup finely chopped pistachios
3 tbsps. panko breadcrumbs
1 tbsp. Dijon mustard
2 tsps. chopped fresh oregano
1 tsp. chopped fresh rosemary
Salt and freshly ground black pepper, to taste

1. Preheat the air fryer oven to 380ºF (193ºC).
2. In a food processor, put the pistachios, rosemary, breadcrumbs, oregano, olive oil, salt, and black pepper. Pulse to combine until smooth.
3. Season the lamb rack with salt and black pepper on a clean work surface, then arrange it in the air fryer basket.
4. Place the air fryer basket onto the baking pan, and slide the baking pan into Rack Position 2, select Convection Broil and set time to 12 minutes, until lightly browned. Turn the lamb halfway through the cooking time.
5. Take the lamb on a plate and coat with Dijon mustard on the fat side, then season with the pistachios mixture over the lamb rack to coat well.
6. Place the lamb rack back to the air fryer oven and broil for another 8 minutes or until the internal temperature of the rack reaches at least 145ºF (63ºC).
7. Transfer the lamb rack from the air fryer oven with tongs and let cool for 5 minutes before sling to serve.

## Pork and Veggies Kebabs

Prep time: 1 hour 20 minutes | Cook time: 8 minutes per batch | Serves 4

**For the Pork:**
1 pound (454 g) pork steak, cut in cubes
¼ cup soy sauce
3 tbsps. steak sauce
1 tbsp. white wine vinegar
2 tsps. smoked paprika
1 tsp. powdered chili
1 tsp. red chili flakes
1 tsp. garlic salt
**For the Vegetable:**
Cooking spray
1 yellow squash, deseeded and cut in cubes
1 green squash, deseeded and cut in cubes
1 green pepper, cut in cubes
1 red pepper, cut in cubes
Salt and ground black pepper, to taste
**Special Equipment:**
4 bamboo skewers, soaked in water for at least 30 minutes

1. In a large bowl, combine the ingredients for the pork. Press the pork to dunk in the marinade. Wrap the bowl in plastic and refrigerate for at least an hour.
2. Preheat the air fryer oven to 370ºF (188ºC) and spray the baking pan lightly with cooking spray.
3. Transfer the pork from the marinade and run the skewers through the pork and vegetables alternatively. Season with salt and pepper to taste.
4. Place the skewers in the baking pan and spray lightly with cooking spray. Slide the baking pan into Rack Position 2, select Roast and set time to 8 minutes, until the pork is browned and the vegetables are lightly charred and soft. Flip the skewers halfway through. You may need to cook in batches to avoid overcrowding.
5. Serve hot.

## Pork Butt with Garlicky Coriander-Parsley Sauce

Prep time: 1 hour 15 minutes | Cook time: 30 minutes | Serves 4

1 tbsp. olive oil
1 pound (454 g) pork butt, cut into pieces 2-inches long
1 egg white, well whisked
1 tbsp. soy sauce
1 tsp. golden flaxseed meal
1 tsp. lemon juice, preferably freshly squeezed
Salt and ground black pepper, to taste
**Garlicky Coriander-Parsley Sauce:**
⅓ cup extra-virgin olive oil
⅓ cup fresh coriander leaves
⅓ cup fresh parsley leaves
3 garlic cloves, minced
1 tsp. lemon juice
½ tbsp. salt

1. In a large bowl, combine the flaxseed meal, egg white, soy sauce, lemon juice, salt, black pepper, and olive oil. Dip the pork strips in and press to submerge.
2. Wrap the bowl in plastic and refrigerate to marinate for a minimum of an hour.
3. Preheat the air fryer oven to 380ºF (193ºC).
4. Place the marinated pork strips in the air fryer basket. Then put the air fryer basket onto the baking pan, and slide the baking pan into Rack Position 2, select Air Fry and set time to 30 minutes, until cooked through and well browned. Flip the strips halfway through.
5. At the same time, in a small bowl, combine the ingredients for the sauce. Stir to mix well. Place the bowl in the refrigerator to chill until ready to serve.
6. Serve hot with the chilled sauce.

## Sumptuous Pepperoni Pizza Tortilla Rolls

Prep time: 10 minutes | Cook time: 6 minutes | Serves 4

Cooking spray
1 tsp. butter
8 flour tortillas
8 thin slices deli ham
24 pepperoni slices
1 cup shredded Mozzarella cheese
4 ounces (113 g) fresh white mushrooms, chopped
½ cup pizza sauce
½ medium onion, slivered
½ red or green bell pepper, julienned

1. Preheat the air fryer oven to 390ºF (199ºC).
2. Place butter, onions, bell pepper, and mushrooms in a baking pan. Slide the baking pan into Rack Position 1, select Convection Bake and set time to 3 minutes. Stir and bake for about 3 to 4 minutes longer until just crisp and tender. Remove pan and keep aside.
3. To assemble rolls, lay about 2 tsps. of pizza sauce on one half of each tortilla. Place a slice of ham and 3 slices of pepperoni on top. Divide sautéed vegetables among tortillas and top with cheese.
4. Roll up tortillas, secure with toothpicks if needed, and spritz lightly with oil.
5. Put 4 rolls in the air fryer basket. Then place the air fryer basket onto the baking pan, and slide the baking pan into Rack Position 2, select Air Fry and set time to 4 minutes. Turn and air fry for 4 minutes, until heated through and lightly browned.
6. Repeat step 5 to air fry the remaining pizza rolls.
7. Serve hot.

## Homemade Char Siew

Prep time: 10 minutes | Cook time: 20 minutes | Serves 4 to 6

Olive oil, for brushing the pan
1 strip of pork shoulder butt with a good amount of fat marbling
**Marinade:**
1 tsp. sesame oil

4 tbsps. raw honey
2 tbsps. Hoisin sauce
1 tbsp. rose wine
1 tsp. low-sodium dark soy sauce
1 tsp. light soy sauce

1. In a Ziploc bag, combine all the marinade ingredients together. Place the pork in bag, making sure all sections of pork strip are engulfed in the marinade. Chill for 3 to 24 hours.
2. Remove the strip 30 minutes before planning to cook and preheat the air fryer oven to 350ºF (177ºC).
3. Place foil on the air fryer basket and coat with olive oil. Arrange the marinated pork strip onto the air fryer basket.
4. Place the air fryer basket onto the baking pan, and slide the baking pan into Rack Position 2, select Convection Broil and set time to 20 minutes.
5. Glaze with marinade every 5 to 10 minutes.
6. Remove strip and let cool a few minutes before slicing.
7. Serve hot.

## Lollipop Lamb Chops with Mint Pesto

Prep time: 15 minutes | Cook time: 7 minutes | Serves 4

2 tbsps. vegetable oil
½ cup olive oil
8 lamb chops (1 rack)
¼ cup packed fresh parsley
¾ cup packed fresh mint
⅓ cup shelled pistachios
¼ cup grated Parmesan cheese

½ small clove garlic
1 tbsp. dried rosemary, chopped
1 tbsp. dried thyme
½ tsp. lemon juice
¼ tsp. salt
Salt and freshly ground black pepper, to taste

1. Make the pesto: in a food processor, combine the garlic, parsley and mint and process until finely chopped. Place the lemon juice, Parmesan cheese, pistachios and salt. Process until all the ingredients have turned into a paste. With the processor running, gently pour the olive oil in. Scrape the sides of the processor by using a spatula and process for another

30 seconds.
2. Preheat the air fryer oven to 400ºF (204ºC).
3. Coat both sides of the lamb chops with vegetable oil and sprinkle with salt, pepper, rosemary and thyme, pressing the herbs into the meat gently with the fingers. Take the lamb chops to the baking pan.
4. Slide the baking pan into Rack Position 2, select Roast and set time to 5 minutes. Flip the chops over and air fry for another 2 minutes.
5. Drizzle the mint pesto on the lamb chops and serve warm.

## Spicy Mongolian Flank Steak

Prep time: 20 minutes | Cook time: 15 minutes | Serves 4

1½ pounds (680 g) flank steak, thinly sliced on the bias into ¼-inch strips
**Marinade:**
1 clove garlic, smashed
2 tbsps. soy sauce
Pinch crushed red pepper flakes
**Sauce:**
1 tbsp. vegetable oil

¾ cup soy sauce
¾ cup chicken stock
½ cup cornstarch, divided
2 cloves garlic, minced
3 dried red chili peppers
5 to 6 tbsps. brown sugar
1 bunch scallions, sliced into 2-inch pieces
1 tbsp. finely grated fresh ginger

1. Marinate the beef in the soy sauce, red pepper flakes and garlic for one hour.
2. In the meantime, make the sauce. In a small saucepan over medium heat, add the oil, ginger, garlic, and dried chili peppers and sauté for just a minute or two. Pour in the soy sauce, chicken stock and brown sugar and continue to simmer for several minutes. Dissolve 3 tbsps. of cornstarch in 3 tbsps. of water and stir this into the saucepan. Stir the sauce over medium heat until it thickens. Keep this aside.
3. Preheat the air fryer oven to 400ºF (204ºC).
4. Transfer the beef from the marinade and take it to a zipper sealable plastic bag with the remaining cornstarch. Shake it around to completely coat the beef and remove the coated strips of beef to the air fryer basket, shaking off any excess cornstarch. Spritz the strips lightly with vegetable oil on all sides.
5. Place the air fryer basket onto the baking pan, and slide the baking pan into Rack Position 2, select Air Fry and set time to 15 minutes, flipping to toss the beef strips throughout the cooking process. Put the scallions for the last 4 minutes of the cooking. Take the hot beef strips and scallions to a bowl and toss with the sauce, coating all the beef strips with the sauce. Serve hot.

## Classic Beef Spring Rolls

Prep time: 10 minutes | Cook time: 8 minutes | Serves 20

1 tbsp. sesame oil
1 packet spring roll sheets
1 cup ground beef
1 cup fresh mix vegetables

⅓ cup noodles
1 small onion, diced
3 garlic cloves, minced
2 tbsps. cold water
1 tsp. soy sauce

1. Cook the noodle in enough hot water to make them soft, drain them and cut them to make them shorter.
2. In a frying pan over medium heat, cook the beef, soy sauce, mixed vegetables, onion, and garlic in sesame oil until the beef is cooked through. Take the pan off the heat and throw in the noodles. Mix well to incorporate everything.
3. Unroll a spring roll sheet and lay it flat. Sprinkle the filling diagonally across it and roll it up, brushing the edges lightly with water to act as an adhesive. Repeat this process until you have used up all the sheets and the filling.
4. Preheat the air fryer oven to 350ºF (177ºC).
5. Coat each spring roll with a light brushing of oil and take to the air fryer basket.
6. Place the air fryer basket onto the baking pan, and slide the baking pan into Rack Position 2, select Air Fry and set time to 8 minutes. Serve warm.

## Garlic Lamb Loin Chops with Horseradish Cream Sauce

Prep time: 10 minutes | Cook time: 13 minutes | Serves 4

**For the Lamb:**
2 tbsps. vegetable oil
4 lamb loin chops
1 clove garlic, minced
½ tsp. kosher salt
½ tsp. black pepper
**For the Horseradish**

**Cream Sauce:**
½ cup mayonnaise
1 to 1½ tbsps. prepared horseradish
1 tbsp. Dijon mustard
2 tsps. sugar
Cooking spray

1. Preheat the air fryer oven to 325ºF (163ºC). Spray the air fryer basket lightly with cooking spray.
2. Put the lamb chops on a plate. Rub with the oil and season with the garlic, salt and black pepper. Let stand to marinate for 30 minutes at room temperature.
3. Make the horseradish cream sauce: In a bowl, mix the horseradish, mustard, mayonnaise, and sugar

until well combined. Keep half of the sauce aside until ready to serve.
4. Place the marinated chops in the prepared air fryer basket. Put the air fryer basket onto the baking pan, and slide the baking pan into Rack Position 2, select Air Fry and set time to 10 minutes, flipping the chops halfway through.
5. Take the chops from the air fryer oven to the bowl of the horseradish sauce. Roll to coat well.
6. Arrange the coated chops in the air fryer basket again. Turn the temperature to 400ºF (204ºC) and air fry for 3 minutes, until the internal temperature reaches 145ºF (63ºC) on a meat thermometer (for medium-rare).
7. Serve warm with the horseradish cream sauce.

## Cheesy Stuffed Beef and Pork Meatballs

Prep time: 15 minutes | Cook time: 12 minutes | Serves 4 to 6

1 tbsp. olive oil
¾ pound (340 g) ground beef
¾ pound (340 g) ground pork
2 eggs, lightly beaten
¾ cup bread crumbs
5 ounces (142 g) sharp or aged provolone cheese, cut into 1-inch cubes
¼ cup grated Parmesan

cheese
¼ cup finely chopped fresh parsley
1 small onion, finely chopped
1 to 2 cloves garlic, minced
½ tsp. dried oregano
1½ tsps. salt
Freshly ground black pepper, to taste

1. In a skillet over medium-high heat, add the oil and cook the onion and garlic until soft, but not browned.
2. Take the onion and garlic to a large bowl and add the beef, pork, bread crumbs, Parmesan cheese, oregano, parsley, salt, pepper and eggs. Combine well until all the ingredients are mixed. Distribute the mixture into 12 evenly sized balls. Make one meatball at a time, by pressing a hole in the meatball mixture with the finger and pushing a piece of provolone cheese into the hole. Then mold the meat back into a ball, enclosing the cheese.
3. Preheat the air fryer oven to 380ºF (193ºC).
4. Working in two batches, take six of the meatballs to the air fryer basket. Then place the air fryer basket onto the baking pan, and slide the baking pan into Rack Position 2, select Air Fry and set time to 12 minutes, flipping and turning the meatballs twice during the cooking time. Repeat with the remaining 6 meatballs. Serve hot.

## Spicy Lahmacun

Prep time: 20 minutes | Cook time: 10 minutes per batch | Serves 4

| | |
|---|---|
| 4 (6-inch) flour tortillas | 2 tsps. tomato paste |
| **For the Meat Topping:** | ¼ tsp. ground cumin |
| 4 ounces (113 g) ground lamb or 85% lean ground beef | ¼ tsp. sweet paprika |
| | ⅛ to ¼ tsp. red pepper flakes |
| ¼ cup finely chopped green bell pepper | ⅛ tsp. ground allspice |
| | ⅛ tsp. kosher salt |
| ¼ cup chopped fresh parsley | ⅛ tsp. black pepper |
| | **For Serving:** |
| 1 small plum tomato, deseeded and chopped | 1 tsp. extra-virgin olive oil |
| 1 garlic clove, minced | ¼ cup chopped fresh mint |
| 2 tbsps. chopped yellow onion | 1 lemon, cut into wedges |

1. Preheat the air fryer oven to 400ºF (204ºC).
2. In a medium bowl, combine all the ingredients for the meat topping until well mixed.
3. Spread the tortillas on a clean work surface. Scoop the meat mixture on the tortillas and spread all over.
4. Work in batches, one at a time. Put the tortillas in the air fryer basket. Then place the air fryer basket onto the baking pan, and slide the baking pan into Rack Position 2, select Air Fry and set time to 10 minutes, until the edge of the tortilla is golden and the meat is lightly browned.
5. Take them to a serving dish. Garnish with chopped fresh mint and drizzle with olive oil. Squeeze the lemon wedges on top and serve hot.

## Breaded Pork with Aloha Salsa

Prep time: 20 minutes | Cook time: 8 minutes | Serves 4

| | |
|---|---|
| Cooking spray | **Aloha Salsa:** |
| 1 pound (454 g) boneless, thin pork cutlets (⅜- to ½-inch thick) | 1 cup fresh pineapple, chopped in small pieces |
| | ¼ cup green or red bell pepper, chopped |
| 2 eggs | ¼ cup red onion, finely chopped |
| ¼ cup cornstarch | |
| ¼ cup flour | 1 tsp. low-sodium soy sauce |
| ¼ cup panko bread crumbs | ½ tsp. ground cinnamon |
| 2 tbsps. milk | ⅛ tsp. crushed red pepper |
| 4 tsps. sesame seeds | |
| Lemon pepper and salt, to taste | ⅛ tsp. ground black pepper |

1. Stir together all ingredients for salsa in a medium bowl. Cover and refrigerate while cooking the pork.
2. Preheat the air fryer oven to 390ºF (199ºC).
3. In a shallow dish, beat the eggs and milk.
4. Mix the flour, panko, and sesame seeds in another shallow dish.
5. Season pork cutlets with lemon pepper and salt.
6. Dip pork cutlets in cornstarch, egg mixture, and then panko coating. Spritz both sides lightly with cooking spray.
7. Put the pork cutlets in the air fryer basket. Then place the air fryer basket onto the baking pan, and slide the baking pan into Rack Position 2, select Air Fry and set time to 3 minutes. Flip cutlets over, spraying both sides, and continue air frying for about 5 minutes or until well done.
8. Serve the cutlets with salsa on the side.

## Orange Glazed Pork Tenderloin

Prep time: 15 minutes | Cook time: 20 minutes | Serves 3 to 4

| | |
|---|---|
| 1 pound (454 g) pork tenderloin | 2 tsps. grated fresh ginger |
| ½ cup orange juice | ½ tsp. soy sauce |
| ¼ cup white wine | Salt and freshly ground black pepper, to taste |
| Zest of 1 orange | |
| 2 tbsps. brown sugar | Fresh parsley, for garnish |
| 2 tsps. cornstarch | Oranges, halved, for garnish |
| 2 tsps. Dijon mustard | |

1. In a small saucepan, combine the brown sugar, cornstarch, Dijon mustard, orange juice, ginger, soy sauce, white wine and orange zest and bring the mixture to a boil on the stovetop. Lower the heat and simmer when you air fry the pork tenderloin or until the sauce has thickened.
2. Preheat the air fryer oven to 370ºF (188ºC).
3. Sprinkle all sides of the pork tenderloin with salt and black pepper. Take the tenderloin to the air fryer basket.
4. Place the air fryer basket onto the baking pan, and slide the baking pan into Rack Position 2, select Air Fry and set time to 20 minutes, until the internal temperature reaches 145ºF (63ºC). Turn the tenderloin over halfway through the cooking process and baste with the sauce.
5. Take the tenderloin to a cutting board and allow it to cool for 5 minutes. Slice the pork at a slight angle and serve hot with orange halves and fresh parsley.

## Spaghetti Squash and Beef Lasagna

Prep time: 5 minutes | Cook time: 1 hour 15 minutes | Serves 6

4 pounds (1.8 kg) ground beef
2 large spaghetti squash, cooked (about 2¾ pounds / 1.2 kg)
1 (2½-pound / 1.1-kg)

large jar Marinara sauce
30 ounces whole-milk ricotta cheese
25 slices Mozzarella cheese

1. Preheat the air fryer oven to 375ºF (191ºC).
2. Slice the spaghetti squash and arrange it face down inside a baking pan. Fill with water until covered.
3. Slide the baking pan into Rack Position 1, select Convection Bake and set time to 45 minutes, until skin is soft.
4. In a skillet over medium-high heat, sear the ground beef for 5 minutes or until browned, then pour in the marinara sauce and heat until warm. Keep aside.
5. Scrape the flesh off the cooked squash to resemble strands of spaghetti.
6. Spread the lasagna in a large greased pan in alternating layers of spaghetti squash, beef sauce, Mozzarella, ricotta. Repeat until all the ingredients have been used.
7. Bake for 30 minutes and serve hot!

## Crusted Pork Rack with Macadamia Nuts

Prep time: 5 minutes | Cook time: 35 minutes | Serves 2

2 tbsps. olive oil
1 pound (454 g) rack of pork
1 cup chopped macadamia nuts
1 egg

1 clove garlic, minced
1 tbsp. breadcrumbs
1 tbsp. rosemary, chopped
Salt and ground black pepper, to taste

1. Preheat the air fryer oven to 350ºF (177ºC).
2. In a small bowl, combine the garlic and olive oil. Stir to mix well.
3. On a clean work surface, coat the pork rack with the garlic oil and season with salt and black pepper on both sides.
4. In a shallow dish, combine the macadamia nuts, breadcrumbs, and rosemary. In a large bowl, whisk the egg.
5. Dredge the pork in the egg, then roll the pork over the macadamia nut mixture to coat evenly. Shake the

excess off.
6. Place the pork in the air fryer basket. Then put the air fryer basket onto the baking pan, and slide the baking pan into Rack Position 2, select Air Fry and set time to 15 minutes. Turn the pork over and air fry the other side for 15 minutes. Raise the temperature to 390ºF (199ºC) and fry for another 5 minutes or until the pork is well browned.
7. Serve hot.

## Lamb Meatballs with Tomato Sauce

Prep time: 20 minutes | Cook time: 8 minutes | Serves 4

**Meatballs:**
1 pound (454 g) ground lamb
1 egg yolk
½ cup crumbled feta cheese, for garnish
½ small onion, finely diced
1 clove garlic, minced
2 tbsps. milk
2 tbsps. fresh parsley, finely chopped (plus more for garnish)
2 tsps. fresh oregano,

finely chopped
Salt and freshly ground black pepper, to taste
**Tomato Sauce:**
Olive oil, for greasing
1 (28-ounce / 794-g) can crushed tomatoes
1 clove garlic, smashed
2 tbsps. butter
¼ tsp. ground cinnamon
Pinch crushed red pepper flakes
Salt, to taste

1. In a large bowl, combine all ingredients for the meatballs and mix just until everything is combined. Shape the mixture into 1½-inch balls or shape the meat between two spoons to make quenelles.
2. Preheat the air fryer oven to 400ºF (204ºC).
3. When the air fryer oven is preheating, start the quick tomato sauce. Place the butter, garlic and red pepper flakes in a sauté pan over medium heat on the stovetop. Let the garlic sizzle a little, but before the butter browns, put the cinnamon and tomatoes. Bring to a simmer and simmer for about 15 minutes. Sprinkle with salt to taste.
4. Spray the bottom of the air fryer basket lightly with olive oil and take the meatballs to the air fryer basket in one layer, air frying in batches if necessary.
5. Place the air fryer basket onto the baking pan, and slide the baking pan into Rack Position 2, select Air Fry and set time to 8 minutes, flipping once during the cooking time to turn the meatballs over.
6. To serve, scoop a pool of the tomato sauce onto plates and put the meatballs. Scatter the feta cheese on top and garnish with more fresh parsley. Serve warm.

## Classic Walliser Pork Schnitzel

Prep time: 5 minutes | Cook time: 14 minutes | Serves 2

Cooking spray
2 pork schnitzel, halved
2 eggs
½ cup pork rinds
½ tbsp. fresh parsley
⅓ tbsp. cider vinegar
½ tsp. fennel seed
½ tsp. mustard
1 tsp. garlic salt
⅓ tsp. ground black pepper

1. Preheat the air fryer oven to 350ºF (177ºC) and spray the air fryer basket lightly with cooking spray.
2. Place the pork rinds, parsley, fennel seeds, and mustard in a food processor. Pour in the vinegar and season with salt and ground black pepper to taste. Pulse until well combined and smooth.
3. Put the pork rind mixture in a large bowl. Whisk the eggs in a separate bowl.
4. Dip the pork schnitzel in the whisked eggs, then dip in the pork rind mixture to coat evenly. Shake the excess off.
5. Spread the schnitzel in the air fryer basket and spray with cooking spray. Place the air fryer basket onto the baking pan, and slide the baking pan into Rack Position 2, select Air Fry and set time to 14 minutes, until golden and crispy. Flip the schnitzel halfway through.
6. Serve hot.

## Bacon-Wrapped Sausage with Relish

Prep time: 1 hour 15 minutes | Cook time: 32 minutes | Serves 4

8 pork sausages
8 bacon strips
**Relish:**
8 large tomatoes, chopped
1 small onion, peeled
1 clove garlic, peeled
3 tbsps. chopped parsley
2 tbsps. sugar
1 tbsp. white wine vinegar
1 tsp. smoked paprika
Salt and ground black pepper, to taste

1. In a food processor, purée the tomatoes, onion, and garlic until well mixed and smooth.
2. Add the purée in a saucepan and drizzle with white wine vinegar. Season with salt and ground black pepper. Simmer over medium heat for about 10 minutes.
3. Place the parsley, paprika, and sugar to the saucepan and cook for about 10 more minutes or until it has a thick consistency. Keep stirring during the cooking. Refrigerate for an hour to chill.
4. Preheat the air fryer oven to 350ºF (177ºC).
5. Wrap the sausage with bacon strips and secure with toothpicks, then arrange them in the air fryer basket.
6. Put the air fryer basket onto the baking pan, and slide the baking pan into Rack Position 2, select Air Fry and set time to 12 minutes, until the bacon is crispy and browned. Gently flip the bacon-wrapped sausage halfway through.
7. Take the bacon-wrapped sausage on a plate and dunk with the relish or just serve with the relish alongside.

## Chinese Char Siu

Prep time: 8 hours 10 minutes | Cook time: 15 minutes | Serves 4

Cooking spray
1 pound (454 g) fatty pork shoulder, cut into long, 1-inch-thick pieces
¼ cup honey
2 tbsps. soy sauce
1 tbsp. Shaoxing wine (rice cooking wine)
1 tbsp. sugar
1 tbsp. hoisin sauce
2 tsps. minced garlic
2 tsps. minced fresh ginger
1 tsp. Chinese five-spice powder

1. In a microwave-safe bowl, combine all the ingredients, except for the pork shoulder. Stir to mix well. Microwave until the honey has dissolved. Stir periodically.
2. Pierce the pork pieces generously by using a fork, then place the pork in a large bowl. Pour in half of the honey mixture. Keep the remaining sauce aside until ready to serve.
3. Press the pork pieces into the mixture to coat well and wrap the bowl in plastic and refrigerate to marinate for at least 8 hours.
4. Preheat the air fryer oven to 400ºF (204ºC). Spray the air fryer basket lightly with cooking spray.
5. Discard the marinade and take the pork pieces in the air fryer basket.
6. Place the air fryer basket onto the baking pan, and slide the baking pan into Rack Position 2, select Air Fry and set time to 15 minutes, until well browned. Flip the pork pieces halfway through the cooking time.
7. At the same time, microwave the remaining marinade on high for a minute or until it has a thick consistency. Stir periodically.
8. Take the pork from the air fryer oven and let cool for 10 minutes before serving with the thickened marinade.

## Quick Beef Steak Fingers

Prep time: 5 minutes | Cook time: 8 minutes | Serves 4

| | |
|---|---|
| Cooking spray | Salt and ground black |
| 4 small beef cube steaks | pepper, to taste |
| ½ cup flour | |

1. Preheat the air fryer oven to 390ºF (199ºC).
2. Cut the beef cube steaks into 1-inch-wide strips.
3. Season with salt and pepper to taste.
4. Roll in flour to coat all the sides.
5. Spray the air fryer basket lightly with cooking spray.
6. Arrange the steak strips in the air fryer basket in a single layer. Spray top of steak strips lightly with cooking spray.
7. Place the air fryer basket onto the baking pan, and slide the baking pan into Rack Position 2, select Air Fry and set time to 4 minutes. Flip strips over, and spray with cooking spray.
8. Air fry for 4 more minutes and test with fork for doneness. Steak fingers should be crispy outside with no red juices inside.
9. Repeat steps 5 to 7 to air fry the remaining strips.
10. Serve hot.

## Simple Lamb Kofta

Prep time: 25 minutes | Cook time: 10 minutes | Serves 4

| | |
|---|---|
| 1 pound (454 g) ground lamb | 1 tsp. cumin |
| 2 tbsps. mint, chopped | ½ tsp. ground coriander |
| 1 tbsp. ras el hanout (North African spice) | Salt and ground black pepper, to taste |
| 1 tsp. onion powder | **Special Equipment:** |
| 1 tsp. garlic powder | 4 bamboo skewers |

1. In a large bowl, mix the ground lamb, ras el hanout, coriander, onion powder, garlic powder, cumin, mint, salt, and ground black pepper. Stir to combine well.
2. Take the mixture into sausage molds and sit the bamboo skewers in the mixture. Refrigerate for 15 minutes.
3. Preheat air fryer oven to 380ºF (193ºC). Spray the baking pan lightly with cooking spray.
4. Put the lamb skewers in the baking pan and spray lightly with cooking spray.
5. Slide the baking pan into Rack Position 2, select Roast and set time to 10 minutes, until the lamb is well browned. Flip the lamb skewers halfway through.
6. Serve hot.

## Ritzy Skirt Steak Fajitas with Guacamole

Prep time: 15 minutes | Cook time: 30 minutes | Serves 4

| | |
|---|---|
| 2 tbsps. olive oil | ½ tsp. hot sauce |
| 8 flour tortillas | ½ tsp. salt |
| 1 pound (454 g) skirt steak | Salt and freshly ground black pepper, to taste |
| ¼ cup lime juice | **Toppings:** |
| 1 onion, sliced | Shredded lettuce |
| 1 red pepper, sliced | Crumbled Queso Fresco |
| 1 green pepper, sliced | (or grated Cheddar |
| 1 clove garlic, minced | cheese) |
| 2 tbsps. chopped fresh cilantro | Diced tomatoes |
| 1 tsp. chili powder | Sliced black olives |
| ½ tsp. ground cumin | Guacamole |
| | Sour cream |

1. In a shallow dish, combine the olive oil, lime juice, garlic, cumin, hot sauce, salt and cilantro. Place the skirt steak and turn it over several times to coat all sides. Pierce the steak with a needle-style meat tenderizer or paring knife. Marinate the steak in the refrigerator for at least 3 hours, or overnight. When you are ready to cook, transfer the steak from the refrigerator and allow to cool at room temperature for 30 minutes.
2. Preheat the air fryer oven to 400ºF (204ºC).
3. Toss the onion slices with the chili powder and a little olive oil and take them to the air fryer basket. Then place the air fryer basket onto the baking pan, and slide the baking pan into Rack Position 2, select Air Fry and set time to 5 minutes. Put the red and green peppers to the air fryer basket with the onions, sprinkle with salt and pepper and air fry for another 8 minutes, until the onions and peppers are tender. Transfer the vegetables to a dish and cover with aluminum foil to keep warm.
4. Arrange the skirt steak in the air fryer basket and pour the marinade over the top. Air fry at 400ºF (204ºC) for about 12 minutes. Flip the steak over and air fry for another 5 minutes. Remove the cooked steak to a cutting board and let the steak rest for several minutes. If the peppers and onions need to be heated, take them back to the air fryer oven for just 1 to 2 minutes.
5. Thinly cut the steak at an angle, cutting against the grain of the steak. Place the onions and peppers, the warm tortillas and the fajita toppings on the side of steak.

## Authentic Pork and Pinto Bean Gorditas

Prep time: 20 minutes | Cook time: 21 minutes | Serves 4

Cooking spray
1 pound (454 g) lean ground pork
1 (15-ounce / 425-g) can pinto beans, drained and rinsed
4 cups shredded lettuce
5 (12-inch) flour tortillas
2 cups grated Cheddar cheese
4 (8-inch) crispy corn tortilla shells
1 tomato, diced
½ cup taco sauce
½ cup water
⅓ cup sliced black olives
2 tbsps. chili powder
2 tbsps. ground cumin
2 tsps. paprika
1 tsp. dried oregano
Sour cream, for serving
Tomato salsa, for serving
1 tsp. garlic powder
Salt and freshly ground black pepper, to taste

1. Preheat the air fryer oven to 400ºF (204ºC). Spray the air fryer basket lightly with cooking spray.
2. Place the ground pork in the air fryer basket. Then put the air fryer basket onto the baking pan, and slide the baking pan into Rack Position 2, select Air Fry and set time to 10 minutes, stirring several times to gently break up the meat. In a small bowl, combine the chili powder, cumin, oregano, paprika, garlic powder and water. Stir the spice mixture into the browned pork. Stir in the beans and taco sauce and air fry for an additional minute. Take the pork mixture to a bowl. Sprinkle with salt and freshly ground black pepper to taste.
3. Scatter ½ cup of the grated cheese in the center of the flour tortillas, leaving a 2-inch border around the edge free of cheese and filling. Distribute the pork mixture evenly among the four tortillas, putting it on top of the cheese. Arrange a crunchy corn tortilla on top of the pork and top with shredded lettuce, diced tomatoes, and black olives. Cut the remaining flour tortilla into 4 quarters. These quarters of tortilla will serve as the bottom of the gordita. Place one quarter tortilla on top of each gordita and fold the edges of the bottom flour tortilla up over the sides, enclosing the filling. When holding the seams down, coat the bottom of the gordita with olive oil and arrange the seam side down on the countertop while you finish the remaining three gorditas.
4. Set the temperature to 380ºF (193ºC).
5. Air fry one gordita at a time. Take the gordita carefully to the air fryer oven, seam side down. Spritz the top tortilla lightly with oil and air fry for 5 minutes. Gently turn the gordita over and air fry for another 4 to 5 minutes until both sides are browned. When cooked all four gorditas, layer them back into the air fryer oven for another minute to make sure they are all warm before serving with sour cream and salsa.

## Hearty Sweet and Sour Pork and Pineapple

Prep time: 20 minutes | Cook time: 14 minutes | Serves 2 to 4

Vegetable or canola oil
¾ pound (340 g) boneless pork, cut into 1-inch cubes
1½ cups large chunks of red and green peppers
1 cup cubed pineapple
1 egg
¼ cup orange juice
½ cup ketchup
⅓ cup all-purpose flour
⅓ cup cornstarch
1 clove garlic, minced
2 tbsps. milk
2 tbsps. rice wine vinegar or apple cider vinegar
2 tbsps. brown sugar
1 tbsp. soy sauce
2 tsps. Chinese five-spice powder
Chopped scallions, for garnish
1 tsp. salt
Freshly ground black pepper, to taste

1. Set up a dredging station with two bowls. In one large bowl, combine the flour, cornstarch, Chinese five-spice powder, salt and pepper. In a second bowl, whisk the egg and milk together. Dredge the pork cubes in the flour mixture first, then dunk them into the egg and then back into the flour to coat on all the sides. Spritz the coated pork cubes lightly with vegetable or canola oil.
2. Preheat the air fryer oven to 400ºF (204ºC).
3. Coat the pepper chunks with a little oil and put the bacon in the air fryer basket. Then place the air fryer basket onto the baking pan, and slide the baking pan into Rack Position 2, select Air Fry and set time to 5 minutes, flipping halfway through the cooking time.
4. When the peppers are cooking, start making the sauce. In a medium saucepan, combine the ketchup, rice wine vinegar, brown sugar, orange juice, soy sauce, and garlic and bring the mixture to a boil on the stovetop. Lower the heat and simmer for about 5 minutes. When the peppers have finished air frying, place them to the saucepan along with the pineapple chunks. Simmer the peppers and pineapple in the sauce for an additional 2 minutes. Set aside and keep warm.
5. Place the dredged pork cubes to the air fryer basket and air fry at 400ºF (204ºC) for about 6 minutes, flipping to turn the cubes over for the last minute of the cooking process.
6. When ready to serve, toss the cooked pork with the pineapple, peppers and sauce. Garnish with chopped scallions and serve warm.

BBQ Pork Ribs, page 97

Citrus Pork Loin Roast, page 92

Mustard Lamb Rack with Pistachio, page 79

Balsamic Ribeye Steaks with Rosemary, page 90

## Crispy Lechon Kawali

Prep time: 10 minutes | Cook time: 30 minutes | Serves 4

Cooking spray
1 pound (454 g) pork belly, cut into three thick chunks
3 cups water
6 garlic cloves
2 bay leaves
2 tbsps. soy sauce
1 tsp. kosher salt
1 tsp. ground black pepper

1. Add all the ingredients in a pressure cooker, then cover the lid and cook on high for about 15 minutes.
2. Natural release the pressure and release any remaining pressure, take the tender pork belly on a clean work surface. Let cool under room temperature until you can handle.
3. Preheat the air fryer oven to 400ºF (204ºC). Generously spray the air fryer basket with cooking spray.
4. Slice each chunk into two slices, then arrange the pork slices in the air fryer basket.
5. Place the air fryer basket onto the baking pan, and slide the baking pan into Rack Position 2, select Air Fry and set time to 15 minutes, until the pork fat is crispy. Spay the pork with more cooking spray, if necessary.
6. Serve hot.

## Spicy Pork Leg Roast with Candy Onions

Prep time: 10 minutes | Cook time: 52 minutes | Serves 4

2 tsps. sesame oil
2 pounds (907 g) pork leg roast, scored
½ pound (227 g) candy onions, sliced
4 cloves garlic, finely chopped
2 chili peppers, minced
1 rosemary sprig, chopped
1 thyme sprig, chopped
1 tsp. dried sage, crushed
1 tsp. cayenne pepper
Sea salt and ground black pepper, to taste

1. Preheat the air fryer oven to 400ºF (204ºC).
2. Combine the sesame oil, sage, cayenne pepper, rosemary, thyme, salt and black pepper in a mixing bowl until well mixed. Place the pork leg in another bowl, and brush with the seasoning mixture.
3. Put the seasoned pork leg in a baking pan. Slide the baking pan into Rack Position 2, select Roast and set time to 40 minutes, until lightly browned, flipping

halfway through. Place the candy onions, garlic and chili peppers to the pan and roast for an additional 12 minutes.
4. Take the pork leg to a plate. Let rest for 5 minutes and slice. Spread the juices left in the pan over the pork and serve hot with the candy onions.

## Crunchy Pork Schnitzels with Sour Cream and Dill Sauce

Prep time: 5 minutes | Cook time: 24 minutes | Serves 4 to 6

2 tbsps. olive oil
6 boneless, center cut pork chops (about 1½ pounds / 680 g), fat trimmed, pound to ½-inch thick
2 eggs
1½ cups toasted breadcrumbs
½ cup flour
½ cup milk
3 tbsps. melted butter
Lemon wedges, for serving
1 tsp. paprika
1½ tsps. salt
Freshly ground black pepper, to taste
**Sour Cream and Dill Sauce:**
1 cup chicken stock
⅓ cup sour cream
1½ tbsps. cornstarch
1½ tbsps. chopped fresh dill
Salt and ground black pepper, to taste

1. Preheat the air fryer oven to 400ºF (204ºC).
2. In a large bowl, combine the flour with salt and black pepper. Stir to mix well. In a second bowl, whisk the egg with milk. In a third bowl, stir the breadcrumbs and paprika.
3. Dredge the pork chops in the flour bowl, then in the egg milk, and then into the breadcrumbs bowl. Press to coat evenly. Shake the excess off.
4. Working in batches, place one pork chop in the air fryer basket each time, then coat with olive oil and butter on all sides.
5. Put the air fryer basket onto the baking pan, and slide the baking pan into Rack Position 2, select Air Fry and set time to 4 minutes, until golden brown and crispy. Flip the chop halfway through the cooking time.
6. Take the cooked pork chop (schnitzel) to the baking pan in the oven and keep warm over low heat when air frying the remaining pork chops.
7. At the same time, combine the chicken stock and cornstarch and bring to a boil over medium-high heat in a small saucepan. Simmer for another 2 minutes.
8. Transfer from the heat, then mix in the sour cream, fresh dill, salt, and black pepper.
9. Take the schnitzels from the air fryer oven to a plate and coat with sour cream and dill sauce. Squeeze the lemon wedges over and slice to serve.

## Cheddar Potato and Prosciutto Salad

Prep time: 10 minutes | Cook time: 7 minutes | Serves 8

**Salad:**
4 pounds (1.8 kg) potatoes, boiled and cubed
2 cups shredded Cheddar cheese
15 slices prosciutto, diced

**Dressing:**
15 ounces (425 g) sour cream
2 tbsps. mayonnaise
1 tsp. dried basil
1 tsp. salt
1 tsp. black pepper

1. Preheat the air fryer oven to 350ºF (177ºC).
2. In the air fryer basket, add the potatoes, prosciutto, and Cheddar. Place the air fryer basket onto the baking pan, and slide the baking pan into Rack Position 2, select Air Fry and set time to 7 minutes.
3. In a separate bowl, combine the mayonnaise, sour cream, salt, pepper, and basil with a whisk.
4. Top the salad with the dressing and serve hot.

## Balsamic Ribeye Steaks with Rosemary

Prep time: 10 minutes | Cook time: 15 minutes | Serves 2

¼ cup butter
2 ribeye steaks
¼ cup rosemary, chopped
1½ tbsps. balsamic

vinegar
1 clove garlic, minced
Salt and ground black pepper, to taste

1. In a skillet over medium heat, melt the butter. Place the garlic and fry until fragrant.
2. Remove the skillet from the heat and put the salt, pepper, and vinegar. Let it to cool.
3. Place the rosemary, then pour the mixture into a Ziploc bag.
4. Arrange the ribeye steaks in the bag and shake well, coating the meat well. Refrigerate for an hour, then let sit for a further 20 minutes.
5. Preheat the air fryer oven to 400ºF (204ºC).
6. Put he ribeye steaks in the air fryer basket. Then place the air fryer basket onto the baking pan, and slide the baking pan into Rack Position 2, select Air Fry and set time to 15 minutes.
7. Remove the steaks from the air fryer oven and plate up.
8. Serve hot.

## Simple Pork Meatballs with Scallion

Prep time: 5 minutes | Cook time: 15 minutes | Serves 4

Cooking spray
1 pound (454 g) ground pork
1 cup scallions, finely chopped
2 cloves garlic, finely minced
1 small sliced red chili,

for garnish
1½ tbsps. Worcestershire sauce
1 tbsp. oyster sauce
1 tsp. turmeric powder
½ tsp. freshly grated ginger root

1. Preheat the air fryer oven to 350ºF (177ºC). Spray the baking pan lightly with cooking spray.
2. In a large bowl, combine all the ingredients, except for the red chili. Toss to mix well.
3. Form the mixture into equally sized balls, then place them in the preheated air fryer oven and spray lightly with cooking spray.
4. Slide the baking pan into Rack Position 2, select Roast and set time to 15 minutes, until the balls are lightly browned. Flip the balls halfway through.
5. Garnish with red chili and serve warm.

## Easy Pork and Vegetable Kabobs

Prep time: 25 minutes | Cook time: 15 minutes | Serves 4

1 tbsp. oregano
1 pound (454 g) pork tenderloin, cubed
1 zucchini, cut into chunks
1 green bell pepper, cut into chunks
1 red onion, sliced
Cooking spray

1 tsp. smoked paprika
Salt and ground black pepper, to taste
**Special Equipment:**
Small bamboo skewers, soaked in water for 20 minutes to keep them from burning while cooking

1. Preheat the air fryer oven to 350ºF (177ºC). Spray the baking pan lightly with cooking spray.
2. Place the pork to a bowl and season with the smoked paprika, salt and black pepper. Thread the seasoned pork cubes and vegetables alternately onto the soaked skewers.
3. Put the skewers in the prepared baking pan and spritz lightly with cooking spray. Slide the baking pan into Rack Position 2, select Roast and set time to 15 minutes, until the pork is well browned and the vegetables are soft, flipping once halfway through.
4. Take the skewers to the serving dishes and garnish with oregano. Serve warm.

## BBQ Kielbasa Sausage with Pineapple and Peppers

Prep time: 15 minutes | Cook time: 10 minutes | Serves 2 to 4

Cooking spray
¾ pound (340 g) kielbasa sausage, cut into ½-inch slices
1 (8-ounce / 227-g) can pineapple chunks in juice, drained
1 cup bell pepper chunks
1 tbsp. soy sauce
1 tbsp. barbecue seasoning

1. Preheat the air fryer oven to 390ºF (199ºC). Spray the air fryer basket lightly with cooking spray.
2. In a large bowl, combine all the ingredients. Toss to mix well.
3. Add the sausage mixture in the air fryer basket.
4. Place the air fryer basket onto the baking pan, and slide the baking pan into Rack Position 2, select Air Fry and set time to 10 minutes, until the sausage is lightly browned and the bell pepper and pineapple are tender, flipping halfway through.
5. Serve hot.

## Spicy Sausage Ratatouille

Prep time: 10 minutes | Cook time: 25 minutes | Serves 4

4 pork sausages
**Ratatouille:**
2 tbsps. olive oil
2 zucchinis, sliced
1 eggplant, sliced
15 ounces (425 g) tomatoes, sliced
1 cup canned butter beans, drained
1 medium red onion, sliced
1 red bell pepper, sliced
2 garlic cloves, minced
1 red chili, chopped
2 tbsps. fresh thyme, chopped
1 tbsp. balsamic vinegar

1. Preheat the air fryer oven to 390ºF (199ºC).
2. Arrange the sausages in the air fryer basket. Then place the air fryer basket onto the baking pan, and slide the baking pan into Rack Position 2, select Air Fry and set time to 10 minutes, until the sausage is lightly browned. Flip the sausages halfway through.
3. At the same time, make the ratatouille: place the vegetable slices on another baking pan alternatively, then put the remaining ingredients on top.
4. Take the air fried sausage to a plate, then slide the baking pan with the ratatouille into Rack Position 1, select Convection Bake and set time to 15 minutes, until the vegetables are soft.

5. Place the sausage on the ratatouille and serve hot.

## Lamb Pita Burger

Prep time: 15 minutes | Cook time: 16 minutes | Serves 3 to 4

2 tsps. olive oil
1 pound (454 g) ground lamb
4 thick pita breads
½ cup black olives, finely chopped
⅓ cup crumbled feta cheese
⅓ onion, finely chopped
1 clove garlic, minced
2 tbsps. fresh parsley, finely chopped
1½ tsps. fresh oregano, finely chopped
½ tsp. salt
Freshly ground black pepper, to taste
tzatziki sauce or some mayonnaise for serving

1. In a medium skillet over medium-high heat, add the olive oil and cook the onion until soft, but not browned for about 4 to 5 minutes. Place the garlic and cook for another minute. Take the onion and garlic to a mixing bowl and add the ground lamb, oregano, parsley, olives, feta cheese, salt and pepper. Carefully mix the ingredients together.
2. Distribute the mixture evenly into 3 or 4 equal portions and then shape the hamburgers, being careful not to over-handle the meat. One good way to do this is to throw the meat back and forth between the hands like a baseball, packing the meat each time you catch it. Flatten the balls tightly into patties, making an indentation in the center of each patty. At the same time, flatten the sides of the patties to make it easier to fit them into the baking pan.
3. Preheat the air fryer oven to 370ºF (188ºC).
4. If you don't have room for all four burgers, work in batches. Put two or three burgers in the baking pan. Slide the baking pan into Rack Position 1, select Convection Bake and set time to 8 minutes. Turn the burgers over and bake for an additional 8 minutes. If you cooked the burgers in batches, take the first batch of burgers back to the air fryer oven for the last two minutes of cooking to re-heat. This will give you a medium-well burger. If you'd prefer a medium-rare burger, shorten the cooking time to approximately 13 minutes. Transfer the burgers to a resting plate and allow the burgers to rest for a few minutes before dressing and serving.
5. When the burgers are resting, bake the pita breads in the air fryer oven for about 2 minutes. Tuck the burgers into the toasted pita breads, or wrap the pitas around the burgers. Serve alongside with a tzatziki sauce or some mayonnaise.

## Homemade Teriyaki Pork and Mushroom Rolls

Prep time: 10 minutes | Cook time: 8 minutes | Serves 6

6 (4-ounce / 113-g) pork belly slices
6 ounces (170 g) Enoki mushrooms
2-inch ginger, chopped

4 tbsps. brown sugar
4 tbsps. soy sauce
4 tbsps. mirin
1 tsp. almond flour

1. Mix the brown sugar, mirin, soy sauce, almond flour, and ginger together in a small bowl until brown sugar dissolves.
2. Take pork belly slices and wrap around a bundle of mushrooms. Coat each roll with teriyaki sauce. Chill for about half an hour.
3. Preheat the air fryer oven to 350ºF (177ºC) and place the marinated pork rolls in the air fryer basket.
4. Put the air fryer basket onto the baking pan, and slide the baking pan into Rack Position 2, select Air Fry and set time to 8 minutes. Flip the rolls halfway through.
5. Serve hot.

## Citrus Pork Loin Roast

Prep time: 10 minutes | Cook time: 45 minutes | Serves 8

Cooking spray
2 pound (907 g) boneless pork loin roast
1 tbsp. lime juice
1 tbsp. orange marmalade

1 tsp. curry powder
1 tsp. coarse brown mustard
1 tsp. dried lemongrass
Salt and ground black pepper, to taste

1. Preheat the air fryer oven to 360ºF (182ºC).
2. In the large bowl, mix the lime juice, marmalade, mustard, curry powder, and lemongrass.
3. Rub mixture all over the surface of the pork loin. Season with salt and pepper to taste.
4. Spritz the air fryer basket lightly with cooking spray and put the pork roast diagonally in the air fryer basket.
5. Place the air fryer basket onto the baking pan, and slide the baking pan into Rack Position 2, select Air Fry and set time to 45 minutes, until the internal temperature reaches at least 145ºF (63ºC).
6. Wrap roast in foil and allow to rest for 10 minutes before slicing.
7. Serve hot.

## Smoked Beef and Peppers

Prep time: 10 minutes | Cook time: 45 minutes | Serves 8

2 tbsps. extra-virgin olive oil
2 pounds (907 g) roast beef, at room temperature
2 jalapeño peppers, thinly sliced

1 tsp. smoked paprika
1 tsp. sea salt flakes
1 tsp. ground black pepper
Few dashes of liquid smoke

1. Preheat the air fryer oven to 330ºF (166ºC).
2. Pat the beef dry with kitchen towels.
3. Massage the extra-virgin olive oil, salt, ground black pepper, and paprika into the meat. Cover with liquid smoke.
4. Arrange the beef in the air fryer basket. Then place the air fryer basket onto the baking pan, and slide the baking pan into Rack Position 2, select Convection Broil and set time to 30 minutes. Turn the roast over and allow to cook for an additional 15 minutes.
5. When cooked through, Top with sliced jalapeños and serve.

## Cheesy Pork Sausage with Cauliflower Mash

Prep time: 5 minutes | Cook time: 27 minutes | Serves 6

Cooking spray
1 pound (454 g) cauliflower, chopped
6 pork sausages, chopped
3 eggs, beaten
⅓ cup Colby cheese

½ onion, sliced
1 tsp. cumin powder
½ tsp. tarragon
½ tsp. sea salt
½ tsp. ground black pepper

1. Preheat the air fryer oven to 365ºF (185ºC). Spray a baking pan lightly with cooking spray.
2. In a saucepan, boil the cauliflower over medium heat until tender. Put the boiled cauliflower in a food processor and pulse until puréed. Take to a large bowl and mix with remaining ingredients until well blended.
3. Place the cauliflower and sausage mixture into the baking pan. Slide the baking pan into Rack Position 1, select Convection Bake and set time to 27 minutes, until lightly browned.
4. Distribute the mixture evenly among six serving dishes and serve hot.

## Mustard London Broil

Prep time: 15 minutes | Cook time: 25 minutes | Serves 8

2 tbsps. olive oil
2 pounds (907 g) London broil
3 large garlic cloves, minced
3 tbsps. whole-grain

mustard
3 tbsps. balsamic vinegar
½ tsp. dried hot red pepper flakes
Sea salt and ground black pepper, to taste

1. Wash and dry the London broil. Use a knife to score its sides.
2. In a small bowl, add the remaining ingredients. Rub this mixture into the broil, coating it evenly. Let marinate for at least 3 hours.
3. Preheat the air fryer oven to 400ºF (204ºC).
4. Put the London broil in the air fryer basket. Then place the air fryer basket onto the baking pan, and slide the baking pan into Rack Position 2, select Air Fry and set time to 15 minutes. Flip the meat and air fry for another 10 minutes before serving.

## Spicy Pork Chops with Mushrooms and Carrots

Prep time: 10 minutes | Cook time: 16 minutes | Serves 4

Cooking spray
2 tbsps. olive oil
1 pound (454 g) boneless pork chops
1 cup mushrooms, sliced
2 carrots, cut into sticks

2 garlic cloves, minced
1 tsp. dried thyme
1 tsp. dried oregano
1 tsp. cayenne pepper
Salt and ground black pepper, to taste

1. Preheat air fryer oven to 360ºF (182ºC). Spray the air fryer basket lightly with cooking spray.
2. Toss together the carrots, mushrooms, garlic, olive oil and salt in a mixing bowl until well combined.
3. Place the pork chops to a different bowl and sprinkle with oregano, thyme, cayenne pepper, salt and black pepper.
4. Arrange the vegetable mixture in the air fryer basket. Put the seasoned pork chops on top. Then place the air fryer basket onto the baking pan, and slide the baking pan into Rack Position 2, select Air Fry and set time to 16 minutes, flipping the pork and stirring once halfway through.
5. Take the pork chops to the serving dishes and allow to cool for about 5 minutes. Serve hot with vegetable on the side.

## Citrus Glazed Carnitas

Prep time: 1 hour 10 minutes | Cook time: 25 minutes | Serves 6

Cooking spray
2½ pounds (1.1 kg) boneless country-style pork ribs, cut into 2-inch pieces
⅓ cup orange juice
3 tbsps. olive brine

1 tbsp. minced fresh oregano leaves
1 tbsp. minced garlic
1 tsp. ground cumin
1 tsp. salt
1 tsp. ground black pepper

1. In a large bowl, combine all the ingredients. Toss to coat the pork ribs evenly. Wrap the bowl in plastic and refrigerate for at least an hour to marinate.
2. Preheat the air fryer oven to 400ºF (204ºC) and spray the air fryer basket lightly with cooking spray.
3. Place the marinated pork ribs in a single layer, in the air fryer basket and spray lightly with cooking spray.
4. Put the air fryer basket onto the baking pan, and slide the baking pan into Rack Position 2, select Air Fry and set time to 25 minutes, until well browned. Flip the ribs halfway through.
5. Serve hot.

## Crunchy Tonkatsu

Prep time: 5 minutes | Cook time: 10 minutes per batch | Serves 4

Cooking spray
4 (4-ounce / 113-g) center-cut boneless pork loin chops (about ½ inch thick)

2 large egg whites
1 cup panko breadcrumbs
⅔ cup all-purpose flour

1. Preheat the air fryer oven to 375ºF (191ºC). Spray the baking pan lightly with cooking spray.
2. In a bowl, pour the flour. In a separate bowl, whisk the egg whites. Spread the breadcrumbs on a large plate.
3. Dredge the pork loin chops in the flour first, press to coat evenly, then shake the excess off and dip the chops in the eggs whites, and then roll the chops over the breadcrumbs. Shake the excess off.
4. Place the pork chops in batches in a single layer in the baking pan and spray lightly with cooking spray.
5. Slide the baking pan into Rack Position 1, select Convection Bake and set time to 10 minutes, until the pork chops are lightly browned and crunchy. Flip the chops halfway through. Repeat this with remaining chops.
6. Serve hot.

## Teriyaki Country-Style Pork Ribs

Prep time: 5 minutes | Cook time: 30 minutes | Serves 4

Cooking spray
4 (8-ounce / 227-g) boneless country-style pork ribs

¼ cup soy sauce
¼ cup honey
1 tsp. garlic powder
1 tsp. ground dried ginger

1. Preheat the air fryer oven to 350ºF (177ºC). Spray the air fryer basket lightly with cooking spray.
2. Make the teriyaki sauce: in a bowl, combine the soy sauce, honey, garlic powder, and ginger. Stir to mix well.
3. Coat the ribs with half of the teriyaki sauce, then place the ribs in the air fryer basket. Spray lightly with cooking spray. You may need to work in batches to avoid overcrowding.
4. Put the air fryer basket onto the baking pan, and slide the baking pan into Rack Position 2, select Air Fry and set time to 30 minutes, until the internal temperature of the ribs reaches at least 145ºF (63ºC). Coat the ribs with remaining teriyaki sauce and flip halfway through.
5. Serve hot.

## Air Fried Panko Wasabi Spam

Prep time: 5 minutes | Cook time: 12 minutes | Serves 3

Cooking spray
2 large eggs
2 cups panko breadcrumbs

6 ½-inch-thick spam slices
⅔ cup all-purpose flour
1½ tbsps. wasabi paste

1. Preheat the air fryer oven to 400ºF (204ºC) and spray the air fryer basket lightly with cooking spray.
2. In a shallow plate, place the flour. In a large bowl, whisk the eggs with wasabi. In a separate shallow plate, put the panko.
3. Dredge the spam slices in the flour first, then dunk in the egg mixture, and then roll the spam over the panko to coat well. Shake the excess off.
4. Place the spam slices in a single layer in the air fryer basket and spray lightly with cooking spray.
5. Put the air fryer basket onto the baking pan, and slide the baking pan into Rack Position 2, select Air Fry and set time to 12 minutes, until the spam slices are golden and crispy. Gently flip the spam slices halfway through.
6. Serve hot.

## Crispy Pork Tenderloin

Prep time: 5 minutes | Cook time: 10 minutes | Serves 6

Cooking spray
1½ pounds (680 g) pork tenderloin, cut into ¼-pound (113-g) sections

2 cups crushed pretzel crumbs
2 large egg whites
1½ tbsps. Dijon mustard

1. Preheat the air fryer oven to 350ºF (177ºC). Spray the baking pan lightly with cooking spray.
2. In a bowl, whisk the egg whites with Dijon mustard until bubbly. In a separate bowl, pour the pretzel crumbs.
3. Dredge the pork tenderloin in the egg white mixture and press to coat well. Shake the excess off and roll the tenderloin over the pretzel crumbs.
4. Place the well-coated pork tenderloin in batches in a single layer in the baking pan and spray lightly with cooking spray.
5. Slide the baking pan into Rack Position 2, select Roast and set time to 10 minutes, until the pork is golden brown and crispy. Flip the pork gently halfway through. Repeat this with remaining pork sections.
6. Serve hot.

## Sweet Pork Chops

Prep time: 15 minutes | Cook time: 12 minutes | Serves 2

1 tbsp. olive oil
2 pork chops
3 tbsps. lemongrass
1 tbsp. chopped shallot
1 tbsp. chopped garlic

1 tbsp. fish sauce
1 tbsp. brown sugar
1 tsp. soy sauce
1 tsp. ground black pepper

1. In a bowl, combine shallot, garlic, fish sauce, lemongrass, soy sauce, brown sugar, olive oil, and pepper. Stir to mix well.
2. Place the pork chops in the bowl. Toss to coat evenly. Put the bowl in the refrigerator to marinate for 2 hours.
3. Preheat the air fryer oven to 400ºF (204ºC).
4. Transfer the pork chops from the bowl and discard the marinade. Take the chops into the air fryer basket.
5. Put the air fryer basket onto the baking pan, and slide the baking pan into Rack Position 2, select Air Fry and set time to 12 minutes, until lightly browned. Flip the pork chops halfway through the cooking time.
6. Take the pork chops from the oven and serve warm.

## Beef and Mushroom Meatloaf

Prep time: 10 minutes | Cook time: 25 minutes | Serves 4

1 pound (454 g) ground beef
1 egg, beaten
1 small onion, chopped
1 mushroom, sliced
3 tbsps. bread crumbs
1 tbsp. thyme
Ground black pepper, to taste

1. Preheat the air fryer oven to 400ºF (204ºC).
2. Mix all the ingredients into a large bowl and mix entirely.
3. Take the meatloaf mixture into the loaf pan and move it to the air fryer oven.
4. Slide the pan into Rack Position 1, select Convection Bake and set time to 25 minutes. Slice up before serving.

## Glazed Pork with Apple

Prep time: 15 minutes | Cook time: 19 minutes | Serves 4

3 tbsps. olive oil, divided
4 pork chops
1 sliced apple
1 small onion, sliced
2 tbsps. apple cider vinegar, divided
½ tsp. thyme
½ tsp. rosemary
¼ tsp. brown sugar
¼ tsp. smoked paprika
Salt and ground black pepper, to taste

1. Preheat the air fryer oven to 350ºF (177ºC).
2. In a baking pan, combine the apple slices, onion, 1 tbsp. of vinegar, thyme, rosemary, brown sugar, and 2 tbsps. of olive oil. Stir to mix well.
3. Slide the baking pan into Rack Position 1, select Convection Bake and set time to 4 minutes.
4. At the same time, combine the remaining vinegar and olive oil, and paprika in a large bowl. Season with salt and ground black pepper to taste. Stir to mix well. Dredge the pork in the mixture and toss to coat evenly.
5. Remove from the air fryer oven and place the pork in the air fryer basket. Put the air fryer basket onto the baking pan, and slide the baking pan into Rack Position 2, select Air Fry and set time to 10 minutes to lightly brown the pork. Flip the pork chops halfway through.
6. Take the pork from the air fryer oven and brush with baked apple mixture on both sides. Place the pork back to the air fryer oven and air fry for another 5 minutes. Flip halfway through.
7. Serve hot.

## Swedish Beef Meatballs with Pasta Sauce

Prep time: 10 minutes | Cook time: 12 minutes | Serves 8

1 pound (454 g) ground beef
1 egg, beaten
2 carrots, shredded
2 bread slices, crumbled
2 cups pasta sauce
1 cup tomato sauce
1 small onion, minced
½ tsp. garlic salt
Pepper and salt, to taste

1. Preheat the air fryer oven to 400ºF (204ºC).
2. Combine the ground beef, egg, carrots, crumbled bread, onion, garlic salt, pepper and salt in a bowl.
3. Distribute the mixture evenly into equal amounts and form each one into a small meatball.
4. Arrange them in the air fryer basket. Then place the air fryer basket onto the baking pan, and slide the baking pan into Rack Position 2, select Air Fry and set time to 7 minutes.
5. Take the meatballs to an oven-safe dish and place the tomato sauce and pasta sauce on top.
6. Put the dish into the air fryer oven and let air fry at 320ºF (160ºC) for 5 more minutes. Serve warm.

## Bacon-Wrapped Hot Dogs with Mayo Sauce

Prep time: 5 minutes | Cook time: 10 minutes | Serves 5

5 pork hot dogs, halved
10 thin slices of bacon
1 tsp. cayenne pepper
**Sauce:**
¼ cup mayonnaise
4 tbsps. low-carb ketchup
1 tsp. rice vinegar
1 tsp. chili powder

1. Preheat the air fryer oven to 390ºF (199ºC).
2. Place the slices of bacon on a clean work surface. One by one, put the halved hot dog on one end of each slice, sprinkle with cayenne pepper and wrap the hot dog with the bacon slices and secure with toothpicks as needed.
3. Work in batches, arrange half the wrapped hot dogs in the air fryer basket. Then place the air fryer basket onto the baking pan, and slide the baking pan into Rack Position 2, select Air Fry and set time to 10 minutes, until the bacon turns browned and crispy.
4. Make the sauce: In a small bowl, stir all the ingredients for the sauce. Wrap the bowl in plastic and set in the refrigerator until ready to serve.
5. Take the hot dogs to a platter and serve warm with the sauce.

# Quick Lamb Satay

Prep time: 5 minutes | Cook time: 8 minutes | Serves 2

Cooking spray
2 boneless lamb steaks
1 tsp. ginger
¼ tsp. cumin
½ tsp. nutmeg
Salt and ground black pepper, to taste

1. In a bowl, combine the cumin, ginger, nutmeg, salt and pepper.
2. Cut the lamb steaks into cubes and massage the spice mixture into each one.
3. Let marinate for about 10 minutes, then take onto metal skewers.
4. Preheat the air fryer oven to 400ºF (204ºC).
5. Spray the skewers with the cooking spray. Slide the baking pan into Rack Position 2, select Roast and set time to 8 minutes.
6. Remove them from the air fryer oven and serve warm.

# Kielbasa Sausage with Pierogies

Prep time: 15 minutes | Cook time: 30 minutes | Serves 3 to 4

1 tsp. olive oil
1 pound (454 g) light Polish kielbasa sausage, cut into 2-inch chunks
1 (13-ounce / 369-g) package frozen mini pierogies
1 sweet onion, sliced
2 tbsps. butter, cut into
small cubes
2 tsps. vegetable or olive oil
1 tsp. sugar
Chopped scallions, for garnish
Salt and freshly ground black pepper, to taste

1. Preheat the air fryer oven to 400ºF (204ºC).
2. Coat the sliced onions with olive oil, salt and pepper and take them to the air fryer basket. Dot the onions with pieces of butter. Place the air fryer basket onto the baking pan, and slide the baking pan into Rack Position 2, select Air Fry and set time to 2 minutes. Then scatter the sugar over the onions and stir. Pour any melted butter from the bottom of the air fryer oven drawer over the onions. Continue to air fry for an additional 13 minutes, stirring every few minutes to air fry the onions evenly.
3. Place the kielbasa chunks to the onions and toss well. Air fry for 5 minutes more, flipping halfway through the cooking time. Take the kielbasa and onions to a bowl and cover with aluminum foil to keep warm.
4. Toss the frozen pierogies with the vegetable or olive oil and take them to the air fryer basket. Air fry at 400ºF (204ºC) for about 8 minutes, flipping twice during cooking.
5. When the pierogies have finished cooking, take the kielbasa and onions back to the air fryer oven and gently toss with the pierogies. Air fry for 2 minutes more and then transfer everything to a serving platter. Serve with the chopped scallions garnished.

# Sake Marinated Steak

Prep time: 5 minutes | Cook time: 12 minutes | Serves 4

1 tbsp. olive oil
¾ pound (340 g) flank steak
2 cloves garlic, pressed
1½ tbsps. sake
1 tbsp. brown miso paste
1 tsp. honey

1. Add all the ingredients in a Ziploc bag. Shake to cover the steak evenly with the seasonings and refrigerate for at least 1 hour.
2. Preheat the air fryer oven to 400ºF (204ºC). Spray all sides of the steak lightly with cooking spray. Arrange the steak in the in the air fryer basket.
3. Place the air fryer basket onto the baking pan, and slide the baking pan into Rack Position 2, select Air Fry and set time to 12 minutes, turning the steak twice during the cooking time. Serve hot.

# Air Fried Lamb Ribs with Mint

Prep time: 5 minutes | Cook time: 18 minutes | Serves 4

1 pound (454 g) lamb ribs
2 tbsps. mustard
1 cup Greek yogurt
¼ cup mint leaves,
chopped
1 tsp. rosemary, chopped
Salt and ground black pepper, to taste

1. Preheat the air fryer oven to 350ºF (177ºC).
2. Brush the lamb ribs with mustard, and sprinkle with rosemary, salt, and pepper to taste.
3. Put the lamb ribs in the air fryer basket. Then place the air fryer basket onto the baking pan, and slide the baking pan into Rack Position 2, select Air Fry and set time to 18 minutes.
4. At the same time, combine the mint leaves and yogurt in a bowl.
5. Transfer the lamb ribs from the air fryer oven when cooked and serve hot with the mint yogurt.

## BBQ Pork Ribs

Prep time: 5 minutes | Cook time: 30 minutes | Serves 4

1 tsp. sesame oil
1 pound (454 g) pork ribs, chopped
1 tbsp. barbecue dry rub
1 tbsp. apple cider vinegar
1 tsp. mustard

1. In a large bowl, combine the dry rub, mustard, apple cider vinegar, and sesame oil, then coat the ribs with this mixture. Refrigerate the ribs for 20 minutes.
2. Preheat the air fryer oven to 360ºF (182ºC).
3. When the ribs are ready, arrange them in the baking pan. Slide the baking pan into Rack Position 2, select Roast and set time to 15 minutes. Flip them over and roast on the other side for another 15 minutes.
4. Serve hot.

## Cheesy Pepperoni and Bell Pepper Pockets

Prep time: 5 minutes | Cook time: 8 minutes | Serves 4

Olive oil, for misting
24 slices pepperoni
4 bread slices, 1-inch thick
1 ounce (28 g) roasted
red peppers, drained and patted dry
1 ounce (28 g) Pepper Jack cheese, cut into 4 slices

1. Preheat the air fryer oven to 360ºF (182ºC).
2. Spritz both sides of bread slices lightly with olive oil.
3. Stand slices upright and cut a deep slit in the top to create a pocket (almost to the bottom crust, but not all the way through).
4. Stuff each bread pocket with 6 slices of pepperoni, a large strip of roasted red pepper, and a slice of cheese.
5. Arrange the bread pockets in the air fryer basket, standing up. Place the air fryer basket onto the baking pan, and slide the baking pan into Rack Position 2, select Air Fry and set time to 8 minutes, until filling is heated through and bread is lightly browned.
6. Serve warm.

## Two-Cheese Beef Meatballs

Prep time: 5 minutes | Cook time: 15 minutes | Serves 6

1 pound (454 g) ground beef
½ cup Mozzarella cheese
½ cup grated Parmesan
cheese
1 tbsp. minced garlic
1 tsp. freshly ground pepper

1. Preheat the air fryer oven to 400ºF (204ºC).
2. Mix all the ingredients together in a bowl.
3. Roll the meat mixture into 5 generous meatballs.
4. Put the meatballs in the air fryer basket. Then place the air fryer basket onto the baking pan, and slide the baking pan into Rack Position 2, select Air Fry and set time to 15 minutes, until the internal temperature of the meatball reaches at least 165ºF (74ºC).
5. Serve hot.

## Simple Beef Schnitzel

Prep time: 5 minutes | Cook time: 12 minutes | Serves 1

2 tbsps. olive oil
1 thin beef schnitzel
1 egg, beaten
½ cup friendly bread crumbs
Pepper and salt, to taste

1. Preheat the air fryer oven to 350ºF (177ºC).
2. Combine the bread crumbs, oil, pepper, and salt in a shallow dish.
3. Place the beaten egg in a second shallow dish.
4. Dredge the schnitzel in the egg before rolling it in the bread crumbs.
5. Arrange the coated schnitzel in the air fryer basket. Then place the air fryer basket onto the baking pan, and slide the baking pan into Rack Position 2, select Air Fry and set time to 12 minutes. Flip the schnitzel halfway through.
6. Serve hot.

# Chapter 7 Casseroles, Frittatas and Quiches

## Cheese and Asparagus Frittata

Prep time: 5 minutes | Cook time: 25 minutes | Serves 2 to 4

1 tsp. vegetable oil
6 eggs, beaten
1 cup asparagus spears, cut into 1-inch pieces
2 ounces (57 g) goat cheese, crumbled
1 tbsp. milk
1 tbsp. minced chives, optional
Kosher salt and pepper, to taste

1. Preheat the air fryer oven to 400ºF (204ºC).
2. Place the asparagus spears to a small bowl and drizzle with the vegetable oil. Toss until evenly coated and take to a cake pan.
3. Slide the baking pan into Rack Position 1, select Convection Bake and set time to 5 minutes, until the asparagus become soft and slightly wilted. Remove then pan from the air fryer oven.
4. In a medium bowl, stir together the milk and eggs. Pour the mixture over the asparagus in the pan. Scatter with the goat cheese and the chives (if using) over the eggs. Sprinkle with a pinch of salt and pepper to season.
5. Put the pan back to the air fryer oven and bake at 320ºF (160ºC) for about 20 minutes or until the top is lightly golden and the eggs are set.
6. Transfer the frittata to a serving dish. Slice and serve hot.

## Sumptuous Vegetable Frittata with Cheese

Prep time: 15 minutes | Cook time: 20 minutes | Serves 2

2 tsps. olive oil
4 eggs
1 large zucchini, sliced
1 cup baby spinach
2 asparagus, sliced thinly
⅓ cup sliced mushrooms
1 small red onion, sliced
⅓ cup crumbled feta
cheese
⅓ cup grated Cheddar cheese
¼ cup chopped chives
⅓ cup milk
Salt and ground black pepper, to taste

1. Preheat the air fryer oven to 380ºF (193ºC). Line a baking pan with parchment paper.
2. In a large bowl, whisk together the eggs, milk, salt,

and ground black pepper. Set aside.
3. In a nonstick skillet over medium heat, heat the olive oil until shimmering.
4. Place the zucchini, asparagus, spinach, mushrooms, and onion to the skillet and sauté for about 5 minutes or until soft.
5. Pour the sautéed vegetables into the prepared baking pan, then spread the egg mixture over and sprinkle with cheeses.
6. Slide the baking pan into Rack Position 1, select Convection Bake and set time to 15 minutes, until the eggs are set the edges are lightly browned.
7. Transfer the frittata from the air fryer oven and garnish with chives before serving.

## Classic Chicken Divan

Prep time: 5 minutes | Cook time: 24 minutes | Serves 4

Cooking spray
4 chicken breasts
1 head broccoli, cut into florets
1 cup shredded Cheddar cheese
½ cup croutons
½ cup cream of mushroom soup
Salt and ground black pepper, to taste

1. Preheat the air fryer oven to 390ºF (199ºC). Spay the baking pan lightly with cooking spray.
2. Place the chicken breasts in the baking pan and season with salt and ground black pepper.
3. Slide the baking pan into Rack Position 1, select Convection Bake and set time to 14 minutes, until well browned and soft. Flip the breasts halfway through the cooking time.
4. Transfer the breasts from the air fryer oven and let cool for a few minutes on a plate, then cut the breasts into bite-size pieces.
5. In a large bowl, combine the chicken, broccoli, mushroom soup, and Cheddar cheese. Stir to mix well.
6. Spray the baking pan lightly with cooking spray. Add the chicken mixture into the pan. Spread the croutons over the mixture.
7. Arrange the baking pan in the air fryer oven. Bake for about 10 minutes or until the croutons are lightly browned and the mixture is set.
8. Transfer the chicken from the air fryer oven and serve hot.

## Ritzy Vegetable Frittata with Cheese

Prep time: 15 minutes | Cook time: 21 minutes | Serves 2

| | |
|---|---|
| ½ tbsp. olive oil | ¼ cup milk |
| 4 eggs | 5 tbsps. feta cheese, crumbled |
| 1 zucchini, sliced | |
| ½ bunch asparagus, sliced | 4 tbsps. Cheddar cheese, grated |
| ½ cup mushrooms, sliced | ¼ bunch chives, minced |
| ½ cup spinach, shredded | Sea salt and ground black pepper, to taste |
| ½ cup red onion, sliced | |

1. Mix the eggs, milk, salt and pepper in a bowl.
2. In a nonstick pan over a medium heat, sauté the vegetables for about 6 minutes with the olive oil.
3. Place some parchment paper in the base of a baking tin. Pour in the vegetables, followed by the egg mixture. Put the feta and grated Cheddar on top.
4. Preheat the air fryer oven to 320ºF (160ºC).
5. Slide the baking tin into Rack Position 1, select Convection Bake and set time to 15 minutes. Transfer the frittata from the air fryer oven and let cool for about 5 minutes.
6. Garnish with the minced chives and serve warm.

## Sumptuous Chili Beef and Bean Casserole

Prep time: 15 minutes | Cook time: 31 minutes | Serves 4

| | |
|---|---|
| 1 tbsp. olive oil | ½ cup chopped celery |
| 1 pound (454 g) ground beef | 1½ cups vegetable broth |
| 1 (8-ounce / 227-g) can cannellini beans | 2 garlic cloves, minced |
| | ½ tbsp. chili powder |
| 1 can diced tomatoes | 1 tsp. chopped cilantro |
| ½ cup finely chopped bell pepper | ½ tsp. parsley |
| | Salt and ground black pepper, to taste |
| 1 onion, chopped | |

1. Preheat the air fryer oven to 350ºF (177ºC).
2. In a nonstick skillet over medium heat, heat the olive oil until shimmering.
3. Place the bell pepper, celery, onion, and garlic to the skillet and sauté for about 5 minutes or until the onion is tender.
4. Put the ground beef and sauté for another 6 minutes or until lightly browned.
5. Mix in the tomatoes, parsley, chili powder, cilantro and vegetable broth, then cook for another 10 minutes. Stir frequently.
6. Pour them in the air fryer basket, then mix in the beans and season with salt and ground black pepper to taste.
7. Arrange the air fryer basket onto the baking pan, and slide the baking pan into Rack Position 2, select Convection Broil and set time to 10 minutes, until the vegetables are soft and the beef is well browned.
8. Transfer the baking pan from the air fryer oven and serve hot.

## Mini Sausage Quiche Cups

Prep time: 15 minutes | Cook time: 16 minutes | Makes 10 quiche cups

| | |
|---|---|
| Cooking spray | Cheddar cheese, grated |
| 4 ounces (113 g) ground pork sausage | ¾ cup milk |
| | **Special Equipment:** |
| 3 eggs | 20 foil muffin cups |
| 4 ounces (113 g) sharp | |

1. Preheat the air fryer oven to 390ºF (199ºC). Spray the air fryer basket lightly with cooking spray.
2. Distribute sausage evenly into 3 portions and form each into a thin patty.
3. Arrange patties in the air fryer basket. Place the air fryer basket onto the baking pan, and slide the baking pan into Rack Position 2, select Air Fry and set time to 6 minutes.
4. When sausage is cooking, prepare the egg mixture. In a large bowl, combine the eggs and milk and whisk until well blended. Keep aside.
5. When sausage has cooked completely, take patties from the air fryer basket, drain well, and crumble the meat into small pieces with a fork.
6. Double the foil cups into 10 sets. Transfer paper liners from the top muffin cups and spritz the foil cups with cooking spray.
7. Distribute crumbled sausage evenly among the 10 muffin cup sets.
8. Top each with grated cheese, divided evenly among the cups.
9. Arrange 5 cups in the baking pan.
10. Place the egg mixture into each cup, filling until each cup is at least ⅔ full.
11. Slide the baking pan into Rack Position 1, select Convection Bake and set time to 8 minutes. It's okay if a knife inserted into the center doesn't have any raw egg on it when removed.
12. Repeat the steps 8 through 11 for the remaining quiches.
13. Serve hot.

## Corn, Chorizo, and Potato Frittata

Prep time: 8 minutes | Cook time: 12 minutes |
Serves 4

2 tbsps. olive oil
4 eggs
1 large potato, boiled and
cubed
1 chorizo, sliced
½ cup corn

½ cup feta cheese,
crumbled
1 tbsp. chopped parsley
Salt and ground black
pepper, to taste

1. Preheat the air fryer oven to 330ºF (166ºC).
2. In a nonstick skillet over medium heat, heat the olive oil until shimmering.
3. Place the chorizo and cook for about 4 minutes or until golden brown.
4. In a bowl, whisk the eggs, then season with salt and ground black pepper to taste.
5. Mix the remaining ingredients in the egg mixture, then pour the chorizo and its fat into a baking pan. Pour in the egg mixture.
6. Slide the baking pan into Rack Position 1, select Convection Bake and set time to 8 minutes, until the eggs are set.
7. Serve hot.

## Feta Kale Frittata

Prep time: 5 minutes | Cook time: 11 minutes |
Serves 2

Cooking spray
1 tsp. olive oil
4 large eggs, beaten
1 cup kale, chopped

3 tbsps. crumbled feta
2 tbsps. water
Kosher salt, to taste

1. Preheat the air fryer oven to 360ºF (182ºC). Spray the air fryer basket lightly with cooking spray.
2. Place the kale to the air fryer basket and drizzle with olive oil. Then put the air fryer basket onto the baking pan, and slide the baking pan into Rack Position 2, select Convection Broil and set time to 3 minutes.
3. At the same time, combine the eggs with salt and water in a large bowl. Stir to mix well.
4. Make the frittata: When the broiling time is complete, transfer the kale from the basket to the baking pan, then pour the eggs and sprinkle with feta cheese. Lower the temperature to 300ºF (149ºC).
5. Slide the baking pan into Rack Position 1, select Convection Bake and set time to 8 minutes, until the eggs are set and the cheese melts.
6. Transfer the frittata from the air fryer oven and serve the frittata hot.

## Smoked Trout Frittata

Prep time: 8 minutes | Cook time: 17 minutes |
Serves 4

Cooking spray
2 tbsps. olive oil
1 cup diced smoked trout
1 egg, beaten
1 onion, sliced

6 tbsps. crème fraiche
2 tbsps. chopped fresh
dill
½ tbsp. horseradish
sauce

1. Preheat the air fryer oven to 350ºF (177ºC). Spray a baking pan lightly with cooking spray.
2. In a nonstick skillet over medium heat, heat the olive oil until shimmering.
3. Place the onion and sauté for about 3 minutes or until tender.
4. In a large bowl, combine the egg, horseradish sauce, and crème fraiche. Stir to mix well, then mix in the sautéed onion, smoked trout, and dill.
5. Put the mixture in the prepared baking pan, then place the pan in the preheated air fryer oven.
6. Slide the baking pan into Rack Position 1, select Convection Bake and set time to 14 minutes, until the egg is set and the edges are lightly browned.
7. Serve hot.

## Mexican Taco Beef and Chile Casserole

Prep time: 10 minutes | Cook time: 15 minutes |
Serves 4

Cooking spray
1 pound (454 g) 85%
lean ground beef
2 large eggs
1 cup shredded Mexican
cheese blend

1 (7-ounce / 198-g) can
diced mild green chiles
½ cup milk
2 tbsps. all-purpose flour
1 tbsp. taco seasoning
½ tsp. kosher salt

1. Preheat the air fryer oven to 350ºF (177ºC). Spray a baking pan lightly with cooking spray.
2. In a large bowl, toss the ground beef with taco seasoning to mix well. Place the seasoned ground beef in the prepared baking pan.
3. In a medium bowl, combing the remaining ingredients. Whisk to mix well, then pour the mixture over the ground beef.
4. Slide the baking pan into Rack Position 1, select Convection Bake and set time to 15 minutes, until a toothpick inserted in the center comes out clean.
5. Transfer the casserole from the air fryer oven and let cool for about 5 minutes, then slice to serve.

## Cheesy Prosciutto Casserole

Prep time: 5 minutes | Cook time: 10 minutes | Serves 2

Nonstick cooking spray
1 cup day-old whole grain bread, cubed
3 large eggs, beaten
1 ounce (28 g) prosciutto, roughly chopped
1 ounce (28 g) Pepper
Jack cheese, roughly chopped
2 tbsps. water
1 tbsp. chopped fresh chives
⅛ tsp. kosher salt

1. Preheat the air fryer oven to 360ºF (182ºC).
2. Spritz a baking pan lightly with nonstick cooking spray, then put the bread cubes in the pan. Take the baking pan to the air fryer oven.
3. Stir together the beaten eggs and water in a medium bowl, then stir in the kosher salt, cheese, prosciutto, and chives.
4. Pour the egg mixture over the bread cubes. Slide the baking pan into Rack Position 1, select Convection Bake and set time to 10 minutes, or until the eggs are set and the top is golden brown.
5. Serve hot.

## Broccoli, Tomato and Carrot Quiche

Prep time: 6 minutes | Cook time: 14 minutes | Serves 4

Cooking spray
4 eggs
2 cups steamed broccoli florets
2 medium tomatoes, diced
1 steamed carrot, diced
1 cup grated Cheddar
cheese
1 cup whole milk
¼ cup crumbled feta cheese
1 tsp. dried thyme
1 tsp. chopped parsley
Salt and ground black pepper, to taste

1. Preheat the air fryer oven to 350ºF (177ºC). Spray a baking pan lightly with cooking spray.
2. In a bowl, whisk together the eggs, thyme, salt, and ground black pepper and fold in the milk while mixing.
3. Arrange the carrots, broccoli, and tomatoes in the prepared baking pan, then lay the feta cheese and ½ cup Cheddar cheese. Pour the egg mixture over, then sprinkle with remaining Cheddar on top.
4. Slide the baking pan into Rack Position 1, select Convection Bake and set time to 14 minutes, until the eggs are set and the quiche is puffed.
5. Transfer the quiche from the air fryer oven and garnish with chopped parsley, then slice to serve.

## Cheesy Frittata with Parsley

Prep time: 10 minutes | Cook time: 20 minutes | Serves 4

Cooking spray
4 large eggs
½ cup shredded Cheddar cheese
½ cup half-and-half
2 tbsps. chopped fresh
parsley
2 tbsps. chopped scallion greens
½ tsp. kosher salt
½ tsp. ground black pepper

1. Preheat the air fryer oven to 300ºF (149ºC). Spray a baking pan lightly with cooking spray.
2. In a large bowl, whisk together all the ingredients, then pour the mixture into the prepared baking pan.
3. Slide the baking pan into Rack Position 1, select Convection Bake and set time to 20 minutes.
4. Serve hot.

## Tater Tot and Sausage Breakfast Casserole

Prep time: 5 minutes | Cook time: 17 to 19 minutes | Serves 4

Cooking spray
4 eggs
1 pound (454 g) frozen tater tots, thawed
12 ounces (340 g)
ground chicken sausage
1 cup milk
¾ cup grated Cheddar cheese
Salt and pepper, to taste

1. In a medium bowl, whisk together the eggs and milk. Sprinkle with salt and pepper to taste and stir until mixed well. Set it aside.
2. In a skillet over medium-high heat, spray with cooking spray. Add the ground sausage in the skillet and break it into smaller pieces by using a spatula or spoon. Cook for about 3 to 4 minutes until the sausage starts to brown, stirring occasionally. Turn off the heat and set it aside.
3. Preheat the air fryer oven to 400ºF (204ºC). Spritz a baking pan with cooking spray.
4. Place the tater tots in the baking pan. Slide the baking pan into Rack Position 1, select Convection Bake and set time to 6 minutes. Stir in the egg mixture and cooked sausage. Bake for an additional 6 minutes.
5. Sprinkle the cheese on top of the tater tots. Continue to bake for another 2 to 3 minutes until the cheese is bubbly and melted.
6. Allow the mixture to cool for 5 minutes and serve hot.

Cheddar Hash Brown Casserole, page 105

Cheesy Breakfast Sausage Quiche, page 104

Mexican Taco Beef and Chile Casserole, page 101

Smoked Trout Frittata, page 101

## Cheesy Breakfast Sausage Quiche

Prep time: 5 minutes | Cook time: 25 minutes | Serves 4

Cooking spray
12 large eggs
12 ounces (340 g) sugar-free breakfast sausage
2 cups shredded

Cheddar cheese
1 cup heavy cream
Salt and black pepper, to taste

1. Preheat the air fryer oven to 375ºF (191ºC). Spray a casserole dish lightly with cooking spray.
2. In a large bowl, beat together the eggs, heavy cream, salt and pepper until creamy. Stir in the breakfast sausage and Cheddar cheese.
3. Place the sausage mixture into the prepared casserole dish. Slide the casserole dish into Rack Position 1, select Convection Bake and set time to 25 minutes, until the top of the quiche is golden brown and the eggs are set.
4. Transfer the quiche the air fryer oven and let rest for 5 to 10 minutes before serving.

## Ricotta Pork Gratin

Prep time: 15 minutes | Cook time: 21 minutes | Serves 4

Cooking spray
2 tbsps. olive oil
2 pounds (907 g) pork tenderloin, cut into serving-size pieces
1 cup Ricotta cheese
1½ cups chicken broth

1 tbsp. mustard
1 tsp. dried marjoram
¼ tsp. chili powder
1 tsp. coarse sea salt
½ tsp. freshly ground black pepper

1. Preheat the air fryer oven to 350ºF (177ºC). Spray a baking pan lightly with cooking spray.
2. In a nonstick skillet over medium-high heat, heat the olive oil until shimmering.
3. Place the pork and sauté for about 6 minutes or until lightly browned.
4. Take the pork to the prepared baking pan and season with marjoram, chili powder, salt, and ground black pepper.
5. In a large bowl, combine the remaining ingredients. Stir to mix well. Pour the mixture over the pork in the pan.
6. Slide the baking pan into Rack Position 1, select Convection Bake and set time to 15 minutes, until frothy and the cheese melts. Stir the mixture halfway through.
7. Serve hot.

## Classic Mediterranean Quiche

Prep time: 10 minutes | Cook time: 30 minutes | Serves 4

Cooking spray
4 eggs
1 cup crumbled feta cheese
½ cup chopped tomatoes
½ cup milk
¼ cup chopped Kalamata

olives
¼ cup chopped onion
½ tbsp. chopped oregano
½ tbsp. chopped basil
Salt and ground black pepper, to taste

1. Preheat air fryer oven to 340ºF (171ºC). Spray a baking pan lightly with cooking spray.
2. In a large bowl, whisk the eggs with remaining ingredients. Stir to mix well.
3. Place the mixture into the prepared baking pan.
4. Slide the baking pan into Rack Position 1, select Convection Bake and set time to 30 minutes, until the eggs are set and a toothpick inserted in the center comes out clean. Check the doneness of the quiche during the last 10 minutes of baking.
5. Serve hot.

## Crustless Broccoli and Pepper Fontina Quiche

Prep time: 5 minutes | Cook time: 10 minutes | Serves 4

Cooking spray
6 eggs
1 cup broccoli florets
1¼ cups grated Fontina cheese
¾ cup chopped roasted

red peppers
¾ cup heavy cream
½ tsp. salt
Freshly ground black pepper, to taste

1. Preheat the air fryer oven to 325ºF (163ºC). Spray a baking pan lightly with cooking spray
2. Place the broccoli florets and roasted red peppers to the pan and sprinkle the grated Fontina cheese on top.
3. Beat together the eggs and heavy cream in a bowl. Season with salt and pepper. Add the egg mixture over the top of the cheese. Wrap the pan in foil.
4. Slide the baking pan into Rack Position 1, select Convection Bake and set time to 8 minutes. Remove the foil and continue to cook for an additional 2 minutes until the quiche is golden brown.
5. Let rest for 5 minutes before cutting into wedges and serve right away.

## Shrimp and Spinach Frittata

Prep time: 6 minutes | Cook time: 14 minutes | Serves 4

| | |
|---|---|
| Cooking spray | ½ cup Monterey Jack |
| 4 whole eggs | cheese, grated |
| ½ cup shrimp, cooked | ½ cup rice, cooked |
| and chopped | 1 tsp. dried basil |
| ½ cup baby spinach | Salt, to taste |

1. Preheat the air fryer oven to 360ºF (182ºC). Spray a baking pan lightly with cooking spray.
2. In a large bowl, whisk the eggs with basil and salt until bubbly, then mix in the shrimp, spinach, rice, and cheese.
3. Pour the mixture into the baking pan. Slide the baking pan into Rack Position 1, select Convection Bake and set time to 14 minutes, until the eggs are set and the frittata is golden brown.
4. Slice to serve.

## Crusted Cheese Quiche

Prep time: 20 minutes | Cook time: 1 hour | Serves 8

| | |
|---|---|
| **Crust:** | cheese |
| 1¼ cups blanched | 1 cup shredded Swiss |
| almond flour | cheese |
| 1¼ cups grated | ½ cup chicken broth |
| Parmesan cheese | ⅓ cup minced leeks |
| 1 large egg, beaten | 1 tbsp. unsalted butter, |
| ¼ tsp. fine sea salt | melted |
| **Filling:** | Chopped green onions, |
| Cooking spray | for garnish |
| 4 large eggs, beaten | ¾ tsp. fine sea salt |
| 4 ounces (113 g) cream | ⅛ tsp. cayenne pepper |

1. Preheat the air fryer oven to 325ºF (163ºC). Spray a pie pan lightly with cooking spray.
2. In a large bowl, combine the flour, egg, Parmesan, and salt. Stir to mix until a satiny and firm dough forms.
3. Place the dough between two grease parchment papers, then roll the dough into a ¹⁄₁₆-inch thick circle.
4. Make the crust: Take the dough into the prepared pie pan and press to coat the bottom well.
5. Slide the pie pan into Rack Position 1, select Convection Bake and set time to 12 minutes, until the edges of the crust are lightly browned.
6. At the same time, in a large bowl, combine the ingredient for the filling, except for the green onions.
7. Add the filling over the cooked crust and cover the edges of the crust with aluminum foil. Bake for another 15 minutes, then lower the heat to 300ºF (149ºC) and bake for an additional 30 minutes or until a toothpick inserted in the center comes out clean.
8. Transfer the pie pan from the air fryer oven and let cool for 10 minutes before serving.

## Simple Mac and Cheese

Prep time: 10 minutes | Cook time: 10 minutes | Serves 2

| | |
|---|---|
| 1 cup grated Cheddar | 1 tbsp. grated Parmesan |
| cheese | cheese |
| 1 cup cooked macaroni | Salt and ground black |
| ½ cup warm milk | pepper, to taste |

1. Preheat the air fryer oven to 350ºF (177ºC).
2. Mix all the ingredients, except for Parmesan in a baking pan.
3. Slide the baking pan into Rack Position 1, select Convection Bake and set time to 10 minutes.
4. Put the Parmesan cheese on top and serve hot.

## Cheddar Hash Brown Casserole

Prep time: 15 minutes | Cook time: 30 minutes | Serves 4

| | |
|---|---|
| Cooking spray | ½ cup sour cream |
| 1 (10.5-ounce / 298-g) | ½ cup shredded sharp |
| can cream of chicken | Cheddar cheese |
| soup | 3 tbsps. butter, melted |
| 3½ cups frozen hash | 1 tsp. salt |
| browns, thawed | 1 tsp. freshly ground |
| 1 cup minced onion | black pepper |

1. Place the hash browns in a large bowl and sprinkle with salt and black pepper. Put the melted butter, cream of chicken soup, and sour cream and stir until incorporated well. Combine in the minced onion and cheese and stir well.
2. Preheat the air fryer oven to 325ºF (163ºC). Spray a baking pan lightly with cooking spray.
3. Arrange the hash brown mixture evenly into the baking pan.
4. Slide the baking pan into Rack Position 1, select Convection Bake and set time to 30 minutes, until browned.
5. Allow to cool for 5 minutes before serving.

# Greek Vegetables Frittata

Prep time: 7 minutes | Cook time: 8 minutes | Serves 2

Cooking spray
4 eggs, lightly beaten
2 cups spinach, chopped
1 cup chopped mushrooms

3 ounces (85 g) feta cheese, crumbled
2 tbsps. heavy cream
A handful of fresh parsley, chopped
Salt and ground black pepper, to taste

1. Preheat the air fryer oven to 350ºF (177ºC). Spray a baking pan lightly with cooking spray.
2. In a large bowl, whisk together all the ingredients. Stir to mix well.
3. Place the mixture in the prepared baking pan.
4. Slide the baking pan into Rack Position 1, select Convection Bake and set time to 8 minutes, until the eggs are set.
5. Serve hot.

# Shrimp and Cauliflower Casserole

Prep time: 15 minutes | Cook time: 22 minutes | Serves 4

Cooking spray
2 tbsps. sesame oil
1 pound (454 g) shrimp, cleaned and deveined
2 cups cauliflower, cut into florets

1 cup tomato paste
2 green bell pepper, sliced
1 shallot, sliced

1. Preheat the air fryer oven to 360ºF (182ºC). Spray a baking pan lightly with cooking spray.
2. Place the shrimp and vegetables in the baking pan. Then pour the sesame oil over the vegetables. Put the tomato paste over the vegetables.
3. Slide the baking pan into Rack Position 1, select Convection Bake and set time to 10 minutes. Stir with a large spoon and bake for another 12 minutes.
4. Serve hot.

# Chapter 8 Wraps and Sandwiches

## Simple Pork and Carrot Momos

Prep time: 20 minutes | Cook time: 10 minutes per batch | Serves 4

2 tbsps. olive oil
1 pound (454 g) ground pork
16 wonton wrappers
1 shredded carrot

1 onion, chopped
1 tsp. soy sauce
Salt and ground black pepper, to taste

1. Preheat the air fryer oven to 320ºF (160ºC).
2. In a nonstick skillet over medium heat, heat the olive oil until shimmering.
3. Place the ground pork, carrot, onion, soy sauce, salt, and ground black pepper and sauté for about 10 minutes or until the pork is well browned and carrots are soft.
4. Unfold the wrappers on a clean work surface, then distribute the cooked pork and vegetables on the wrappers. Fold the edges around the filling to form momos. Nip the top to seal the momos.
5. Put the momos in the air fryer basket and spray lightly with cooking spray. Then place the air fryer basket onto the baking pan, and slide the baking pan into Rack Position 2, select Air Fry and set time to 10 minutes. Work in batches to avoid overcrowding.
6. Serve hot.

## Quick Turkey Sliders with Chive Mayo

Prep time: 10 minutes | Cook time: 15 minutes | Serves 6

Cooking spray
12 burger buns
**For the Turkey Sliders:**
¾ pound (340 g) turkey, minced
¼ cup pickled jalapeno, chopped
1 to 2 cloves garlic, minced
2 tbsps. chopped scallions

1 tbsp. oyster sauce
1 tbsp. chopped fresh cilantro
Sea salt and ground black pepper, to taste
**For the Chive Mayo:**
1 cup mayonnaise
Zest of 1 lime
1 tbsp. chives
1 tsp. salt

1. Preheat the air fryer oven to 365ºF (185ºC) and spray the air fryer basket lightly with cooking spray.

2. In a large bowl, combine the ingredients for the turkey sliders. Stir to mix well. Form the mixture into 6 balls, then bash the balls into patties.
3. Place the patties in the air fryer basket and spray lightly with cooking spray. Put the air fryer basket onto the baking pan, and slide the baking pan into Rack Position 2, select Air Fry and set time to 15 minutes. Flip the patties halfway through.
4. At the same time, combine all the ingredients for the chive mayo in a small bowl. Stir to mix well.
5. Brush the patties with chive mayo, then assemble the patties between two buns to make the sliders. Serve hot.

## Juicy Korean Bulgogi Burgers

Prep time: 15 minutes | Cook time: 10 minutes | Serves 4

**For the Burgers:**
Cooking spray
1 tbsp. toasted sesame oil
1 pound (454 g) 85% lean ground beef
4 hamburger buns
¼ cup chopped scallions
2 tbsps. gochujang
1 tbsp. soy sauce
2 tsps. minced garlic

2 tsps. minced fresh ginger
2 tsps. sugar
½ tsp. kosher salt
**For the Korean Mayo:**
1 tbsp. toasted sesame oil
¼ cup mayonnaise
¼ cup chopped scallions
2 tsps. sesame seeds
1 tbsp. gochujang

1. In a large bowl, combine the ingredients for the burgers, except for the buns. Stir to mix well, then wrap the bowl in plastic and refrigerate to marinate for at least an hour.
2. Preheat the air fryer oven to 350ºF (177ºC) and spray the air fryer basket lightly with cooking spray.
3. Distribute the meat mixture into four portions and shape into four balls. Bash the balls into patties.
4. Place the patties in the air fryer basket and spray lightly with cooking spray. Put the air fryer basket onto the baking pan, and slide the baking pan into Rack Position 2, select Air Fry and set time to 10 minutes. Flip the patties halfway through.
5. At the same time, combine all the ingredients for the Korean mayo in a small bowl. Stir to mix well.
6. Transfer the patties from the air fryer oven and assemble with the buns, then brush the Korean mayo over the patties to make the burgers. Serve hot.

## Simple Crab Wontons

Prep time: 10 minutes | Cook time: 10 minutes per batch | Serves 6 to 8

Cooking spray
24 wonton wrappers, thawed if frozen
**For the Filling:**
1½ tsps. toasted sesame oil
5 ounces (142 g) lump crab meat, drained and patted dry

4 ounces (113 g) cream cheese, at room temperature
2 scallions, sliced
1 tsp. Worcestershire sauce
Kosher salt and ground black pepper, to taste

1. Preheat the air fryer oven to 350ºF (177ºC). Spray the air fryer basket lightly with cooking spray.
2. Place all the ingredients for the filling in a medium-size bowl, and stir until well mixed. Prepare a small bowl of water alongside.
3. Lay the wonton wrappers on a clean work surface. Scoop 1 tsp. of the filling in the center of each wrapper. Wet the edges with a touch of water. Fold each wonton wrapper diagonally in half over the filling to form a triangle.
4. Place the wontons in the air fryer basket. Spray the wontons lightly with cooking spray. Work in batches, 6 to 8 at a time. Put the air fryer basket onto the baking pan, and slide the baking pan into Rack Position 2, select Air Fry and set time to 10 minutes, until crispy and golden brown. Flip once halfway through.
5. Serve hot.

## Ketchup Sloppy Joes

Prep time: 10 minutes | Cook time: 17 to 19 minutes | Makes 4 large sandwiches or 8 sliders

Cooking spray
1 pound (454 g) very lean ground beef
⅓ cup ketchup
¼ cup water
1 tbsp. lemon juice
1½ tsps. brown sugar
1¼ tsps. low-sodium

Worcestershire sauce
1 tsp. onion powder
½ tsp. vinegar
⅛ tsp. dry mustard
½ tsp. celery seed
½ tsp. salt (optional)
Hamburger or slider buns, for serving

1. Preheat the air fryer oven to 390ºF (199ºC). Spritz the baking pan lightly with cooking spray.
2. Break raw ground beef into small chunks and pile into the baking pan. Slide the baking pan into Rack Position 2, select Roast and set time to 5 minutes. Stir to break apart and roast for another 3 minutes.

Stir and roast for 2 to 4 minutes longer, or until meat is well done.
3. Transfer the meat from the air fryer oven, drain, and fork to crumble into small pieces with a knife.
4. Give the baking pan a quick rinse to remove any bits of meat.
5. Put all the remaining ingredients, except for the buns, in the baking pan and mix together. Place the meat and stir well.
6. Adjust the temperature to 330ºF (166ºC). Slide the baking pan into Rack Position 1, select Convection Bake and set time to 5 minutes. Stir and bake for another 2 minutes.
7. Scoop onto buns. Serve warm.

## Golden Chicken Empanadas

Prep time: 25 minutes | Cook time: 24 minutes | Makes 12 empanadas

Cooking spray
2 purchased refrigerated pie crusts, from a minimum 14.1-ounce box
1 cup boneless, skinless rotisserie chicken breast meat, chopped finely
⅔ cup shredded Cheddar

cheese
1 large egg
¼ cup salsa verde
2 tbsps. water
1 tsp. ground cumin
1 tsp. ground black pepper

1. Preheat the air fryer oven to 350ºF (177ºC) and spray the baking pan lightly with cooking spray.
2. In a large bowl, combine the chicken meat, salsa verde, Cheddar, cumin, and black pepper. Stir to mix well. Keep aside.
3. Unfold the pie crusts on a clean work surface, then with a large cookie cutter, cut out 3½-inch circles as much as possible.
4. Roll the remaining crusts to a ball and flatten into a circle which has the same thickness of the original crust. Cut out more 3½-inch circles until you have 12 circles in total.
5. Make the empanadas: Distribute the chicken mixture in the middle of each circle, about 1½ tbsps. each. Dab the edges of the circle with water. Fold the circle in half over the filling to shape like a half-moon and press to seal, or you can press with a fork.
6. In a small bowl, whisk the egg with water.
7. Place six of the empanadas in the baking pan and spray with with cooking spray. Brush with whisked egg. Slide the baking pan into Rack Position 2, select Roast and set time to 12 minutes. Turn the empanadas halfway through.
8. Serve hot.

# Herbed Beef Burgers

Prep time: 15 minutes | Cook time: 10 minutes | Serves 4

| | |
|---|---|
| Cooking spray | 1 tsp. dried red pepper |
| 1 pound (454 g) 85% | flakes |
| lean ground beef | 1 tsp. kosher salt |
| 4 hamburger buns | 2 tsps. ground black |
| 1 tsp. coriander seeds | pepper |
| 1 tsp. cumin seeds | 2 tbsps. Worcestershire |
| 1 tsp. mustard seeds | sauce |
| 1 tsp. dried minced garlic | Mayonnaise, for serving |

1. Preheat the air fryer oven to 350ºF (177ºC) and spray the baking pan lightly with cooking spray.
2. In a food processor, place the seeds, garlic, red pepper flakes, salt, and ground black pepper. Pulse to coarsely ground the mixture.
3. Add the ground beef in a large bowl. Pour in the seed mixture and drizzle with Worcestershire sauce. Stir to combine well.
4. Distribute the mixture into four parts and form each part into a ball, then bash each ball into a patty.
5. Place the patties in the baking pan. Slide the baking pan into Rack Position 1, select Convection Bake and set time to 10 minutes. Turn the patties with tongs halfway through.
6. Assemble the buns with the patties, then coat the mayo over the patties to make the burgers. Serve warm.

# Pork and Cabbage Gyoza

Prep time: 10 minutes | Cook time: 10 minutes per batch | Makes 48 gyozas

| | |
|---|---|
| Cooking spray | ½ cup minced scallions |
| 1 pound (454 g) ground | 1 tbsp. minced garlic |
| pork | 1 tsp. minced fresh |
| 48 to 50 wonton or | chives |
| dumpling wrappers | 1 tsp. soy sauce |
| 1 small head Napa | 1 tsp. minced fresh |
| cabbage (about 1 pound | ginger |
| / 454 g), sliced thinly and | 1 tsp. granulated sugar |
| minced | 2 tsps. kosher salt |

1. Make the filling: In a large bowl, combine all the ingredients, except for the wrappers. Stir to mix well.
2. On a clean work surface, unfold a wrapper, then dab the edges with a little water. Spoon up 2 tsps. of the filling mixture in the center.
3. Make the gyoza: Fold the wrapper over to filling and press the edges to seal. Pleat the edges if desired.

Repeat this with remaining wrappers and fillings.
4. Preheat the air fryer oven to 360ºF (182ºC) and spray the air fryer basket lightly with cooking spray.
5. Place the gyozas in the air fryer basket and spray lightly with cooking spray. Put the air fryer basket onto the baking pan, and slide the baking pan into Rack Position 2, select Air Fry and set time to 6 minutes. Turn the gyozas halfway through. Work in batches to avoid overcrowding.
6. Serve hot.

# Black Bean, Sweet Potato and Spinach Burritos

Prep time: 15 minutes | Cook time: 1 hour | Makes 6 burritos

| | |
|---|---|
| Cooking spray | 1½ cups baby spinach, |
| 1 tbsp. vegetable oil | divided |
| 6 large flour tortillas | ¾ cup grated Cheddar |
| 6 eggs, scrambled | cheese, divided |
| 2 sweet potatoes, peeled | ¼ cup salsa |
| and cut into a small dice | ¼ cup sour cream |
| 1 (16-ounce / 454-g) | Kosher salt and ground |
| can refried black beans, | black pepper, to taste |
| divided | |

1. Preheat the air fryer oven to 400ºF (204ºC).
2. In a large bowl, add the sweet potatoes, then drizzle with vegetable oil and season with salt and black pepper to taste. Toss to coat well.
3. Put the potatoes in the air fryer basket. Then place the air fryer basket onto the baking pan, and slide the baking pan into Rack Position 2, select Air Fry and set time to 10 minutes, flipping halfway through.
4. Unfold the tortillas on a clean work surface. Distribute the black beans, spinach, air fried sweet potatoes, scrambled eggs, and cheese evenly on top of the tortillas.
5. Fold the long side of the tortillas over the filling, then fold in the shorter side to wrap the filling to make the burritos.
6. Work in batches, wrap the burritos in the aluminum foil and place in the air fryer oven to air fry at 350ºF (177ºC) for about 20 minutes. Turn the burritos halfway through.
7. Remove the burritos from the air fryer oven and return to the air fryer oven. Spray lightly with cooking spray and air fry for another 5 minutes or until lightly browned. Repeat with remaining burritos.
8. Transfer the burritos from the air fryer oven and coat with sour cream and salsa. Serve hot.

## Baked Cheese and Hot Capicola Sandwich

Prep time: 5 minutes | Cook time: 8 minutes | Serves 2

4 thick slices sourdough bread
4 thick slices Brie cheese
8 slices hot capicola
2 tbsps. mayonnaise

1. Preheat the air fryer oven to 350ºF (177ºC).
2. Coat the mayonnaise on one side of each slice of bread. Put 2 slices of bread in the baking pan, mayonnaise-side down.
3. Arrange the slices of Brie and capicola on the bread and cover with the remaining two slices of bread, mayonnaise-side up.
4. Slide the baking pan into Rack Position 1, select Convection Bake and set time to 8 minutes, until the cheese has melted.
5. Serve hot.

## Crab Cake Sandwich with Cajun Mayo

Prep time: 15 minutes | Cook time: 10 minutes | Serves 4

**Crab Cakes:**
Cooking spray
10 ounces (283 g) lump crab meat
½ cup panko bread crumbs
¼ cup minced fresh parsley
1 large egg, beaten
1 large egg white
1 tbsp. mayonnaise
1 tbsp. fresh lemon juice
1 tsp. Dijon mustard
½ tsp. Old Bay seasoning
⅛ tsp. sweet paprika
⅛ tsp. kosher salt
Freshly ground black pepper, to taste
**Cajun Mayo:**
¼ cup mayonnaise
1 tbsp. minced dill pickle
1 tsp. fresh lemon juice
¾ tsp. Cajun seasoning
**For Serving:**
4 whole wheat potato buns or gluten-free buns
4 Boston lettuce leaves

1. For the crab cakes: Combine the panko, whole egg, egg white, mayonnaise, mustard, parsley, lemon juice, Old Bay, paprika, salt, and pepper to taste in a large bowl and mix well. Fold in the crab meat, being careful not to over mix. Carefully shape into 4 round patties, about ½ cup each, ¾ inch thick. Spritz both sides lightly with oil.
2. Preheat the air fryer oven to 370ºF (188ºC).
3. Working in batches, arrange the crab cakes in the baking pan. Slide the baking pan into Rack Position 1, select Convection Bake and set time to 10 minutes, flipping halfway, until the edges are golden.
4. At the same time, for the Cajun mayo: Combine the mayonnaise, pickle, lemon juice, and Cajun seasoning in a small bowl.
5. To serve: Put a lettuce leaf on each bun bottom and top with a crab cake and a generous tbsp. of Cajun mayonnaise. Place the bun top and serve hot.

## Mexican-Style Chicken and Cauliflower Burgers

Prep time: 15 minutes | Cook time: 20 minutes | Serves 6 to 8

Cooking spray
4 skinless and boneless chicken breasts
1 small head of cauliflower, sliced into florets
6 to 8 brioche buns, sliced lengthwise
1 egg
2 tomatoes, sliced
1 jalapeño pepper
2 lettuce leaves, chopped
¾ cup taco sauce
3 tbsps. smoked paprika
1 tbsp. thyme
1 tbsp. oregano
1 tbsp. mustard powder
1 tsp. cayenne pepper
Salt and ground black pepper, to taste

1. Preheat the air fryer oven to 350ºF (177ºC) and spray the air fryer basket lightly with cooking spray.
2. Add the cauliflower florets, jalapeño pepper, paprika, thyme, oregano, mustard powder and cayenne pepper in a blender, and blend until the mixture has a texture similar to breadcrumbs.
3. Take ¾ of the cauliflower mixture to a medium bowl and keep aside. Beat the egg in a different bowl and set aside.
4. Place the chicken breasts to the blender with remaining cauliflower mixture. Season with salt and pepper to taste. Blend until finely chopped and well mixed.
5. Transfer the mixture from the blender and shape into 6 to 8 patties. One by one, dredge each patty in the reserved cauliflower mixture, then into the egg. Dunk them in the cauliflower mixture again for additional coating.
6. Arrange the coated patties in the air fryer basket and spray lightly with cooking spray. Place the air fryer basket onto the baking pan, and slide the baking pan into Rack Position 2, select Air Fry and set time to 20 minutes. Flip halfway through to ensure even cooking.
7. Take the patties to a clean work surface and assemble with the buns, tomato slices, chopped lettuce leaves and taco sauce to make burgers. Serve hot and enjoy.

## Potato Samosas with Chutney

Prep time: 30 minutes | Cook time: 1 hour 10 minutes | Makes 16 samosas

**Dough:**
4 cups all-purpose flour, plus more for flouring the work surface
½ cup cold unsalted butter, cut into cubes
¼ cup plain yogurt
1 cup ice water
2 tsps. kosher salt
**Filling:**
Cooking spray
2 tbsps. vegetable oil
2 cups mashed potatoes
½ cup peas, thawed if frozen
1 onion, diced
1 clove garlic, minced

2 tbsps. yogurt
1½ tsps. coriander
1½ tsps. cumin
1 tsp. turmeric
1 tsp. kosher salt
**Chutney:**
2 tbsps. vegetable oil
1 cup mint leaves, lightly packed
2 cups cilantro leaves, lightly packed
1 green chile pepper, deseeded and minced
½ cup minced onion
Juice of 1 lime
1 tsp. granulated sugar
1 tsp. kosher salt

1. In a food processor, put the flour, yogurt, butter, and salt. Pulse to combine until grainy. Add the water and pulse until a smooth and firm dough forms.
2. Take the dough on a clean and lightly floured working surface. Knead the dough and form it into a ball. Cut in half and flatten the halves into 2 discs. Wrap them in plastic and let sit in refrigerator until ready to use.
3. At the same time, make the filling: In a saucepan over medium heat, heat the vegetable oil.
4. Add the onion and sauté for about 5 minutes or until lightly browned.
5. Place the coriander, cumin, turmeric, garlic, and salt and sauté for 2 minutes or until fragrant.
6. Add the peas, potatoes, and yogurt and stir to combine well. Remove from the heat and let cool.
7. At the same time, combine the ingredients for the chutney in a food processor. Pulse to mix well until glossy. Place the chutney in a bowl and refrigerate until ready to use.
8. Make the samosas: Remove the dough discs from the refrigerator and cut each disc into 8 parts. Form each part into a ball, then roll the ball into a 6-inch circle. Slice the circle in half and roll each half into a cone.
9. Spoon up 2 tbsps. of the filling into the cone, press the edges of the cone to seal and form into a triangle. Repeat with remaining dough and filling.
10. Preheat the air fryer oven to 360ºF (182ºC) and spray the air fryer basket lightly with cooking spray.
11. Put four samosas each batch in the air fryer basket and spray with cooking spray. Place the air fryer basket onto the baking pan, and slide the baking pan into Rack Position 2, select Air Fry and set time to

15 minutes, until golden brown and crispy. Flip the samosas halfway through.
12. Serve the samosas with the chutney.

## Italian Lettuce Chicken Sandwiches

Prep time: 10 minutes | Cook time: 10 minutes | Serves 4

2 boneless, skinless chicken breasts, cut into 1-inch cubes
4 pita pockets, split
2 cups torn butter lettuce
1 cup chopped cherry

tomatoes
1 small red onion, sliced
1 red bell pepper, sliced
⅓ cup Italian salad dressing, divided
½ tsp. dried thyme

1. Preheat the air fryer oven to 380ºF (193ºC).
2. Put the chicken, onion, and bell pepper in the baking pan. Drizzle with 1 tbsp. of the Italian salad dressing, add the thyme, and toss well.
3. Slide the baking pan into Rack Position 1, select Convection Bake and set time to 10 minutes, until the chicken is 165ºF (74ºC) on a food thermometer, stirring once during the cooking time.
4. Take the chicken and vegetables to a bowl and toss with the remaining salad dressing.
5. Assemble sandwiches with the pita pockets, butter lettuce, and cherry tomatoes. Serve hot.

## Easy Pork and Turkey Sandwiches

Prep time: 20 minutes | Cook time: 8 minutes | Makes 4 sandwiches

Cooking spray
8 slices ciabatta bread, about ¼-inch thick
1 tbsp. brown mustard
**Toppings:**
6 to 8 ounces (170 to 227 g) thinly sliced leftover roast pork

4 ounces (113 g) thinly sliced deli turkey
⅓ cup bread and butter pickle slices
2 to 3 ounces (57 to 85 g) Pepper Jack cheese slices

1. Preheat the air fryer oven to 390ºF (199ºC).
2. Spray one side of each slice of bread with cooking spray on a clean work surface. Spread the other side of each slice of bread evenly with brown mustard.
3. Top each bread slice with the roast pork, turkey, pickle slices, cheese, finished with remaining bread slices. Arrange in the baking pan.
4. Slide the baking pan into Rack Position 2, select Toast and set time to 8 minutes.
5. Let rest for 5 minutes and serve warm.

Simple Pork and Carrot Momos, page 108

Cheesy Chicken Taquitos, page 115

Ketchup Sloppy Joes, page 109

Simple Crab Wontons, page 109

## Easy Parmesan Eggplant Hoagies

Prep time: 15 minutes | Cook time: 12 minutes | Makes 3 hoagies

| | |
|---|---|
| Cooking spray | open lengthwise, warmed |
| 6 peeled eggplant slices | ¼ cup jarred pizza sauce |
| (about ½ inch thick and 3 | 6 tbsps. grated Parmesan |
| inches in diameter) | cheese |
| 3 Italian sub rolls, split | |

1. Preheat the air fryer oven to 350ºF (177ºC) and spray the air fryer basket lightly with cooking spray.
2. Place the eggplant slices in the air fryer basket and spray with cooking spray.
3. Put the air fryer basket onto the baking pan, and slide the baking pan into Rack Position 2, select Air Fry and set time to 10 minutes, until lightly wilted and tender. Turn the slices halfway through.
4. Distribute and spread the pizza sauce and cheese on top of the eggplant slice and air fry over 375ºF (191ºC) for another 2 minutes or until the cheese melts.
5. Assemble each sub roll with two slices of eggplant and serve hot.

## Cheesy Muffin Tuna Sandwiches

Prep time: 8 minutes | Cook time: 6 minutes | Serves 4

| | |
|---|---|
| 1 (6-ounce / 170-g) can | ¼ cup mayonnaise |
| chunk light tuna, drained | 2 green onions, minced |
| 6 thin slices Provolone or | 3 tbsps. softened butter |
| Muenster cheese | 2 tbsps. mustard |
| 3 English muffins, split | 1 tbsp. lemon juice |
| with a fork | |

1. Preheat the air fryer oven to 390ºF (199ºC).
2. Combine the tuna, mayonnaise, mustard, lemon juice, and green onions in a small bowl. Set it aside.
3. Butter the cut side of the English muffins. Put in the baking pan, butter-side up. Slide the baking pan into Rack Position 1, select Convection Bake and set time to 3 minutes, until light golden brown. Transfer the muffins from the air fryer oven.
4. Top each muffin with one slice of cheese and take back to the air fryer oven. Bake for 3 minutes or until the cheese melts and starts to brown.
5. Transfer the muffins from the air fryer oven and place the tuna mixture on top. Serve warm.

## Veggies Pita Sandwiches

Prep time: 10 minutes | Cook time: 10 minutes | Serves 4

| | |
|---|---|
| 1 tsp. olive oil | crosswise |
| 1 baby eggplant, peeled | ½ cup shredded carrot |
| and chopped | ½ cup diced red onion |
| 1 red bell pepper, sliced | ⅓ cup low-fat Greek |
| 2 low-sodium whole- | yogurt |
| wheat pita breads, halved | ½ tsp. dried tarragon |

1. Preheat the air fryer oven to 390ºF (199ºC).
2. Stir together the eggplant, red bell pepper, red onion, carrot, and olive oil in the air fryer basket. Then place the air fryer basket onto the baking pan, and slide the baking pan into Rack Position 2, select Convection Broil and set time to 8 minutes, stirring once, until the vegetables are tender. Drain if necessary.
3. Thoroughly mix the yogurt and tarragon in a small bowl until well combined.
4. Stir the yogurt mixture into the vegetables. Stuff one-fourth of this mixture into each pita pocket.
5. Arrange the sandwiches in the baking pan. Slide the baking pan into Rack Position 1, select Convection Bake and set time to 2 minutes, until the bread is toasted.
6. Serve hot.

## Pork Sliders with Scallion

Prep time: 10 minutes | Cook time: 14 minutes | Makes 6 sliders

| | |
|---|---|
| Cooking spray | 2 tbsps. minced peeled |
| 1 pound (454 g) ground | fresh ginger |
| pork | 1½ tbsps. fish sauce |
| 6 slider buns, split open | 1 tbsp. Thai curry paste |
| lengthwise, warmed | 1 tbsp. light brown sugar |
| ¼ cup thinly sliced | 1 tsp. ground black |
| scallions, white and | pepper |
| green parts | |

1. Preheat the air fryer oven to 375ºF (191ºC) and spray the air fryer basket lightly with cooking spray.
2. In a large bowl, combine all the ingredients, except for the buns. Stir to mix well.
3. Distribute and form the mixture into six balls, then bash the balls into six 3-inch-diameter patties.
4. Place the patties in the air fryer basket and spray lightly with cooking spray. Put the air fryer basket onto the baking pan, and slide the baking pan into Rack Position 2, select Air Fry and set time to 14 minutes, until well browned. Flip the patties halfway through.
5. Assemble the buns with patties to make the sliders and serve hot.

## Cheesy Chicken Taquitos

Prep time: 15 minutes | Cook time: 12 minutes | Serves 4

Cooking spray
4 flour tortillas
1 cup cooked chicken, shredded
1 cup shredded

Mozzarella cheese
¼ cup Greek yogurt
¼ cup salsa
Salt and ground black pepper, to taste

1. Preheat the air fryer oven to 380ºF (193ºC) and spray the air fryer basket lightly with cooking spray.
2. In a large bowl, combine all the ingredients, except for the tortillas. Stir to mix well.
3. Make the taquitos: Unfold the tortillas on a clean work surface, then spoon up 2 tbsps. of the chicken mixture in the middle of each tortilla. Roll the tortillas up to wrap the filling.
4. Place the taquitos in the air fryer basket and spray lightly with cooking spray.
5. Put the air fryer basket onto the baking pan, and slide the baking pan into Rack Position 2, select Air Fry and set time to 12 minutes, until golden brown and the cheese melts. Turn the taquitos halfway through.
6. Serve hot.

## Fast Cream Cheese Wontons

Prep time: 5 minutes | Cook time: 6 minutes | Serves 4

Cooking spray
2 ounces (57 g) cream cheese, softened

16 square wonton wrappers
1 tbsp. sugar

1. Preheat the air fryer oven to 350ºF (177ºC). Spray the air fryer basket lightly with cooking spray.
2. Stir together the cream cheese and sugar in a mixing bowl until well mixed. Prepare a small bowl of water alongside.
3. Lay the wonton wrappers on a clean work surface. Spoon ¼ tsp. of cream cheese in the center of each wonton wrapper. Dab the water over the wrapper edges. Fold each wonton wrapper diagonally in half over the filling to form a triangle.
4. Place the wontons in the air fryer basket. Spray the wontons lightly with cooking spray. Put the air fryer basket onto the baking pan, and slide the baking pan into Rack Position 2, select Air Fry and set time to 6 minutes. Flip once halfway through to ensure even cooking.
5. Distribute the wontons among four plates. Allow to cool for 5 minutes before serving.

## Cheesy Shrimp Sandwiches

Prep time: 10 minutes | Cook time: 6 minutes | Serves 4

4 slices whole grain or whole-wheat bread
1 (6-ounce / 170-g) can tiny shrimp, drained
1¼ cups shredded Colby, Cheddar, or Havarti

cheese
3 tbsps. mayonnaise
2 tbsps. softened butter
2 tbsps. minced green onion

1. Preheat the air fryer oven to 400ºF (204ºC).
2. Combine the cheese, shrimp, mayonnaise, and green onion in a medium bowl, and mix well.
3. Lay this mixture on two of the slices of bread. Top with the other slices of bread to make two sandwiches. Coat the sandwiches lightly with butter.
4. Put the bread in the baking pan. Slide the baking pan into Rack Position 2, select Toast and set time to 6 minutes, until the bread is browned and crisp and the cheese is melted.
5. Cut in half and serve hot.

## Mixed Greens and Cheese Sandwiches

Prep time: 15 minutes | Cook time: 10 to 13 minutes | Serves 4

Cooking spray
2 tsps. olive oil
1½ cups chopped mixed greens
4 slices low-sodium

whole-wheat bread
2 slices low-sodium low-fat Swiss cheese
2 garlic cloves, thinly sliced

1. Preheat the air fryer oven to 400ºF (204ºC).
2. Mix the greens, garlic, and olive oil in the air fryer basket. Then place the air fryer basket onto the baking pan, and slide the baking pan into Rack Position 2, select Air Fry and set time to 5 minutes, stirring once, until the vegetables are soft. Drain, if necessary.
3. Make 2 sandwiches, dividing half of the greens and 1 slice of Swiss cheese between 2 slices of bread. Spritz the outsides of the sandwiches lightly with cooking spray.
4. Put the sandwiches in the baking pan. Slide the baking pan into Rack Position 1, select Convection Bake and set time to 6 minutes, turning with tongs halfway through, until the bread is toasted and the cheese melts.
5. Cut each sandwich in half and serve warm.

## Brie Pear Sandwiches

Prep time: 10 minutes | Cook time: 6 minutes | Serves 4 to 8

2 tbsps. butter, melted slices
1 large ripe pear, cored 8 slices oat nut bread
and cut into ½-inch-thick 8 ounces (227 g) Brie

1. Preheat the air fryer oven to 360ºF (182ºC).
2. Make the sandwiches: Spread each of 4 slices of bread with ¼ of the Brie. Place the pear slices and remaining 4 bread slices on the Brie.
3. Coat the melted butter lightly on both sides of each sandwich.
4. Put the sandwiches in the baking pan. You may need to cook in batches to avoid overcrowding.
5. Slide the baking pan into Rack Position 2, select Toast and set time to 6 minutes, until the cheese is melted. Repeat this process with the remaining sandwiches.
6. Serve hot.

## Homemade PB&J Sandwiches

Prep time: 5 minutes | Cook time: 6 minutes | Serves 4

Cooking spray ½ cup cornflakes,
2 medium bananas, cut crushed
into ½-inch-thick slices ¼ cup shredded coconut
8 slices oat nut bread or 6 tbsps. peanut butter
any whole-grain, oversize 6 tbsps. pineapple
bread preserves
1 egg, beaten

1. Preheat the air fryer oven to 360ºF (182ºC).
2. Mix the cornflake crumbs and coconut in a shallow dish.
3. For each sandwich, coat one bread slice with 1½ tbsps. of peanut butter. Top with banana slices. Coat another bread slice with 1½ tbsps. of preserves. Combine to make a sandwich.
4. With a pastry brush, brush top of sandwich lightly with beaten egg. Scatter with about 1½ tbsps. of crumb coating, pressing it in to make it stick. Spritz lightly with cooking spray.
5. Flip sandwich over and repeat to coat and spritz lightly the other side.
6. Working 2 at a time, put the sandwiches in the baking pan. Slide the baking pan into Rack Position 2, select Toast and set time to 6 minutes, until coating is golden brown and crispy.
7. Cut the cooked sandwiches in half and serve hot.

## Cheesy Lamb Hamburgers

Prep time: 15 minutes | Cook time: 16 minutes | Makes 4 burgers

Cooking spray 1½ tsps. minced garlic
1½ pounds (680 g) 1½ tsps. tomato paste
ground lamb 1 tsp. ground dried ginger
4 kaiser rolls or 1 tsp. ground coriander
hamburger buns, split ¼ tsp. salt
open lengthwise, warmed ¼ tsp. cayenne pepper
¼ cup crumbled feta

1. Preheat the air fryer oven to 375ºF (191ºC) and spray the air fryer basket lightly with cooking spray.
2. In a large bowl, combine all the ingredients, except for the buns. Coarsely stir to mix well.
3. Form the mixture into four balls, then pound the balls into four 5-inch diameter patties.
4. Place the patties in the air fryer basket and spray lightly with cooking spray. Put the air fryer basket onto the baking pan, and slide the baking pan into Rack Position 2, select Air Fry and set time to 16 minutes. Turn the patties halfway through.
5. Assemble the buns with patties and serve warm.

## Bell Pepper, Bacon and Tomato Sandwiches

Prep time: 10 minutes | Cook time: 6 minutes | Serves 4

3 pita pockets, cut in half ⅓ cup spicy barbecue
1¼ cups torn butter sauce
lettuce leaves 1 red bell pepper, sliced
2 tomatoes, sliced 1 yellow bell pepper,
8 slices cooked bacon, sliced
cut into thirds 2 tbsps. honey

1. Preheat the air fryer oven to 350ºF (177ºC).
2. Combine the barbecue sauce and the honey in a small bowl. Coat this mixture lightly onto the bacon slices and the red and yellow pepper slices.
3. Place the bacon and peppers into the air fryer basket. Arrange the air fryer basket onto the baking pan, and slide the baking pan into Rack Position 2, select Convection Broil and set time to 4 minutes. Then flip and cook for another 2 minutes or until the bacon is browned and the peppers are soft.
4. Fill the pita halves with the bacon, peppers, any remaining barbecue sauce, tomatoes, and lettuce, and serve hot.

# Turkey Hamburgers with Peppers

Prep time: 10 minutes | Cook time: 20 minutes | Serves 4

Cooking spray
1 cup leftover turkey, cut into bite-sized chunks
4 hamburger buns
½ cup sour cream
1 leek, sliced
2 bell peppers, deseeded and chopped

1 Serrano pepper, deseeded and chopped
2 tbsps. Tabasco sauce
1 heaping tbsp. fresh cilantro, chopped
1 tsp. hot paprika
¾ tsp. kosher salt
½ tsp. ground black pepper

1. Preheat the air fryer oven to 385ºF (196ºC). Spray a baking pan lightly with cooking spray.
2. In a large bowl, mix all the ingredients, except for the buns. Toss to combine well.
3. Add the mixture in the baking pan. Slide the baking pan into Rack Position 2, select Roast and set time to 20 minutes, until the turkey is well browned and the leek is soft.
4. Assemble the hamburger buns with the turkey mixture and serve hot.

# Crispy Mexican Potato Taquitos

Prep time: 5 minutes | Cook time: 6 minutes per batch | Makes 12 taquitos

Cooking spray
12 corn tortillas

2 cups mashed potatoes
½ cup shredded Mexican cheese

1. Preheat the air fryer oven to 400ºF (204ºC). Line the air fryer basket with parchment paper.
2. Combine the potatoes and cheese in a bowl until well mixed. Microwave the tortillas on high heat for 30 seconds, or until softened. Pour some water into another bowl and set alongside.
3. Lay the tortillas on a clean work surface. Spoon 3 tbsps. of the potato mixture in the center of each tortilla. Roll up tightly and secure with toothpicks if necessary.
4. Put the filled tortillas, seam side down, in the air fryer basket. Spray the tortillas lightly with cooking spray. Place the air fryer basket onto the baking pan, and slide the baking pan into Rack Position 2, select Air Fry and set time to 6 minutes, flipping once halfway through the cooking time. You may need to cook in batches to avoid overcrowding.
5. Serve immediately.

# Chapter 9 Appetizers and Snacks

## Funny Mini Pigs in a Blanket

Prep time: 5 minutes | Cook time: 14 minutes | Serves 4 to 6

1 (8-ounce / 227-g) tube refrigerated crescent roll dough
24 cocktail smoked sausages

6 slices deli-sliced Cheddar cheese, each cut into 8 rectangular pieces

1. Preheat the air fryer oven to 350ºF (177ºC).
2. Unroll the crescent roll dough into one large sheet. If your crescent roll dough has perforated seams, pinch or roll all the perforated seams together. Slice the large sheet of dough into 4 rectangles. Then make one slice lengthwise in the middle and 2 slices horizontally to cut each rectangle into 6 pieces. You should have 24 pieces of dough.
3. Cut a deep slit lengthwise down the center of the cocktail sausage. Stuff two pieces of cheese into the slit in the sausage. Roll one piece of crescent dough around the stuffed cocktail sausage, leaving the ends of the sausage exposed. Pinch the seam together. Repeat this process with the remaining sausages.
4. Working in 2 batches, put the sausages seam-side down in the air fryer basket. Then place the air fryer basket onto the baking pan, and slide the baking pan into Rack Position 2, select Air Fry and set time to 7 minutes. Serve immediately.

## Mozzarella Ham Stuffed Mushrooms

Prep time: 15 minutes | Cook time: 12 minutes | Serves 8

1 to 2 tsps. olive oil
16 fresh Baby Bella mushrooms, stemmed removed
4 ounces (113 g) Mozzarella cheese, cut into pieces

½ cup diced ham
2 green onions, chopped
2 tbsps. bread crumbs
½ tsp. garlic powder
¼ tsp. ground oregano
¼ tsp. ground black pepper

1. In a food processor, process the cheese, ham, green onions, bread crumbs, garlic powder, oregano, and pepper until finely chopped.
2. With the food processor running, gently drizzle in 1 to 2 tsps. olive oil until a thick paste has formed. Take the mixture to a bowl.
3. Evenly distribute the mixture into the mushroom caps and lightly press down the mixture.
4. Preheat the air fryer oven to 390ºF (199ºC).
5. Spread the mushrooms in the air fryer basket in a single layer. You'll need to cook in batches to avoid overcrowding.
6. Place the air fryer basket onto the baking pan, and slide the baking pan into Rack Position 2, select Convection Broil and set time to 12 minutes, until the mushrooms are lightly browned and soft.
7. Transfer from the oven to a plate and repeat this process with the remaining mushrooms.
8. Allow the mushrooms to rest for 5 minutes and serve hot.

## Spicy Mushroom and Sausage Empanadas

Prep time: 5 minutes | Cook time: 12 minutes | Serves 4

Cooking spray
½ pound (227 g) Kielbasa smoked sausage, chopped
½ package puff pastry dough, at room temperature
1 egg, beaten

4 chopped canned mushrooms
2 tbsps. chopped onion
½ tsp. ground cumin
¼ tsp. paprika
Salt and black pepper, to taste

1. Preheat air fryer oven to 360ºF (182ºC). Spray the air fryer basket lightly with cooking spray.
2. In a bowl, combine the sausage, mushrooms, onion, cumin, paprika, salt, and pepper and stir to mix well.
3. Make the empanadas: Put the puff pastry dough on a lightly floured surface. Slice circles into the dough with a glass. Add 1 tbsp. of the sausage mixture into the center of each pastry circle. Gently fold each in half and pinch the edges to seal. With a fork, crimp the edges. Coat them with the beaten egg and spray with cooking spray.
4. Arrange the empanadas in the air fryer basket. Place the air fryer basket onto the baking pan, and slide the baking pan into Rack Position 2, select Air Fry and set time to 12 minutes. Turn the empanadas halfway through the cooking time.
5. Let them cool for 5 minutes and serve immediately.

## Old Bay Chicken Wings

Prep time: 10 minutes | Cook time: 14 minutes | Serves 4

Cooking spray
2 pounds (907 g) chicken wings, patted dry
2 tbsps. Old Bay seasoning
2 tsps. baking powder
2 tsps. salt

1. Preheat the air fryer oven to 400ºF (204ºC). Spray lightly the baking pan with cooking spray.
2. In a large zip-top plastic bag, combine the Old Bay seasoning, baking powder, and salt. Place the chicken wings, seal, and shake until the wings are evenly coated in the seasoning mixture.
3. Arrange the chicken wings in the baking pan in a single layer and lightly spray with cooking spray. You may need to cook in batches to avoid overcrowding.
4. Put the bread in the baking pan. Slide the baking pan into Rack Position 2, select Roast and set time to 14 minutes, turning the wings halfway through, until the wings are lightly browned and the internal temperature reaches at least 165ºF (74ºC) on a meat thermometer.
5. Transfer from the oven to a plate and repeat this with the remaining chicken wings.
6. Serve warm.

## Panko Coated Chicken Wings

Prep time: 1 hour 20 minutes | Cook time: 18 minutes | Serves 4

2 pounds (907 g) chicken wings
**Marinade:**
1 cup buttermilk
½ tsp. salt
½ tsp. black pepper
**Coating:**
Cooking spray
1 cup panko bread crumbs
1 cup flour
2 tbsps. poultry seasoning
2 tsps. salt

1. In a large bowl, whisk together all the ingredients for the marinade.
2. Place the chicken wings to the marinade and toss well. Take to the refrigerator to marinate for at least an hour.
3. Preheat the air fryer oven to 360ºF (182ºC). Spray the air fryer basket lightly with cooking spray.
4. In a shallow bowl, thoroughly combine all the ingredients for the coating.
5. Transfer the chicken wings from the marinade and shake off any excess. Roll them in the coating mixture.

6. Arrange the chicken wings in the air fryer basket in a single layer. You'll need to cook in batches to avoid overcrowding.
7. Spray the wings lightly with cooking spray. Place the air fryer basket onto the baking pan, and slide the baking pan into Rack Position 2, select Air Fry and set time to 18 minutes, until the wings are crisp and golden brown on the outside. Gently flip the wings halfway through the cooking time.
8. Transfer from the oven to a plate and repeat this process with the remaining wings.
9. Serve warm.

## Italian Breaded Rice Balls with Olives

Prep time: 20 minutes | Cook time: 10 minutes | Makes 8 rice balls

Cooking spray
2 eggs
1½ cups cooked sticky rice
¾ cup panko bread crumbs
⅓ cup Italian bread crumbs
8 black olives, pitted
1 ounce (28 g) Mozzarella cheese, cut into tiny pieces (small enough to stuff into olives)
½ tsp. Italian seasoning blend
¾ tsp. salt, divided

1. Preheat air fryer oven to 390ºF (199ºC).
2. Stuff each black olive with a piece of Mozzarella cheese. Keep aside.
3. Combine the cooked sticky rice, Italian seasoning blend, and ½ tsp. of salt in a bowl, and stir to mix well. Shape the rice mixture into a log with your hands and distribute it into 8 equal portions. Mold each portion around a black olive and roll into a ball.
4. Take to the freezer to chill for about 10 to 15 minutes until firm.
5. Place the Italian bread crumbs in a shallow dish. Whisk the eggs in a separate shallow dish. In a third shallow dish, mix the panko bread crumbs and remaining salt.
6. One by one, roll the rice balls in the Italian bread crumbs, then dunk in the whisked eggs, finally coat them evenly with the panko bread crumbs.
7. Put the rice balls in the air fryer basket and spray both sides lightly with cooking spray.
8. Place the air fryer basket onto the baking pan, and slide the baking pan into Rack Position 2, select Air Fry and set time to 10 minutes, until the rice balls are golden brown. Turn the balls halfway through the cooking time.
9. Serve hot.

# Cajun Breaded Dill Pickle Chips

Prep time: 5 minutes | Cook time: 10 minutes | Makes 16 slices

Cooking spray
2 large dill pickles, sliced into 8 rounds each
½ cup panko bread crumbs
¼ cup all-purpose flour
1 large egg, beaten
2 tsps. Cajun seasoning

1. Preheat the air fryer oven to 390ºF (199ºC).
2. Put the panko bread crumbs, all-purpose flour, and egg into 3 separate shallow bowls, then stir the Cajun seasoning into the flour.
3. Dredge each pickle chip in the flour mixture, then the egg, and finally the bread crumbs. Shake off any excess, then arrange each coated pickle chip on a plate.
4. Spray the air fryer basket lightly with cooking spray, then put 8 pickle chips in the air fryer basket. Place the air fryer basket onto the baking pan, and slide the baking pan into Rack Position 2, select Air Fry and set time to 5 minutes. Repeat with the remaining pickle chips.
5. Transfer the chips and let cool slightly on a wire rack before serving.

# Classic Muffuletta Sliders with Olive Spread

Prep time: 10 minutes | Cook time: 6 minutes per batch | Makes 8 sliders

Cooking spray
8 slider buns, split in half
¼ pound (113 g) thinly sliced pastrami
¼ pound (113 g) thinly sliced deli ham
4 ounces (113 g) low-fat Mozzarella cheese, grated
1 tbsp. sesame seeds

**Olive Mix:**
½ cup sliced green olives with pimentos
¼ cup chopped kalamata olives
¼ cup sliced black olives
1 tsp. red wine vinegar
¼ tsp. basil
⅛ tsp. garlic powder

1. Preheat the air fryer oven to 360ºF (182ºC).
2. In a small bowl, combine all the ingredients for the olive mix and stir well.
3. In a medium bowl, stir together the ham, pastrami, and cheese and divide the mixture evenly into 8 equal portions.
4. Assemble the sliders: Top each bottom bun with 1 portion of meat and cheese, 2 tbsps. of olive mix, finished by the remaining buns. Spray the tops lightly with cooking spray. Sprinkle the sesame seeds on top.
5. Working in batches, place the sliders in the baking pan. Slide the baking pan into Rack Position 1, select Convection Bake and set time to 6 minutes, until the cheese melts.
6. Take to a large plate and repeat this process with the remaining sliders.
7. Serve hot.

# Italian Spinach and Mushroom Calzones

Prep time: 15 minutes | Cook time: 26 to 27 minutes | Serves 4

Cooking spray
2 tbsps. olive oil
1 pound (454 g) spinach, chopped
1 (13-ounce / 369-g) pizza crust
1½ cups marinara sauce
1 cup ricotta cheese, crumbled
¼ cup chopped mushrooms
1 onion, chopped
2 garlic cloves, minced
1 tbsp. Italian seasoning
½ tsp. oregano
Salt and black pepper, to taste

Make the Filling:
1. In a pan over medium heat, heat the olive oil until shimmering.
2. Place the onion, garlic, and mushrooms and sauté for about 4 minutes, or until softened.
3. Stir in the spinach and sauté for about 2 to 3 minutes, or until the spinach is wilted. Scatter with the oregano, Italian seasoning, salt, and pepper and mix well.
4. Put the marinara sauce and cook for 5 minutes, stirring occasionally, or until the sauce is thickened.
5. Transfer the pan from the heat and stir in the ricotta cheese. Keep aside.

Make the Calzones:
6. Preheat the air fryer oven to 375ºF (191ºC). Spray the baking pan lightly with cooking spray.
7. Roll the pizza crust out with a rolling pin on a lightly floured work surface, then slice it into 4 rectangles.
8. Scoop ¼ of the filling into each rectangle and fold in half. Crimp the edges with a fork to seal. Spray them lightly with cooking spray.
9. Arrange the calzones in the baking pan. Slide the baking pan into Rack Position 1, select Convection Bake and set time to 15 minutes, flipping once, until the calzones are golden brown and crisp.
10. Take the calzones to a paper towel-lined plate and serve hot.

## Crunchy Fish Fingers

Prep time: 5 minutes | Cook time: 12 minutes | Serves 4

1 pound (454 g) cod fillets, cut into 1-inch strips
2 eggs
2 cups flour
1 cup bread crumbs
1 cup cornmeal
2 tbsps. milk
1 tsp. seafood seasoning
Salt and black pepper, to taste

1. Preheat air fryer oven to 400ºF (204ºC).
2. In a shallow bowl, beat the eggs with the milk. Combine the flour, cornmeal, seafood seasoning, salt, and pepper in another shallow bowl. On a plate, put the bread crumbs.
3. Dredge the cod strips, one at a time, in the flour mixture, then in the egg mixture, finally in the bread crumb to coat well.
4. Place the cod strips in the air fryer basket. Then place the air fryer basket onto the baking pan, and slide the baking pan into Rack Position 2, select Air Fry and set time to 12 minutes.
5. Take the cod strips to a paper towel-lined plate and serve hot.

## Breaded Beef with Cheese Pasta Sauce

Prep time: 10 minutes | Cook time: 14 minutes | Serves 4

2 tbsps. olive oil
1 pound (454 g) sirloin tip, cut into 1-inch cubes
1½ cups soft bread
crumbs
1 cup cheese pasta sauce
½ tsp. dried marjoram

1. Preheat the air fryer oven to 360ºF (182ºC).
2. Toss the beef with the pasta sauce to coat well in a medium bowl.
3. Combine the bread crumbs, oil, and marjoram, and mix well in a shallow bowl. Drop the beef cubes, one at a time, into the bread crumb mixture to coat evenly.
4. Working in two batches, put the beef in the air fryer basket. Then place the air fryer basket onto the baking pan, and slide the baking pan into Rack Position 2, select Air Fry and set time to 7 minutes, flipping once during the cooking time, until the beef is at least 145ºF (63ºC) and the outside is crisp and brown.
5. Serve warm.

## Appetizing Gold Ravioli

Prep time: 10 minutes | Cook time: 6 minutes | Serves 4

Cooking spray
8 ounces (227 g) ravioli
½ cup panko bread crumbs
¼ cup aquafaba
2 tsps. nutritional yeast
1 tsp. dried oregano
1 tsp. garlic powder
1 tsp. dried basil
Salt and ground black pepper, to taste

1. Cover the air fryer basket with aluminum foil and coat with a light brushing of oil.
2. Preheat the air fryer oven to 400ºF (204ºC). In a small bowl, combine the panko bread crumbs, nutritional yeast, oregano, basil, and garlic powder. Season with salt and pepper to taste.
3. Place the aquafaba in a separate bowl. Dunk the ravioli in the aquafaba before coating it in the panko mixture. Spray lightly with cooking spray and arrange in the air fryer basket.
4. Put the air fryer basket onto the baking pan, and slide the baking pan into Rack Position 2, select Air Fry and set time to 6 minutes, flipping halfway.
5. Serve warm.

## Spiced Pita Chips

Prep time: 5 minutes | Cook time: 5 to 6 minutes | Serves 4

Cooking spray
2 whole 6-inch pitas, whole grain or white
¼ tsp. garlic powder
¼ tsp. ground oregano
¼ tsp. ground thyme
¼ tsp. dried basil
¼ tsp. marjoram
¼ tsp. salt

1. Preheat the air fryer oven to 330ºF (166ºC).
2. In a small bowl, mix all the seasonings together.
3. Slice each pita half into 4 wedges. Break apart wedges at the fold.
4. Coat one side of pita wedges with oil. Scatter with half of seasoning mix.
5. Flip pita wedges over, coat the other side with oil, and scatter with remaining seasonings.
6. Arrange pita wedges in the baking pan. Slide the baking pan into Rack Position 1, select Convection Bake and set time to 2 minutes.
7. Flip and bake for another 2 minutes. Flip again, and if needed, bake for about 1 or 2 more minutes, or until crisp. Watch carefully as they will cook very quickly at this point.
8. Serve immediately.

# Cheddar Stuffed Jalapeño Poppers

Prep time: 5 minutes | Cook time: 10 minutes | Serves 4

8 jalapeño peppers
¼ cup shredded Cheddar cheese
½ cup whipped cream cheese

1. Preheat the air fryer oven to 360ºF (182ºC).
2. With a paring knife, carefully cut off the jalapeño tops, then spoon out the ribs and seeds. Keep aside.
3. Combine the whipped cream cheese and shredded Cheddar cheese in a medium bowl. Arrange the mixture in a sealable plastic bag, and with a pair of scissors, cut off one corner from the bag. Carefully squeeze some cream cheese mixture into each pepper until almost full.
4. Arrange a piece of parchment paper on the bottom of the air fryer basket and put the poppers on top, distributing evenly. Place the air fryer basket onto the baking pan, and slide the baking pan into Rack Position 2, select Air Fry and set time to 10 minutes.
5. Let the poppers rest for 5 to 10 minutes before serving.

# Crispy Root Veggie Chips

Prep time: 10 minutes | Cook time: 8 minutes | Serves 2

Cooking spray
1 tsp. olive oil
1 parsnip, washed
1 small turnip, washed
1 small beet, washed
½ small sweet potato,
washed
**Herb Salt:**
2 tsps. finely chopped fresh parsley
¼ tsp. kosher salt

1. Preheat the air fryer oven to 360ºF (182ºC).
2. Peel and thinly slice the parsnip, turnip, beet, and sweet potato, then put the vegetables in a large bowl, add the olive oil, and toss well.
3. Spritz the air fryer basket lightly with cooking spray, then arrange the vegetables in the air fryer basket. Place the air fryer basket onto the baking pan, and slide the baking pan into Rack Position 2, select Air Fry and set time to 8 minutes, gently flipping halfway through.
4. When the chips cook, make the herb salt by combining the kosher salt and parsley in a small bowl.
5. Transfer the chips and put on a serving plate, then scatter the herb salt on top and let cool for about 2 to 3 minutes before serving.

# Caramelized Peaches

Prep time: 10 minutes | Cook time: 10 to 13 minutes | Serves 4

Cooking spray
4 peaches, cut into wedges
2 tbsps. sugar
¼ tsp. ground cinnamon

1. Preheat the air fryer oven to 350ºF (177ºC). Spritz the air fryer basket with cooking spray.
2. In a medium bowl, toss the peaches with the sugar and cinnamon until evenly coated.
3. Place the peaches in the air fryer basket in a single layer. You may need to cook in batches to avoid overcrowding.
4. Spray the peaches lightly with cooking spray. Place the air fryer basket onto the baking pan, and slide the baking pan into Rack Position 2, select Air Fry and set time to 5 minutes. Turn the peaches and air fry for an additional 5 to 8 minutes, or until the peaches are caramelized.
5. Repeat this with the remaining peaches.
6. Allow the peaches to rest for 5 minutes and serve hot.

# Cheesy Bruschetta with Tomato

Prep time: 5 minutes | Cook time: 6 minutes | Serves 6

Cooking spray
1 tsp. olive oil
4 tomatoes, diced
1 loaf French bread, cut into 1-inch-thick slices
⅓ cup shredded fresh basil
¼ cup shredded Parmesan cheese
1 tbsp. balsamic vinegar
1 tbsp. minced garlic
1 tsp. salt
1 tsp. freshly ground black pepper

1. Preheat the air fryer oven to 250ºF (121ºC).
2. In a medium bowl, mix together the tomatoes and basil. Place the cheese, vinegar, olive oil, garlic, salt, and pepper and stir until well incorporated. Keep aside.
3. Spray the baking pan lightly with cooking spray. Working in batches, arrange the bread slices in the baking pan in a single layer. Spritz the slices lightly with cooking spray.
4. Slide the baking pan into Rack Position 1, select Convection Bake and set time to 3 minutes.
5. Transfer from the oven to a plate. Repeat step 3 to 4 with the remaining bread slices.
6. Place a generous spoonful of the tomato mixture and serve warm.

## Cheesy Apple Roll-Ups

Prep time: 5 minutes | Cook time: 5 minutes | Makes 8 roll-ups

2 tbsps. butter, melted
8 slices whole wheat sandwich bread

4 ounces (113 g) Colby Jack cheese, grated
½ small apple, chopped

1. Preheat the air fryer oven to 390ºF (199ºC).
2. Transfer the crusts from the bread and flatten the slices with a rolling pin. Don't be gentle. Press hard so that bread will be very thin.
3. Place cheese and chopped apple on the bread, dividing the ingredients evenly.
4. Roll up each slice tightly and secure each with one or two toothpicks.
5. Coat outside of rolls with melted butter.
6. Arrange in the baking pan. Slide the baking pan into Rack Position 1, select Convection Bake and set time to 5 minutes, until outside is crisp and nicely browned.
7. Serve warm.

## Parmesan Crab Meat and Spinach Cups

Prep time: 10 minutes | Cook time: 10 minutes | Makes 30 cups

Cooking spray
30 mini frozen phyllo shells, thawed
1 (6-ounce / 170-g) can crab meat, drained to yield ⅓ cup meat
½ cup grated Parmesan cheese

¼ cup frozen spinach, thawed, drained, and chopped
1 clove garlic, minced
3 tbsps. plain yogurt
½ tsp. Worcestershire sauce
¼ tsp. lemon juice

1. Preheat the air fryer oven to 390ºF (199ºC).
2. Take any bits of shell that might remain in the crab meat.
3. In a large bowl, mix the spinach, crab meat, garlic, and cheese together.
4. Stir in the lemon juice, yogurt, and Worcestershire sauce and mix well.
5. Scoop a tsp. of filling into each phyllo shell.
6. Spritz the baking pan lightly with cooking spray and place half the shells in the baking pan. Slide the baking pan into Rack Position 1, select Convection Bake and set time to 5 minutes. Repeat this process with the remaining shells.
7. Serve hot.

## Cheesy Bruschetta

Prep time: 5 minutes | Cook time: 6 to 8 minutes | Serves 4

1 tbsp. olive oil
4 frozen hash brown patties
⅓ cup chopped cherry tomatoes
3 tbsps. diced fresh

Mozzarella
2 tbsps. grated Parmesan cheese
1 tbsp. minced fresh basil
1 tbsp. balsamic vinegar

1. Preheat the air fryer oven to 400ºF (204ºC).
2. Arrange the hash brown patties in the air fryer basket in a single layer. Then place the air fryer basket onto the baking pan, and slide the baking pan into Rack Position 2, select Air Fry and set time to 7 minutes, until the potatoes are crisp, hot, and golden brown.
3. At the same time, in a small bowl, combine the olive oil, tomatoes, Mozzarella, Parmesan, vinegar, and basil.
4. When the potatoes are cooked, gently remove from the oven and place on a serving plate. Place the tomato mixture and serve warm.

## Cheesy Artichoke-Spinach Dip

Prep time: 10 minutes | Cook time: 10 minutes | Makes 3 cups

Cooking spray
1 (14-ounce / 397-g) can artichoke hearts packed in water, drained and chopped
1 (10-ounce / 284-g) package frozen spinach, thawed and drained
¼ cup nonfat plain Greek

yogurt
¼ cup shredded part-skim Mozzarella cheese
¼ cup grated Parmesan cheese
2 tbsps. mayonnaise
1 tsp. minced garlic
¼ tsp. freshly ground black pepper

1. Preheat the air fryer oven to 360ºF (182ºC).
2. In a paper towel, wrap the artichoke hearts and spinach and squeeze out any excess liquid, then take the vegetables to a large bowl.
3. Place the minced garlic, plain Greek yogurt, mayonnaise, Mozzarella, Parmesan, and black pepper to the large bowl, stirring to combine well.
4. Spritz the air fryer basket lightly with cooking spray, then put the dip mixture in the air fryer basket. Place the air fryer basket onto the baking pan, and slide the baking pan into Rack Position 2, select Air Fry and set time to 10 minutes.
5. Transfer the dip from the air fryer oven and let cool in the pan on a wire rack for 10 minutes before serving.

Italian Artichoke Hearts, page 126

Swiss Waffle Fries Poutine, page 130

Simple Tortilla Chips, page 129

Hot Chicken Bites, page 130

## Italian Artichoke Hearts

Prep time: 5 minutes | Cook time: 8 minutes | Serves 14

Cooking spray
14 whole artichoke hearts, packed in water
1 egg
½ cup all-purpose flour
⅓ cup panko bread crumbs
1 tsp. Italian seasoning

1. Preheat the air fryer oven to 380ºF (193ºC)
2. Squeeze excess water from the artichoke hearts and put them on paper towels to dry.
3. Beat the egg in a small bowl. Place the flour in another small bowl. Combine the bread crumbs and Italian seasoning in a third small bowl, and stir well.
4. Spray the air fryer basket lightly with cooking spray.
5. Dunk the artichoke hearts in the flour, then the egg, and then the bread crumb mixture.
6. Arrange the breaded artichoke hearts in the air fryer basket. Spritz them lightly with cooking spray. Put the air fryer basket onto the baking pan, and slide the baking pan into Rack Position 2, select Air Fry and set time to 8 minutes, flipping once halfway through.
7. Allow to cool for 5 minutes before serving.

## Honey Nut Mix with Sesame Seeds

Prep time: 10 minutes | Cook time: 2 minutes | Makes 4 cups

Cooking spray
1 cup cashews
1 cup almonds
1 cup mini pretzels
1 cup rice squares cereal
1 tbsp. buttery spread, melted
2 tsps. honey
2 tsps. sesame seeds
¼ tsp. cayenne pepper
¼ tsp. kosher salt
¼ tsp. freshly ground black pepper

1. Preheat the air fryer oven to 360ºF (182ºC).
2. Combine the buttery spread, honey, cayenne pepper, sesame seeds, kosher salt, and black pepper in a large bowl, then add the cashews, almonds, pretzels, and rice squares, tossing to coat well.
3. Spritz a baking pan lightly with cooking spray, then pour the mixture into the pan. Slide the baking pan into Rack Position 1, select Convection Bake and set time to 2 minutes.
4. Transfer the sesame mix from the air fryer oven and let rest in the pan on a wire rack for about 5 minutes before serving.

## Crunchy Artichoke Bites

Prep time: 10 minutes | Cook time: 8 minutes | Serves 4

Cooking spray
14 whole artichoke hearts packed in water
1 egg
½ cup all-purpose flour
⅓ cup panko bread crumbs
1 tsp. Italian seasoning

1. Preheat the air fryer oven to 375ºF (191ºC)
2. Drain the artichoke hearts and pat with paper towels to dry thoroughly.
3. Put the flour on a plate. Beat the egg until frothy in a shallow bowl. Thoroughly mix the bread crumbs and Italian seasoning in a separate shallow bowl.
4. Dredge the artichoke hearts in the flour, then in the beaten egg, and finally roll in the bread crumb mixture until well coated.
5. Arrange the artichoke hearts in the air fryer basket and spray them with cooking spray.
6. Place the air fryer basket onto the baking pan, and slide the baking pan into Rack Position 2, select Air Fry and set time to 8 minutes, turning the artichoke hearts halfway through.
7. Allow the artichoke hearts to rest for 5 minutes before serving.

## Crunchy Green Olives

Prep time: 5 minutes | Cook time: 8 minutes | Serves 4

Cooking spray
1 (5½-ounce / 156-g) jar pitted green olives
1 egg
½ cup all-purpose flour
½ cup bread crumbs
Salt and pepper, to taste

1. Preheat the air fryer oven to 400ºF (204ºC).
2. Transfer the olives from the jar and pat with paper towels to dry.
3. Combine the flour with salt and pepper to taste in a small bowl. In another small bowl, put the bread crumbs. In a third small bowl, beat the egg.
4. Spray the air fryer basket lightly with cooking spray.
5. Dunk the olives in the flour, then the egg, and then the bread crumbs.
6. Arrange the breaded olives in the air fryer basket. It is okay to stack them. Spritz the olives lightly with cooking spray. Place the air fryer basket onto the baking pan, and slide the baking pan into Rack Position 2, select Air Fry and set time to 6 minutes. Turn the olives and air fry for another 2 minutes, or until brown and crisp.
7. Let rest before serving.

## Lemony Endive with Yogurt

Prep time: 5 minutes | Cook time: 10 minutes | Serves 6

| | |
|---|---|
| ½ cup plain and fat-free yogurt | ½ tsp. curry powder |
| 6 heads endive | 1 tsp. garlic powder |
| 3 tbsps. lemon juice | Salt and ground black pepper, to taste |

1. Wash the endives, and cut them in half lengthwise.
2. Mix together the yogurt, lemon juice, garlic powder, curry powder, salt and pepper in a bowl.
3. Spread the endive halves with the marinade, coating them completely. Let stand for at least 30 minutes or up to 24 hours.
4. Preheat the air fryer oven to 320ºF (160ºC).
5. Arrange the endives in the air fryer basket. Then place the air fryer basket onto the baking pan, and slide the baking pan into Rack Position 2, select Air Fry and set time to 10 minutes.
6. Serve warm.

## Crisp Green Tomatoes with Horseradish Sauce

Prep time: 18 minutes | Cook time: 12 minutes | Serves 4

| | Horseradish Sauce: |
|---|---|
| Cooking spray | ¼ cup mayonnaise |
| 1½ pounds (680 g) firm green tomatoes, cut into ¼-inch slices | ¼ cup sour cream |
| | 2 tsps. prepared horseradish |
| 2 eggs | ½ tsp. Worcestershire sauce |
| ½ cup bread crumbs | |
| ½ cup cornmeal | ½ tsp. lemon juice |
| ¼ cup buttermilk | ⅛ tsp. black pepper |
| ¼ tsp. salt | |

1. Preheat air fryer oven to 390ºF (199ºC). Spray the air fryer basket lightly with cooking spray.
2. Whisk together all the ingredients for the horseradish sauce in a small bowl until smooth. Keep aside.
3. Beat the eggs and buttermilk in a shallow dish.
4. Thoroughly combine the bread crumbs, cornmeal, and salt in a separate shallow dish.
5. Dredge the tomato slices, one at a time, in the egg mixture, then roll in the bread crumb mixture until well coated.
6. Working in batches, arrange the tomato slices in the air fryer basket in a single layer. Spritz them lightly with cooking spray.
7. Place the air fryer basket onto the baking pan, and slide the baking pan into Rack Position 2, select Air Fry and set time to 12 minutes, flipping the slices halfway through.
8. Transfer from the oven to a platter and repeat this process with the remaining tomato slices.
9. Drizzle with the prepared horseradish sauce and serve warm.

## Cinnamon Mixed Nuts

Prep time: 5 minutes | Cook time: 20 minutes | Serves 6

| | |
|---|---|
| Cooking spray | 2 tbsps. sugar |
| 2 cups mixed nuts (walnuts, pecans, and almonds) | 2 tbsps. egg white |
| | 1 tsp. ground cinnamon |
| | 1 tsp. paprika |

1. Preheat the air fryer oven to 300ºF (149ºC). Spritz the air fryer basket lightly with cooking spray.
2. In a small bowl, stir together the mixed nuts, egg white, sugar, paprika, and cinnamon until the nuts are completely coated.
3. Place the nuts in the air fryer basket. Then put the air fryer basket onto the baking pan, and slide the baking pan into Rack Position 2, select Convection Broil and set time to 20 minutes. For even cooking, flip halfway through the cooking time.
4. Take the nuts to a bowl and serve hot.

## Simple Prosciutto-Wrapped Asparagus

Prep time: 5 minutes | Cook time: 16 to 24 minutes | Serves 6

| | |
|---|---|
| Cooking spray | 12 asparagus spears, woody ends trimmed |
| 24 pieces thinly sliced prosciutto | |

1. Preheat the air fryer oven to 360ºF (182ºC).
2. Wrap each asparagus spear with 2 slices of prosciutto, then repeat this with the remaining asparagus and prosciutto.
3. Spritz the air fryer basket lightly with cooking spray, then arrange 2 to 3 bundles in the air fryer basket. Place the air fryer basket onto the baking pan, and slide the baking pan into Rack Position 2, select Air Fry and set time to 4 minutes. Repeat this process with the remaining asparagus bundles.
4. Transfer the bundles and let cool on a wire rack for 5 minutes before serving.

## Crispy Mozzarella Sticks

Prep time: 5 minutes | Cook time: 6 to 7 minutes | Serves 4 to 8

8 egg roll wraps
8 Mozzarella string cheese "sticks"

1 egg
1 tbsp. water

1. Preheat the air fryer oven to 390ºF (199ºC).
2. In a small bowl, beat together egg and water.
3. Lay out egg roll wraps and moisten edges with egg wash.
4. Put one piece of string cheese on each wrap near one end.
5. Fold in sides of egg roll wrap gently over ends of cheese, and then roll up.
6. Brush outside of wrap with egg wash and press carefully to seal well.
7. Arrange in the air fryer basket in a single layer. Then place the air fryer basket onto the baking pan, and slide the baking pan into Rack Position 2, select Air Fry and set time to 5 minutes. Air fry for another 1 or 2 minutes, if necessary, or until they are golden brown and crispy.
8. Serve hot.

## Mozzarella Steak Fries with Beef Gravy

Prep time: 5 minutes | Cook time: 20 minutes | Serves 5

Cooking spray
1 (28-ounce / 794-g) bag frozen steak fries
1 cup shredded Mozzarella cheese

½ cup beef gravy
2 scallions, green parts only, chopped
Salt and pepper, to taste

1. Preheat the air fryer oven to 400ºF (204ºC).
2. Put the frozen steak fries in the air fryer basket. Then place the air fryer basket onto the baking pan, and slide the baking pan into Rack Position 2, select Air Fry and set time to 10 minutes. Flip and spray the fries lightly with cooking spray. Season with salt and pepper to taste. Air fry for another 8 minutes.
3. Place the beef gravy into a medium, microwave-safe bowl. Microwave for about 30 seconds, or until the gravy is warm.
4. Scatter the fries with the cheese. Air fry for 2 minutes more, until the cheese is melted.
5. Take the fries to a serving dish. Drizzle the fries with gravy and garnish with scallions. Serve warm.

## Cheddar Potato and Zucchini Tots

Prep time: 5 minutes | Cook time: 20 minutes | Serves 4

Cooking spray
1 large zucchini, grated
1 medium baked potato, skin removed and mashed

1 large egg, beaten
¼ cup shredded Cheddar cheese
½ tsp. kosher salt

1. Preheat the air fryer oven to 390ºF (199ºC).
2. In a paper towel, wrap the grated zucchini and squeeze out any excess liquid. Mix the zucchini, baked potato, egg, shredded Cheddar cheese, and kosher salt in a large bowl.
3. Spritz the air fryer basket lightly with cooking spray, then put individual tbsps. of the zucchini mixture in the air fryer basket. Place the air fryer basket onto the baking pan, and slide the baking pan into Rack Position 2, select Air Fry and set time to 10 minutes. Repeat with the remaining mixture.
4. Transfer the tots and let cool on a wire rack for about 5 minutes before serving.

## Cheesy Crab Toasts

Prep time: 10 minutes | Cook time: 5 minutes | Makes 15 to 18 toasts

1 loaf artisan bread, French bread, or baguette, cut into ⅜-inch-thick slices
1 (6-ounce / 170-g) can flaked crab meat, well drained
¼ cup shredded Cheddar

cheese
¼ cup shredded Parmesan cheese
3 tbsps. light mayonnaise
1 tsp. Worcestershire sauce
½ tsp. lemon juice

1. Preheat the air fryer oven to 360ºF (182ºC).
2. Stir together all the ingredients except the bread slices in a large bowl.
3. Lay the bread slices on a clean work surface. Spread ½ tbsp. of crab mixture onto each slice of bread.
4. Place the bread slices in the baking pan in a single layer. You'll need to cook in batches to avoid overcrowding.
5. Slide the baking pan into Rack Position 2, select Toast and set time to 5 minutes, until the tops are lightly browned.
6. Take to a plate and repeat with the remaining bread slices.
7. Serve hot.

## Simple Tortilla Chips

Prep time: 5 minutes | Cook time: 3 minutes | Serves 2

| | |
|---|---|
| 1 tbsp. olive oil | Salt, to taste |
| 8 corn tortillas | |

1. Preheat the air fryer oven to 390ºF (199ºC).
2. Cut the corn tortillas into triangles. Coat them with a light brushing of olive oil.
3. Arrange the tortilla pieces in the air fryer basket. Then place the air fryer basket onto the baking pan, and slide the baking pan into Rack Position 2, select Air Fry and set time to 3 minutes. You may need to work this in batches.
4. Sprinkle with salt to taste before serving.

## Paprika Kale Chips

Prep time: 5 minutes | Cook time: 12 minutes | Serves 4

| | |
|---|---|
| Cooking spray | removed and chopped |
| 2 tsps. canola oil | ¼ tsp. smoked paprika |
| 5 cups kale, large stems | ¼ tsp. kosher salt |

1. Preheat the air fryer oven to 390ºF (199ºC).
2. Toss the kale, canola oil, smoked paprika, and kosher salt in a large bowl.
3. Spritz the air fryer basket lightly with cooking spray, then arrange half the kale in the air fryer basket. Place the air fryer basket onto the baking pan, and slide the baking pan into Rack Position 2, select Air Fry and set time to 3 minutes.
4. Flip and air fry for another 3 minutes, or until crispy. Repeat this process with the remaining kale.
5. Transfer the kale and let cool on a wire rack for about 3 to 5 minutes before serving.

## Baked Cashews with Rosemary

Prep time: 5 minutes | Cook time: 3 minutes | Makes 2 cups

| | |
|---|---|
| Cooking spray | 2 cups roasted and |
| 1 tsp. olive oil | unsalted whole cashews |
| 2 sprigs of fresh | ½ tsp. honey |
| rosemary (1 chopped | 1 tsp. kosher salt |
| and 1 whole) | |

1. Preheat the air fryer oven to 300ºF (149ºC).
2. Whisk together the chopped rosemary, olive oil, kosher salt, and honey in a medium bowl. Keep aside.
3. Spritz the baking pan lightly with cooking spray, then add the cashews and the whole rosemary sprig in the baking pan. Slide the baking pan into Rack Position 1, select Convection Bake and set time to 3 minutes.
4. Transfer the cashews and rosemary from the air fryer oven, then discard the rosemary and place the cashews to the olive oil mixture, tossing to coat well.
5. Let rest for 15 minutes before serving.

## Crispy Bacon-Wrapped Dates

Prep time: 10 minutes | Cook time: 12 minutes | Serves 6

| | |
|---|---|
| Cooking spray | 6 slices high-quality |
| 12 dates, pitted | bacon, cut in half |

1. Preheat the air fryer oven to 360ºF (182ºC).
2. Wrap each date with half a bacon slice and secure tightly with a toothpick.
3. Spritz the baking pan lightly with cooking spray, then put 6 bacon-wrapped dates in the baking pan. Slide the baking pan into Rack Position 1, select Convection Bake and set time to 6 minutes, until the bacon is crispy. Repeat with the remaining dates.
4. Transfer the dates and let cool on a wire rack for 5 minutes before serving.

## Quick Bacon-Wrapped Dates and Almonds

Prep time: 10 minutes | Cook time: 6 minutes | Makes 16 appetizers

| | |
|---|---|
| 6 to 8 strips turkey | **Special Equipment:** |
| bacon, cut in half | 16 toothpicks, soaked |
| 16 whole dates, pitted | in water for at least 30 |
| 16 whole almonds | minutes |

1. Preheat the air fryer oven to 390ºF (199ºC).
2. Stuff each pitted date with a whole almond on a flat work surface.
3. Wrap half slice of bacon around each date and secure it tightly with a toothpick.
4. Put the bacon-wrapped dates in the air fryer basket. Then place the air fryer basket onto the baking pan, and slide the baking pan into Rack Position 2, select Air Fry and set time to 6 minutes.
5. Take the dates to a paper towel-lined plate to drain. Serve warm.

## Kale Chips with Sesame Seeds

Prep time: 15 minutes | Cook time: 8 minutes | Serves 5

1½ tbsps. olive oil
8 cups deribbed kale leaves, torn into 2-inch pieces

2 tsps. sesame seeds
¾ tsp. chili powder
¼ tsp. garlic powder
½ tsp. paprika

1. Preheat air fryer oven to 350ºF (177ºC).
2. Toss the kale with the olive oil, chili powder, garlic powder, paprika, and sesame seeds until well coated in a large bowl.
3. Place the kale in the air fryer basket. Then put the air fryer basket onto the baking pan, and slide the baking pan into Rack Position 2, select Air Fry and set time to 8 minutes, flipping the kale twice during the cooking time.
4. Serve hot.

## Hot Chicken Bites

Prep time: 10 minutes | Cook time: 12 minutes | Makes 30 bites

Cooking spray
8 ounces boneless and skinless chicken thighs,

cut into 30 pieces
2 tbsps. hot sauce
¼ tsp. kosher salt

1. Preheat the air fryer oven to 390ºF (199ºC).
2. Spritz the baking pan lightly with cooking spray and sprinkle the chicken bites with the kosher salt to taste, then arrange in the baking pan. Slide the baking pan into Rack Position 2, select Roast and set time to 12 minutes.
3. When the chicken bites cook, place the hot sauce into a large bowl.
4. Transfer the bites to the sauce bowl, tossing to coat well. Serve hot.

## Swiss Waffle Fries Poutine

Prep time: 10 minutes | Cook time: 17 minutes | Serves 4

2 tsps. olive oil
2 cups frozen waffle cut fries
1 cup shredded Swiss cheese

1 red bell pepper, chopped
½ cup bottled chicken gravy
2 green onions, sliced

1. Preheat the air fryer oven to 380ºF (193ºC).
2. Coat the waffle fries with the olive oil and arrange in the air fryer basket. Then place the air fryer basket onto the baking pan, and slide the baking pan into Rack Position 2, select Air Fry and set time to 12 minutes, flipping halfway through the cooking time.
3. Transfer the fries from the oven and top with the pepper, green onions, and cheese. Air fry for about 3 minutes, or until the vegetables are crisp and soft.
4. Remove from the air fryer oven and drizzle the gravy over the fries. Air fry for about 2 minutes, or until the gravy is hot.
5. Serve right away.

## Cajun Zucchini Chips

Prep time: 5 minutes | Cook time: 15 to 16 minutes | Serves 4

Cooking spray
2 large zucchinis, cut into

⅛-inch-thick slices
2 tsps. Cajun seasoning

1. Preheat the air fryer oven to 370ºF (188ºC).
2. Spritz the air fryer basket with cooking spray.
3. In a medium bowl, put the zucchini slices and spritz them generously with cooking spray.
4. Scatter the Cajun seasoning over the zucchini and stir to make sure they are well coated with oil and seasoning.
5. Put the slices in a single layer in the air fryer basket, making sure not to overcrowd. You will need to work in several batches.
6. Place the air fryer basket onto the baking pan, and slide the baking pan into Rack Position 2, select Air Fry and set time to 8 minutes. Turn the slices over and air fry for another 7 to 8 minutes, or until they are as crisp and brown as you prefer.
7. Serve hot.

# Honey Chicken Wings

Prep time: 5 minutes | Cook time: 30 minutes | Serves 4

Cooking spray
16 chicken wings and drumettes
1 tbsp. honey

1 tbsp. Sriracha hot sauce
1 garlic clove, minced
½ tsp. kosher salt

1. Preheat the air fryer oven to 360ºF (182ºC).
2. Whisk together the Sriracha hot sauce, honey, minced garlic, and kosher salt in a large bowl, then add the chicken and toss to coat well.
3. Spritz the baking pan lightly with cooking spray, then arrange 8 wings in the baking pan. Slide the baking pan into Rack Position 2, select Roast and set time to 15 minutes, turning halfway through. Repeat with the remaining wings.
4. Transfer the wings and let cool on a wire rack for 10 minutes before serving.

# Barbecue Chicken Sausage Pizza

Prep time: 5 minutes | Cook time: 8 minutes | Serves 1

Cooking spray
1 piece naan bread
½ chicken herby sausage, sliced
¼ cup shredded Monterrey Jack cheese

¼ cup shredded Mozzarella cheese
¼ cup Barbecue sauce
2 tbsps. red onion, thinly sliced
Chopped cilantro or parsley, for garnish

1. Preheat the air fryer oven to 400ºF (204ºC).
2. Spray the bottom of naan bread with cooking spray, then arrange in the baking pan.
3. Coat the bread with the Barbecue sauce. Top with the sausage, cheeses, and finish with the red onion.
4. Slide the baking pan into Rack Position 1, select Convection Bake and set time to 8 minutes, until the cheese is melted.
5. Sprinkle with the chopped cilantro or parsley for garnish before slicing to serve.

# Chapter 10 Desserts

## Black Forest and Cherries Pies

Prep time: 10 minutes | Cook time: 15 minutes | Serves 6

| | |
|---|---|
| 1 (10-by-15-inch) sheet frozen puff pastry, thawed | 2 tbsps. chopped dried cherries |
| 1 egg white, beaten | 2 tbsps. thick, hot fudge sauce |
| 3 tbsps. milk or dark chocolate chips | 2 tbsps. sugar |
| | ½ tsp. cinnamon |

1.  Preheat the air fryer oven to 350ºF (177ºC).
2.  Combine the chocolate chips, fudge sauce, and dried cherries in a small bowl.
3.  Roll out the puff pastry on a floured surface. Cut into 6 squares by using a sharp knife.
4.  Divide the chocolate chip mixture into the center of each puff pastry square. Gently fold the squares in half to make triangles. Firmly press the edges with the tines of a fork to seal.
5.  Coat the triangles on all sides sparingly with the beaten egg white. Scatter the tops with sugar and cinnamon.
6.  Arrange the triangles in the baking pan. Slide the baking pan into Rack Position 1, select Convection Bake and set time to 15 minutes, until the triangles are golden brown. The filling will be hot, so let cool for at least 20 minutes before serving.

## Chocolate Lava Cupcakes

Prep time: 10 minutes | Cook time: 12 minutes | Serves 8

| | |
|---|---|
| Nonstick baking spray with flour | 1 egg yolk |
| ¼ cup safflower oil | ¼ cup hot water |
| 1⅓ cups chocolate cake mix | ⅓ cup sour cream |
| 1 egg | 3 tbsps. peanut butter |
| | 1 tbsp. powdered sugar |

1.  Preheat the air fryer oven to 350ºF (177ºC).
2.  Double up 16 foil muffin cups to make 8 cups. Spritz each with nonstick spray; set aside.
3.  Combine the cake mix, egg, egg yolk, safflower oil, water, and sour cream in a medium bowl and beat until combined.
4.  Combine the peanut butter and powdered sugar in a small bowl, and mix well. Shape this mixture into 8 balls.
5.  Scoop about ¼ cup of the chocolate batter into each muffin cup and top with a peanut butter ball. Scoop remaining batter on top of the peanut butter balls to cover them.
6.  Place the cups in the baking pan, leaving some space between each. Slide the baking pan into Rack Position 1, select Convection Bake and set time to 12 minutes, until the tops look dry and set.
7.  Allow the cupcakes to cool for 10 minutes, then serve hot.

## Simple Apple Fritters

Prep time: 30 minutes | Cook time: 7 minutes | Serves 6

| | |
|---|---|
| Cooking spray | 2 tbsps. butter, melted |
| 1 cup chopped, peeled Granny Smith apple | 1 tsp. ground cinnamon |
| 1 cup all-purpose flour | 1 tsp. baking powder |
| 1 large egg, beaten | ¼ cup confectioners' sugar (optional) |
| ½ cup granulated sugar | 1 tsp. salt |
| 2 tbsps. milk | |

1.  In a small bowl, mix together the apple, granulated sugar, and cinnamon. Let sit for about 30 minutes.
2.  In a medium bowl, combine the flour, baking powder, and salt. Pour in the milk, butter, and egg and stir to incorporate well.
3.  Place the apple mixture into the bowl of flour mixture and use a spatula to stir until a dough forms.
4.  Make the fritters: Divide the dough into 12 equal portions and shape into 1-inch balls on a clean work surface. Flatten them into patties with your hands.
5.  Preheat the air fryer oven to 350ºF (177ºC). Line the baking pan with parchment paper and spritz it lightly with cooking spray.
6.  Take the apple fritters onto the parchment paper, evenly spaced but not too close together. Spritz the fritters lightly with cooking spray.
7.  Slide the baking pan into Rack Position 1, select Convection Bake and set time to 7 minutes, until lightly browned. Flip the fritters halfway through the cooking time.
8.  Transfer from the oven to a plate and serve with the confectioners' sugar sprinkled on top, if desired.

## Pecan Pie with Chocolate Chips

Prep time: 20 minutes | Cook time: 25 minutes | Serves 8

1 (9-inch) unbaked pie crust
**Filling:**
2 large eggs
1½ cups coarsely chopped pecans

1 cup milk chocolate chips
1 cup sugar
½ cup all-purpose flour
⅓ cup butter, melted
2 tbsps. bourbon

1. Preheat the air fryer oven to 350ºF (177ºC).
2. In a large bowl, whisk the eggs and melted butter until creamy.
3. Place the sugar and flour and stir to incorporate well. Mix in the milk chocolate chips, pecans, and bourbon and stir until combined well.
4. With a fork, prick holes in the bottom and sides of the pie crust. Pour the prepared filling into the pie crust. Put the pie crust in the baking pan.
5. Slide the baking pan into Rack Position 1, select Convection Bake and set time to 25 minutes, until a toothpick inserted in the center comes out clean.
6. Let the pie rest for 10 minutes in the oven before serving.

## Air Fried Golden Bananas

Prep time: 5 minutes | Cook time: 7 minutes | Serves 6

Cooking oil
3 bananas, halved crosswise
1 large egg
¼ cup plain bread

crumbs
¼ cup cornstarch
Chocolate sauce, for drizzling

1. Preheat the air fryer oven to 350ºF (177ºC).
2. Beat the egg in a small bowl. Place the cornstarch in another bowl. Put the bread crumbs in a third bowl.
3. Dunk the bananas in the cornstarch, then the egg, and then the bread crumbs.
4. Spritz the air fryer basket lightly with cooking oil.
5. Place the bananas in the air fryer basket and spritz them lightly with cooking oil. Then put the air fryer basket onto the baking pan, and slide the baking pan into Rack Position 2, select Air Fry and set time to 5 minutes.
6. Open the air fryer oven and turn the bananas. Air fry for another 2 minutes.
7. Take the bananas to plates. Drizzle the chocolate sauce over the bananas, and serve hot.

## Sweet Chocolate Donuts

Prep time: 5 minutes | Cook time: 8 minutes | Serves 8

Cooking oil
1 (8-ounce / 227-g) can jumbo biscuits

Chocolate sauce, for drizzling

1. Preheat the air fryer oven to 375ºF (191ºC)
2. Separate the biscuit dough into 8 biscuits and arrange them on a flat work surface. With a small circle cookie cutter or a biscuit cutter, cut a hole in the center of each biscuit. You can also cut the holes with a knife.
3. Spritz the air fryer basket lightly with cooking oil.
4. Place 4 donuts in the air fryer basket. Do not stack. Spritz lightly with cooking oil. Put the air fryer basket onto the baking pan, and slide the baking pan into Rack Position 2, select Air Fry and set time to 4 minutes.
5. Open the air fryer oven and turn the donuts. Air fry for another 4 minutes.
6. Transfer the cooked donuts from the air fryer oven, then repeat steps 4 and 5 for the remaining 4 donuts.
7. Pour chocolate sauce over the donuts and serve warm.

## Almond Blackberry Chocolate Cake

Prep time: 10 minutes | Cook time: 22 minutes | Serves 8

4 eggs
1 cup almond flour
½ cup butter, at room temperature
½ cup cocoa powder

⅓ cup fresh blackberries
2 ounces (57 g) Swerve
1 tsp. orange zest
1 tsp. baking soda
⅓ tsp. baking powder

1. Preheat the air fryer oven to 335ºF (168ºC).
2. Beat the butter and Swerve with an electric mixer or hand mixer, until creamy.
3. One at a time, mix in the eggs and beat again until fluffy.
4. Place the almond flour, baking soda, baking powder, cocoa powder, orange zest and mix well. Pour the butter mixture into the almond flour mixture and stir until well blended. Gently fold in the blackberries.
5. Scrape the batter to a baking pan. Slide the baking pan into Rack Position 1, select Convection Bake and set time to 22 minutes. Check the cake for doneness: It's done if a toothpick inserted into the center of the cake comes out clean.
6. Let the cake cool on a wire rack to room temperature. Serve right away.

## Cinnamon Pecan Pie

Prep time: 10 minutes | Cook time: 35 minutes | Serves 4

| | |
|---|---|
| 1 pie dough | divided |
| 2 eggs | 2 tbsps. sugar |
| ¾ cup maple syrup | ¾ tsp. vanilla extract |
| ½ cup chopped pecans | ½ tsp. cinnamon |
| 3 tbsps. melted butter, | ⅛ tsp. nutmeg |

1. Preheat the air fryer oven to 370ºF (188ºC).
2. Coat the pecans in 1 tbsp. of melted butter in a small bowl.
3. Take the pecans to the air fryer basket. Then place the air fryer basket onto the baking pan, and slide the baking pan into Rack Position 2, select Air Fry and set time to 10 minutes.
4. Place the pie dough in a greased pie pan and put the pecans on top.
5. Mix the rest of the ingredients in a bowl. Pour this over the pecans.
6. Slide the baking pan into Rack Position 1, select Convection Bake and set time to 25 minutes.
7. Serve hot.

## Vanilla Chocolate Coconut Brownies

Prep time: 15 minutes | Cook time: 15 minutes | Serves 8

| | |
|---|---|
| ½ cup coconut oil | 2½ tbsps. water |
| 4 whisked eggs | 1 tbsp. honey |
| 1 cup sugar | ½ tsp. ground anise star |
| ½ cup desiccated coconut | ½ tsp. vanilla extract |
| ½ cup flour | ¼ tsp. ground cinnamon |
| 2 ounces (57 g) dark chocolate | ¼ tsp. coconut extract |
| | Sugar, for dusting |

1. Preheat the air fryer oven to 355ºF (179ºC).
2. In the microwave, melt the coconut oil and dark chocolate.
3. In a large bowl, combine with the sugar, water, eggs, cinnamon, anise, coconut extract, vanilla, and honey.
4. Stir in the flour and desiccated coconut. Incorporate everything well.
5. Grease a baking pan lightly with butter. Take the mixture to the baking pan.
6. Slide the baking pan into Rack Position 1, select Convection Bake and set time to 15 minutes.
7. Transfer from the air fryer oven and let cool slightly.
8. Remove the brownies to a plate. Slice it into squares.
9. Dust with sugar before serving.

## Peach, Apple, and Cranberry Crisp

Prep time: 10 minutes | Cook time: 10 minutes | Serves 8

| | |
|---|---|
| 3 tbsps. softened butter | ½ cup oatmeal |
| 2 peaches, peeled and chopped | ⅓ cup dried cranberries |
| 1 apple, peeled and chopped | ⅓ cup brown sugar |
| | ¼ cup flour |
| | 2 tbsps. honey |

1. Preheat the air fryer oven to 370ºF (188ºC).
2. Combine the apple, peaches, cranberries, and honey in a baking pan, and mix well.
3. In a medium bowl, combine the flour, oatmeal, brown sugar, and butter, and mix until crumbly. Scatter this mixture over the fruit in the baking pan.
4. Slide the baking pan into Rack Position 1, select Convection Bake and set time to 10 minutes, until the fruit is bubbly and the topping is golden brown. Serve hot.

## Vanilla Graham Cracker Cheesecake

Prep time: 10 minutes | Cook time: 20 minutes | Serves 8

| | |
|---|---|
| 2 eggs | softened |
| 1 cup graham cracker crumbs | ¼ cup chocolate syrup |
| ⅓ cup sugar | 3 tbsps. softened butter |
| 1½ (8-ounce / 227-g) packages cream cheese, | 1 tbsp. flour |
| | 1 tsp. vanilla |

1. For the crust: in a small bowl, combine the graham cracker crumbs and butter and mix well. Press into the bottom of a baking pan and place in the freezer to set.
2. For the filling: in a medium bowl, mix the cream cheese and sugar and mix well. Beat in the eggs, one at a time. Place the flour and vanilla.
3. Preheat the air fryer oven to 450ºF (232ºC).
4. Transfer ⅔ cup of the filling to a small bowl and stir in the chocolate syrup until combined well.
5. Place the vanilla filling into the baking pan with the crust. Drop the chocolate filling over the vanilla filling by the spoonful. By using a clean butter knife, stir the fillings in a zigzag pattern to marbleize them.
6. Slide the baking pan into Rack Position 1, select Convection Bake and set time to 20 minutes, until the cheesecake is just set.
7. Let cool on a wire rack for 1 hour, then chill in the refrigerator until the cheesecake is firm.
8. Serve right away.

## Soft Chocolate Molten Cake

Prep time: 5 minutes | Cook time: 10 minutes | Serves 4

| | |
|---|---|
| butter | 3.5 ounces (99 g) |
| 2 eggs | chocolate, melted |
| 3.5 ounces (99 g) butter, melted | 3½ tbsps. sugar |
| | 1½ tbsps. flour |

1. Preheat the air fryer oven to 375ºF (191ºC).
2. Grease four ramekins with a little butter.
3. In a medium bowl, rigorously combine the butter, eggs, and sugar before stirring in the melted chocolate.
4. Gently fold in the flour.
5. Scoop an equal amount of the mixture into each ramekin.
6. Arrange the ramekins in the baking pan. Slide the baking pan into Rack Position 1, select Convection Bake and set time to 10 minutes.
7. Place the ramekins upside-down on plates and let the cakes fall out. Serve warm.

## Chocolate Fudge Pie

Prep time: 15 minutes | Cook time: 25 minutes | Serves 8

| | |
|---|---|
| 1 (9-inch) unbaked pie crust | ½ cup self-rising flour |
| 3 large eggs, beaten | ⅓ cup unsweetened cocoa powder |
| 1½ cups sugar | ¼ cup confectioners' |
| 12 tbsps. (1½ sticks) butter, melted | sugar (optional) |
| | 1½ tsps. vanilla extract |

1. Preheat the air fryer oven to 350ºF (177ºC).
2. In a medium bowl, thoroughly combine the sugar, flour, and cocoa powder. Place the beaten eggs and butter and whisk to combine well. Stir in the vanilla.
3. Place the prepared filling into the pie crust and arrange in a baking pan.
4. Slide the baking pan into Rack Position 1, select Convection Bake and set time to 25 minutes, until just set.
5. Let the pie cool for about 5 minutes. Scatter with the confectioners' sugar, if desired. Serve immediately.

## Oatmeal, Carrot and Cherries Cookie Cups

Prep time: 10 minutes | Cook time: 8 minutes | Makes 16 cups

| | |
|---|---|
| 3 tbsps. unsalted butter, at room temperature | pastry flour |
| 1 egg white | ¼ cup dried cherries |
| ½ cup quick-cooking oatmeal | ¼ cup packed brown sugar |
| ⅓ cup finely grated carrot | 1 tbsp. honey |
| ⅓ cup whole-wheat | ½ tsp. vanilla extract |
| | ½ tsp. baking soda |

1. Preheat the air fryer oven to 350ºF (177ºC)
2. Beat the butter, brown sugar, and honey in a medium bowl, until well combined.
3. Add the vanilla, egg white, and carrot. Beat to combine well.
4. Stir in the pastry flour, oatmeal, and baking soda.
5. Stir in the dried cherries.
6. Double up 32 mini muffin foil cups to make 16 cups. Fill each with about 4 tsps. of dough. Working in batches, put 8 cookie cups in the baking pan. Slide the baking pan into Rack Position 1, select Convection Bake and set time to 8 minutes, until light golden brown and just set. Transfer the cookie cups and repeat with the remaining 8 cookie cups.
7. Serve hot.

## Rich Chocolate Cookie

Prep time: 10 minutes | Cook time: 9 minutes | Serves 4

| | |
|---|---|
| Nonstick baking spray with flour | 1 egg yolk |
| ¾ cup chocolate chips | 3 tbsps. softened butter |
| ½ cup flour | 2 tbsps. ground white chocolate |
| ⅓ cup plus 1 tbsp. brown sugar | ½ tsp. vanilla |
| | ¼ tsp. baking soda |

1. Preheat the air fryer oven to 350ºF (177ºC).
2. Beat the butter and brown sugar together in a medium bowl until fluffy. Stir in the egg yolk.
3. Put the flour, white chocolate, baking soda, and vanilla, and mix well. Stir in the chocolate chips.
4. Line a baking pan with parchment paper. Spritz the parchment paper lightly with nonstick baking spray with flour.
5. Spread the batter into the prepared pan, leaving a ½-inch border on all sides.
6. Slide the baking pan into Rack Position 1, select Convection Bake and set time to 9 minutes, until the cookie is light brown and just barely set.
7. Transfer the pan from the air fryer oven and allow to cool for about 10 minutes. Take the cookie out of the pan, remove the parchment paper, and let rest on a wire rack.
8. Serve right away.

## Fast Chocolate S'mores

Prep time: 5 minutes | Cook time: 3 minutes | Serves 12

| | |
|---|---|
| 12 whole cinnamon graham crackers | 2 (1.55-ounce / 44-g) chocolate bars, broken into 12 pieces |
| 12 marshmallows | |

1. Preheat the air fryer oven to 350ºF (177ºC).
2. Halve each graham cracker into 2 squares.
3. Arrange 6 graham cracker squares in the baking pan. Do not stack. Place a piece of chocolate into each. Slide the baking pan into Rack Position 1, select Convection Bake and set time to 2 minutes.
4. Open the air fryer oven and put a marshmallow onto each piece of melted chocolate. Bake for another minute.
5. Transfer the cooked s'mores from the air fryer oven, then repeat steps 3 and 4 for the remaining s'mores.
6. Place the remaining graham cracker squares on top and serve warm.

## Coffee Almond Chocolate Cake

Prep time: 5 minutes | Cook time: 30 minutes | Serves 8

| | |
|---|---|
| **Dry Ingredients:** | brewed coffee |
| 1½ cups almond flour | 1 stick butter, melted |
| ⅔ cup Swerve | **Topping:** |
| ½ cup coconut meal | 3 tbsps. coconut oil |
| 1 tsp. baking powder | ½ cup confectioner's Swerve |
| ¼ tsp. salt | ¼ cup coconut flour |
| **Wet Ingredients:** | 1 tsp. ground cinnamon |
| 1 egg | ½ tsp. ground cardamom |
| ½ cup hot strongly | |

1. Preheat the air fryer oven to 330ºF (166ºC).
2. Combine the almond flour, coconut meal, Swerve, baking powder, and salt in a medium bowl.
3. Whisk the egg, melted butter, and coffee in a large bowl until smooth.
4. Place the dry mixture to the wet and stir until well incorporated. Take the batter to a greased baking pan.
5. In a small bowl, stir together all the ingredients for the topping. Spread the topping over the batter and smooth the top by using a spatula.
6. Slide the baking pan into Rack Position 1, select Convection Bake and set time to 30 minutes, until the cake springs back when gently pressed with your fingers.
7. Allow to rest for about 10 minutes before serving.

## Pear, Apple and Walnuts Crisp

Prep time: 10 minutes | Cook time: 20 minutes | Serves 6

| | |
|---|---|
| Cooking spray | ¼ cup chopped walnuts |
| ½ pound (227 g) apples, cored and chopped | 1 tbsp. butter |
| ½ pound (227 g) pears, cored and chopped | 1 tsp. ground cinnamon |
| 1 cup flour | 1 tsp. vanilla extract |
| 1 cup sugar | ¼ tsp. ground cloves |
| | Whipped cream, for serving |

1. Preheat the air fryer oven to 340ºF (171ºC).
2. Lightly spray a baking pan with cooking spray and put the apples and pears inside.
3. In a medium bowl, combine the rest of the ingredients, minus the walnuts and the whipped cream, until a coarse, crumbly texture is achieved.
4. Place the mixture over the fruits and spread it evenly. Top with the chopped walnuts.
5. Slide the baking pan into Rack Position 1, select Convection Bake and set time to 20 minutes, until the top turns golden brown.
6. Serve chilled with whipped cream.

## Orange and Hazelnuts Cake

Prep time: 5 minutes | Cook time: 20 minutes | Serves 6

| | |
|---|---|
| Cooking spray | 5 tbsps. liquid monk fruit |
| 1 stick butter, at room temperature | 3 tbsps. sugar-free orange marmalade |
| 2 eggs plus 1 egg yolk, beaten | 1 tsp. baking soda |
| ⅓ cup hazelnuts, roughly chopped | ½ tsp. baking powder |
| 6 ounces (170 g) unbleached almond flour | ½ tsp. ground cinnamon |
| | ½ tsp. ground allspice |
| | ½ ground anise seed |

1. Preheat the air fryer oven to 310ºF (154ºC). Spritz a baking pan lightly with cooking spray.
2. Whisk the butter and liquid monk fruit in a mixing bowl, until the mixture is pale and smooth. Mix in the beaten eggs, hazelnuts, and marmalade and whisk again until entirely incorporated.
3. Pour the almond flour, baking soda, baking powder, allspice, cinnamon, anise seed and stir to mix well.
4. Scrape the batter into the prepared baking pan. Slide the baking pan into Rack Position 1, select Convection Bake and set time to 20 minutes.
5. Take the cake to a wire rack and let cool to room temperature. Serve right away.

Soft Chocolate Molten Cake, page 136

Fast Chocolate S'mores, page 137

Healthy Banana and Walnut Cake, page 141

Sweet Chocolate Donuts, page 134

## Chocolate Pineapple Cake

Prep time: 10 minutes | Cook time: 35 minutes |
Serves 4

½ pound (227 g)
pineapple, chopped
2 cups flour
1 large egg
4 ounces (113 g) butter,
melted

½ cup pineapple juice
¼ cup sugar
1 ounce (28 g) dark
chocolate, grated
2 tbsps. skimmed milk

1. Preheat the air fryer oven to 370ºF (188ºC).
2. Grease a cake tin with a little olive oil or butter.
3. Combine the butter and flour in a bowl to create a
   crumbly consistency.
4. Place the sugar, chopped pineapple, pineapple juice,
   and grated dark chocolate and mix well.
5. Combine the egg and milk in a separate bowl. Put
   this mixture to the flour mixture and stir well until a
   soft dough forms.
6. Place the mixture into the cake tin. Slide the baking
   pan into Rack Position 1, select Convection Bake and
   set time to 35 minutes.
7. Serve hot.

## Orange Almond Cake

Prep time: 5 minutes | Cook time: 17 minutes |
Serves 6

Cooking spray
1 stick butter, melted
2 eggs, beaten
1¼ cups almond flour
¾ cup coconut flour
¾ cup granulated Swerve

⅓ cup coconut milk
2 tbsps. unsweetened
orange jam
½ tsp. baking powder
⅓ tsp. grated nutmeg
¼ tsp. salt

1. Preheat the air fryer oven to 355ºF (179ºC). Spray a
   baking pan lightly with cooking spray. Keep aside.
2. Whisk together the melted butter and granulated
   Swerve in a large mixing bowl, until fluffy.
3. Mix in the beaten eggs and whisk again until smooth.
   Stir in the coconut flour, salt, and nutmeg and
   gently pour in the coconut milk. Place the remaining
   ingredients and stir until well incorporated.
4. Scrape the batter into the baking pan.
5. Slide the baking pan into Rack Position 1, select
   Convection Bake and set time to 17 minutes, until
   the top of the cake springs back when gently pressed
   with your fingers.
6. Transfer from the air fryer oven to a wire rack to cool.
   Serve at room temperature.

## Unsweetened Chocolate Coconut Cake

Prep time: 5 minutes | Cook time: 15 minutes |
Serves 10

Cooking spray
2 eggs, beaten
1¼ cups unsweetened
bakers' chocolate

⅓ cup shredded coconut
1 stick butter
2 tbsps. coconut milk
1 tsp. liquid stevia

1. Preheat the air fryer oven to 330ºF (166ºC). Spray a
   baking pan lightly with cooking spray.
2. In a microwave-safe bowl, place the chocolate,
   butter, and stevia. Microwave for 30 seconds until
   melted. Let the chocolate mixture stand to room
   temperature.
3. Pour the remaining ingredients into the chocolate
   mixture and stir until well incorporated. Place the
   batter into the prepared baking pan.
4. Slide the baking pan into Rack Position 1, select
   Convection Bake and set time to 15 minutes, until a
   toothpick inserted in the center comes out clean.
5. Transfer from the air fryer oven and let cool for about
   10 minutes before serving.

## Coconut Chocolate Cake

Prep time: 5 minutes | Cook time: 15 minutes |
Serves 6

Cooking spray
2 eggs, whisked
1½ cups coconut flour
½ cup unsweetened
chocolate, chopped

½ stick butter, at room
temperature
1 tbsp. liquid stevia
½ tsp. vanilla extract
A pinch of fine sea salt

1. In a microwave-safe bowl, place the chocolate,
   butter, and stevia. Microwave for 30 seconds until
   melted.
2. Allow the chocolate mixture to cool for about 5 to 10
   minutes.
3. Place the remaining ingredients to the bowl of
   chocolate mixture and whisk to incorporate well.
4. Preheat the air fryer oven to 330ºF (166ºC). Spritz a
   baking pan lightly with cooking spray.
5. Scrape the chocolate mixture into the prepared
   baking pan.
6. Slide the baking pan into Rack Position 1, select
   Convection Bake and set time to 15 minutes, until
   the top springs back lightly when gently pressed with
   your fingers.
7. Allow the cake to cool for 5 minutes and serve warm.

## Lemony Blackberry Granola Crisp

Prep time: 5 minutes | Cook time: 20 minutes | Serves 1

| | |
|---|---|
| 2 tbsps. lemon juice | ⅓ cup powdered |
| 2 cup blackberries | erythritol |
| 1 cup crunchy granola | ¼ tsp. xantham gum |

1. Preheat the air fryer oven to 350ºF (177ºC).
2. Combine the lemon juice, erythritol, xantham gum, and blackberries in a bowl. Take to a baking pan and cover with aluminum foil.
3. Slide the baking pan into Rack Position 1, select Convection Bake and set time to 12 minutes.
4. Remove from the air fryer oven. Give the blackberries a good stir and add the granola.
5. Take the granola back to the air fryer oven and bake for another 3 minutes, this time at 320ºF (160ºC). It's okay once the granola has turned brown. Serve warm.

## Fluffy Orange Cake

Prep time: 10 minutes | Cook time: 23 minutes | Serves 8

| | |
|---|---|
| Nonstick baking spray with flour | ¾ cup white sugar |
| ¼ cup safflower oil | ⅓ cup yellow cornmeal |
| 1¼ cups all-purpose flour | ¼ cup powdered sugar |
| 1¼ cups orange juice, divided | 1 tsp. vanilla |
| | 1 tsp. baking soda |

1. Preheat the air fryer oven to 350ºF (177ºC).
2. Spritz a baking pan lightly with nonstick spray and keep aside.
3. Combine the flour, cornmeal, sugar, baking soda, safflower oil, 1 cup of the orange juice, and vanilla in a medium bowl and mix well.
4. Place the batter into the baking pan. Slide the baking pan into Rack Position 1, select Convection Bake and set time to 23 minutes, until a toothpick inserted in the center of the cake comes out clean.
5. Transfer the cake from the oven and place on a cooling rack. With a toothpick, make about 20 holes in the cake.
6. Combine remaining ¼ cup of orange juice and the powdered sugar in a small bowl, and stir well. Drizzle this mixture over the hot cake slowly so the cake absorbs it.
7. Allow to cool completely, then slice into wedges to serve.

## Curry Pears, Peaches and Plums

Prep time: 5 minutes | Cook time: 6 minutes | Serves 6 to 8

| | |
|---|---|
| 2 tbsps. melted butter | 2 plums |
| 2 firm pears | 1 tbsp. honey |
| 2 peaches | 2 to 3 tsps. curry powder |

1. Preheat the air fryer oven to 325ºF (163ºC).
2. Cut the peaches in half, remove the pits, and cut each half in half again. Cut the pears in half, core them, and remove the stem. Cut each half in half again. Do the same with the plums.
3. On the work surface, spread a large sheet of heavy-duty foil. Place the fruit on the foil and drizzle with the butter and honey. Scatter with the curry powder to taste.
4. Wrap the fruit in the foil, making sure to leave some air space in the packet.
5. Place the foil package in the baking pan. Slide the baking pan into Rack Position 1, select Convection Bake and set time to 6 minutes, until the fruit is soft.
6. Serve hot.

## Black and White Chocolate Brownies

Prep time: 10 minutes | Cook time: 20 minutes | Makes 1 dozen brownies

| | |
|---|---|
| Nonstick cooking spray | chips |
| 1 egg | ¼ cup brown sugar |
| ⅓ cup all-purpose flour | 2 tbsps. white sugar |
| ¼ cup cocoa powder | 2 tbsps. safflower oil |
| ¼ cup white chocolate | 1 tsp. vanilla |

1. Preheat the air fryer oven to 340ºF (171ºC). Spray a baking pan lightly with nonstick cooking spray.
2. In a medium bowl, whisk together the egg, brown sugar, and white sugar. Mix in the safflower oil and vanilla and stir to combine well.
3. Place the flour and cocoa powder and stir just until incorporated. Gently fold in the white chocolate chips.
4. Scrape the batter into the prepared baking pan.
5. Slide the baking pan into Rack Position 1, select Convection Bake and set time to 20 minutes, until the brownie springs back when touched lightly with your fingers.
6. Take to a wire rack and allow to cool for about 30 minutes before slicing to serve.

## Lemony Ricotta Cake

Prep time: 5 minutes | Cook time: 25 minutes |
Serves 6

| | |
|---|---|
| 17.5 ounces (496 g) ricotta cheese | 1 lemon, juiced and zested |
| 3 eggs, beaten | 3 tbsps. flour |
| 5.4 ounces (153 g) sugar | 2 tsps. vanilla extract |

1. Preheat the air fryer oven to 320ºF (160ºC).
2. Stir together all the ingredients in a large mixing bowl until the mixture reaches a creamy consistency.
3. Place the mixture into a baking pan. Slide the baking pan into Rack Position 1, select Convection Bake and set time to 25 minutes. until a toothpick inserted in the center comes out clean.
4. Let cool for 10 minutes on a wire rack before serving.

## Cinnamon Pumpkin Pudding

Prep time: 10 minutes | Cook time: 15 minutes |
Serves 4

| | |
|---|---|
| 3 cups pumpkin purée | 1 tbsp. ginger |
| 2 eggs | 1 tbsp. cinnamon |
| 1 cup full-fat cream | 1 tsp. nutmeg |
| 1 cup sugar | 1 tsp. clove |
| 3 tbsps. honey | |

1. Preheat the air fryer oven to 390ºF (199ºC).
2. Stir all the ingredients together to combine in a bowl.
3. Scrape the mixture into a greased baking pan. Slide the baking pan into Rack Position 1, select Convection Bake and set time to 15 minutes. Serve hot.

## Candied Apples

Prep time: 15 minutes | Cook time: 12 minutes |
Serves 4

| | |
|---|---|
| 2 medium Granny Smith apples, peeled and diced | sugar |
| 1 cup packed light brown | 2 tsps. ground cinnamon |

1. Preheat the air fryer oven to 350ºF (177ºC).
2. In a medium bowl, thoroughly combine the brown sugar and cinnamon.
3. Place the apples to the bowl and stir until evenly coated. Take the apples to a baking pan.
4. Slide the baking pan into Rack Position 1, select Convection Bake and set time to 9 minutes. Stir the apples once and bake for another 3 minutes until softened.
5. Serve hot.

## Healthy Banana and Walnut Cake

Prep time: 10 minutes | Cook time: 25 minutes |
Serves 6

| | |
|---|---|
| 2.5 ounces (71 g) butter, melted | 8 ounces (227 g) flour |
| 1 pound (454 g) bananas, mashed | 6 ounces (170 g) sugar |
| | 3.5 ounces (99 g) walnuts, chopped |
| 2 eggs, lightly beaten | ¼ tsp. baking soda |

1. Preheat the air fryer oven to 355ºF (179ºC).
2. In a bowl, combine the butter, flour, sugar, egg, and baking soda with a whisk. Stir in the bananas and walnuts.
3. Take the mixture to a greased baking pan. Slide the baking pan into Rack Position 1, select Convection Bake and set time to 10 minutes.
4. Lower the temperature to 330ºF (166ºC) and bake for an additional 15 minutes. Serve warm.

## Traditional Pound Cake

Prep time: 5 minutes | Cook time: 30 minutes |
Serves 8

| | |
|---|---|
| Cooking spray | ½ tsp. baking powder |
| 1 stick butter, at room temperature | ½ tsp. baking soda |
| | ¼ tsp. salt |
| 4 eggs | A pinch of ground star anise |
| 1½ cups coconut flour | |
| 1 cup Swerve | A pinch of freshly grated nutmeg |
| ½ cup buttermilk | |
| 1 tsp. vanilla essence | |

1. Preheat the air fryer oven to 320ºF (160ºC). Spritz a baking pan lightly with cooking spray.
2. Beat the butter and Swerve with an electric mixer or hand mixer, until creamy. One at a time, mix in the eggs and whisk until fluffy. Place the remaining ingredients and stir to combine well.
3. Take the batter to the prepared baking pan. Slide the baking pan into Rack Position 1, select Convection Bake and set time to 30 minutes, until the center of the cake is springy. Rotate the pan halfway through the cooking time.
4. Let the cake cool in the pan for about 10 minutes before removing and serving.

## Buttery Blackberry Cobbler

Prep time: 15 minutes | Cook time: 22 to 27 minutes | Serves 6

| | |
|---|---|
| Cooking spray | 1 cup self-rising flour |
| 3 cups fresh or frozen blackberries | 8 tbsps. (1 stick) butter, melted |
| 1¾ cups sugar, divided | 1 tsp. vanilla extract |

1. Preheat the air fryer oven to 350ºF (177ºC). Spray a baking pan lightly with cooking spray.
2. In a medium bowl, mix the blackberries, 1 cup of sugar, and vanilla and stir to combine well.
3. In a separate medium bowl, stir together the melted butter, remaining sugar, and flour.
4. Lay the blackberry mixture evenly in the prepared pan and top with the butter mixture.
5. Slide the baking pan into Rack Position 1, select Convection Bake and set time to 22 minutes. Check for doneness and bake for an additional 5 minutes, if needed.
6. Transfer from the air fryer oven and put on a wire rack to cool to room temperature. Serve right away.

## Chocolate Bread Pudding

Prep time: 10 minutes | Cook time: 10 minutes | Serves 8

| | |
|---|---|
| Nonstick cooking spray | ¾ cup chocolate milk |
| 5 slices firm white bread, cubed | 3 tbsps. peanut butter |
| 1 egg | 3 tbsps. brown sugar |
| 1 egg yolk | 2 tbsps. cocoa powder |
| | 1 tsp. vanilla |

1. Preheat the air fryer oven to 330ºF (166ºC). Spray a baking pan lightly with nonstick cooking spray.
2. In a large bowl, whisk together the egg, egg yolk, chocolate milk, brown sugar, peanut butter, cocoa powder, and vanilla until well combined.
3. Gently fold in the bread cubes and stir to mix well. Let the bread soak for about 10 minutes.
4. When ready, take the egg mixture to the prepared baking pan.
5. Slide the baking pan into Rack Position 1, select Convection Bake and set time to 10 minutes, until the pudding is just firm to the touch.
6. Serve when cool.

## Golden Pineapple Rings

Prep time: 5 minutes | Cook time: 6 to 8 minutes | Serves 6

| | |
|---|---|
| 1 medium pineapple, peeled and sliced | 4 tbsps. sugar |
| 1 cup rice milk | ½ tsp. baking soda |
| ⅔ cup flour | ½ tsp. baking powder |
| ¼ cup unsweetened flaked coconut | ½ tsp. ground cinnamon |
| ½ cup water | ½ tsp. vanilla essence |
| | ¼ tsp. ground anise star |
| | Pinch of kosher salt |

1. Preheat the air fryer oven to 380ºF (193ºC).
2. Stir together all the ingredients except the pineapple in a large bowl.
3. Dunk each pineapple slice into the batter until well coated.
4. Arrange the pineapple slices in the air fryer basket. Then place the air fryer basket onto the baking pan, and slide the baking pan into Rack Position 2, select Air Fry and set time to 8 minutes.
5. Transfer from the oven to a plate and let cool for 5 minutes before serving.

## Glazed Apple Wedges with Apricots

Prep time: 5 minutes | Cook time: 16 minutes | Serves 4

| | |
|---|---|
| 2 tbsps. olive oil | chopped |
| 4 large apples, peeled and sliced into 8 wedges | 1 to 2 tbsps. sugar |
| ½ cup dried apricots, | ½ tsp. ground cinnamon |

1. Preheat the air fryer oven to 350ºF (180ºC).
2. In a mixing bowl, toss the apple wedges with the olive oil until well coated.
3. Arrange the apple wedges in the in the air fryer basket. Then place the air fryer basket onto the baking pan, and slide the baking pan into Rack Position 2, select Air Fry and set time to 13 minutes.
4. Scatter with the dried apricots and air fry for an additional 3 minutes.
5. At the same time, thoroughly combine the sugar and cinnamon in a small bowl.
6. Transfer the apple wedges from the oven to a plate. Sprinkle with the sugar mixture and serve warm.

## Simple Coconut Pineapple Sticks

Prep time: 5 minutes | Cook time: 10 minutes | Serves 4

½ fresh pineapple, cut into sticks                    ¼ cup desiccated coconut

1. Preheat the air fryer oven to 400ºF (204ºC).
2. Coat the pineapple sticks in the desiccated coconut and put each one in the air fryer basket. Then place the air fryer basket onto the baking pan, and slide the baking pan into Rack Position 2, select Air Fry and set time to 10 minutes.
3. Serve warm.

## Coconut Chia Pudding

Prep time: 5 minutes | Cook time: 4 minutes | Serves 2

1 tbsp. coconut oil                    1 tsp. butter, melted
1 cup chia seeds                       1 tsp. liquid stevia
1 cup unsweetened coconut milk

1. Preheat the fryer to 360ºF (182ºC).
2. In a large bowl, mix together the chia seeds, coconut milk, and stevia. Pour in the coconut oil and melted butter and stir until well blended.
3. Distribute the mixture evenly between the ramekins, filling only about ⅔ of the way.
4. Put the ramekins in the baking pan. Slide the baking pan into Rack Position 1, select Convection Bake and set time to 4 minutes.
5. Let cool for 5 minutes and serve immediately.

## Beet and Mixed Greens Salad

Prep time: 10 minutes | Cook time: 14 minutes | Serves 4

Cooking spray
1 tsp. olive oil
6 medium red and golden beets, peeled and sliced
8 cups mixed greens
½ cup crumbled feta cheese
¼ tsp. kosher salt
**Vinaigrette:**
2 tsps. olive oil
Juice of 1 lemon
2 tbsps. chopped fresh chives

1. Preheat the air fryer oven to 360ºF (182ºC).
2. Toss the beets, olive oil, and kosher salt in a large bowl.
3. Spritz the air fryer basket lightly with cooking spray, then put the beets in the air fryer basket. Place the air fryer basket onto the baking pan, and slide the baking pan into Rack Position 2, select Air Fry and set time to 14 minutes, until tender.
4. When the beets cook, make the vinaigrette by whisking together the olive oil, lemon juice, and chives in a large bowl.
5. Transfer the beets from the air fryer oven, toss in the vinaigrette, and let cool for about 5 minutes. Place the feta and serve on top of the mixed greens.

## Spinach Spanakopita

Prep time: 5 minutes | Cook time: 25 minutes | Serves 6

6 sheets phyllo dough
½ (10-ounce / 284-g) package frozen spinach, thawed and squeezed dry
1 egg, lightly beaten
½ cup butter, melted
¾ cup crumbled feta
cheese
¼ cup grated Parmesan cheese
¼ cup pine nuts, toasted
⅛ tsp. ground nutmeg
½ tsp. salt
Freshly ground black pepper, to taste

1. In a large bowl, combine all the ingredients, except for the phyllo dough and butter. Whisk to combine well. Keep aside.
2. On a clean work surface, place a sheet of phyllo dough. Brush with melted butter then top with another layer sheet of phyllo. Brush with melted butter, then slice the layered sheets into six 3-inch-wide strips.
3. Top each strip with 1 tbsp. of the spinach mixture, then gently fold the bottom left corner over the mixture towards the right strip edge to make a triangle. Keep folding triangles until each strip is folded over.
4. Coat the triangles with butter and repeat with remaining strips and phyllo dough.
5. Preheat the air fryer oven to 350ºF (177ºC).
6. Arrange six triangles in the baking pan. Slide the baking pan into Rack Position 1, select Convection Bake and set time to 8 minutes. Gently flip the triangles halfway through. Repeat this process with the remaining triangles.
7. Serve hot.

## Chili Purple Potato Chips with Rosemary

Prep time: 10 minutes | Cook time: 12 minutes | Serves 6

1 tsp. olive oil
10 purple fingerling potatoes
1 cup Greek yogurt
2 chipotle chiles, minced
2 tbsps. adobo sauce
1 tbsp. lemon juice
2 tsps. minced fresh rosemary leaves
1 tsp. paprika
¼ tsp. coarse sea salt
⅛ tsp. cayenne pepper

1. Preheat the air fryer oven to 400ºF (204ºC).
2. Combine the yogurt, minced chiles, adobo sauce, paprika, and lemon juice in a medium bowl. Mix well and refrigerate.
3. Wash the potatoes and pat them with paper towels to dry. Using a mandoline, a vegetable peeler, or a very sharp knife, slice the potatoes lengthwise, as thinly as possible.
4. In a medium bowl, combine the potato slices and drizzle with the olive oil; toss to coat well.
5. Working in batches, put the chips in the air fryer basket. Then place the air fryer basket onto the baking pan, and slide the baking pan into Rack Position 2, select Air Fry and set time to 12 minutes. Use tongs to carefully rearrange the chips halfway during the cooking time.
6. Scatter the chips with the rosemary, cayenne pepper, and sea salt. Serve hot with the chipotle sauce for dipping.

## Garlicky Parsnip Fries with Yogurt Dip

Prep time: 10 minutes | Cook time: 10 minutes | Serves 4

Cooking spray
1 tsp. olive oil
3 medium parsnips, peeled, cut into sticks
1 garlic clove, unpeeled
¼ tsp. kosher salt
**Dip:**

¼ cup plain Greek yogurt
1 tbsp. sour cream
⅛ tsp. garlic powder
¼ tsp. kosher salt
Freshly ground black pepper, to taste

1. Preheat the air fryer oven to 360ºF (182ºC). Spray the air fryer basket lightly with cooking spray.
2. In a large bowl, put the parsnip sticks, then season with salt and drizzle with olive oil.
3. Place the parsnip in the air fryer basket. Put the air fryer basket onto the baking pan, and slide the baking pan into Rack Position 2, select Air Fry and set time to 5 minutes. Remove the garlic from the air fryer oven and flip. Air fry for another 5 minutes or until the parsnip sticks are crisp.
4. At the same time, peel the garlic and crush it. Mix the crushed garlic with the ingredients for the dip. Stir to combine well.
5. When the frying is complete, transfer the parsnip fries from the air fryer oven and serve warm with the dipping sauce.

## Glazed Apple Fritters

Prep time: 5 minutes | Cook time: 25 minutes | Makes 15 fritters

**Apple Fritters:**
Cooking spray
2 firm apples, peeled, cored, and diced
1 cup all-purpose flour
2 eggs
¼ cup milk
Juice of 1 lemon
2 tbsps. unsalted butter, melted

2 tbsps. granulated sugar
1½ tsps. baking powder
½ tsp. cinnamon
½ tsp. kosher salt
**Glaze:**
1¼ cups powdered sugar, sifted
¼ cup water
½ tsp. vanilla extract

1. Preheat the air fryer oven to 360ºF (182ºC). Line the air fryer basket with parchment paper.
2. In a small bowl, combine the apples with cinnamon and lemon juice. Toss to coat evenly.
3. In a large bowl, combine the flour, baking powder, and salt. Stir to mix well.

4. In a medium bowl, whisk the egg, milk, butter, and sugar. Stir to mix well.
5. Make a well in the center of the flour mixture, then pour the egg mixture into the well and stir to combine well. Mix in the apple until a dough forms.
6. With an ice cream scoop, scoop 5 balls from the dough in the air fryer basket. Spray lightly with cooking spray.
7. Place the air fryer basket onto the baking pan, and slide the baking pan into Rack Position 2, select Air Fry and set time to 8 minutes. Flip the fritters halfway through. Transfer the fritters from the air fryer oven and repeat with the remaining dough.
8. At the same time, mix the ingredients for the glaze in a separate small bowl. Stir to combine well.
9. Top with the glaze and serve the fritters hot.

## Shrimp, Sausage and Corn Bake

Prep time: 10 minutes | Cook time: 18 minutes | Serves 2

2 tsps. vegetable oil, divided
1 ear corn, husk and silk removed, cut into 2-inch rounds
8 ounces (227 g) red potatoes, unpeeled, cut into 1-inch pieces
8 ounces (227 g) large shrimps (about 12 shrimps), deveined

6 ounces (170 g) andouille or chorizo sausage, cut into 1-inch pieces
2 garlic cloves, minced
1 tbsp. chopped fresh parsley
2 tsps. Old Bay Seasoning, divided
¼ tsp. ground black pepper

1. Preheat the air fryer oven to 400ºF (204ºC).
2. In a large bowl, put the corn rounds and potatoes. Scatter with 1 tsp. of Old Bay seasoning and drizzle with vegetable oil. Toss to coat evenly.
3. Take the corn rounds and potatoes on a baking pan. Slide the baking pan into Rack Position 1, select Convection Bake and set time to 12 minutes, flipping halfway through the cooking time.
4. At the same time, cut slits into the shrimps but be careful not to cut them through. Combine the sausage, shrimps, remaining Old Bay seasoning, and remaining vegetable oil in the large bowl. Toss to coat well.
5. When the baking of the potatoes and corn rounds is complete, place the shrimps and sausage and bake for 6 more minutes or until the shrimps are opaque. Flip halfway through the cooking time.
6. When the baking is finished, transfer them to a plate and spread with parsley before serving.

## Crispy Air Fried Brussels Sprouts

Prep time: 5 minutes | Cook time: 20 minutes | Serves 4

| | |
|---|---|
| 1 tbsp. extra-virgin olive oil | Lemon wedges, for garnish |
| 1 pound (454 g) Brussels sprouts, trimmed and halved | ¼ tsp. salt |
| | ⅛ tsp. ground black pepper |

1. Preheat the air fryer oven to 350ºF (177ºC).
2. In a large bowl, combine the salt, black pepper, and olive oil. Stir to mix well.
3. Place the Brussels sprouts to the bowl of mixture and toss to coat evenly.
4. Spread the Brussels sprouts in the air fryer basket. Then place the air fryer basket onto the baking pan, and slide the baking pan into Rack Position 2, select Air Fry and set time to 20 minutes, flipping two times during the cooking time.
5. Take the cooked Brussels sprouts to a large plate and squeeze the lemon wedges on top. Serve warm.

## Golden Salmon, Carrot and Onion Croquettes

Prep time: 15 minutes | Cook time: 10 minutes | Serves 6

| | |
|---|---|
| Cooking spray | breadcrumbs |
| 1 pound (454 g) chopped salmon fillet | ⅔ cup grated carrots |
| 2 egg whites | ½ cup chopped onion |
| 1 cup almond flour | 2 tbsps. minced garlic cloves |
| 1 cup panko | 2 tbsps. chopped chives |

1. Preheat the air fryer oven to 350ºF (177ºC). Spray the air fryer basket lightly with cooking spray.
2. In a bowl, whisk the egg whites. Place the flour in a second bowl. Pour the breadcrumbs in a third bowl. Keep aside.
3. In a large bowl, combine the salmon, carrots, garlic, onion, and chives. Stir to mix well.
4. Shape the mixture into balls with your hands. Dredge the balls into the flour, then egg, and then breadcrumbs to coat evenly.
5. Place the salmon balls in the air fryer basket and spray with cooking spray.
6. Put the air fryer basket onto the baking pan, and slide the baking pan into Rack Position 2, select Air Fry and set time to 10 minutes, flipping halfway through.
7. Serve hot.

## Fast Devils on Horseback

Prep time: 5 minutes | Cook time: 7 minutes | Serves 12

24 petite pitted prunes (4½ ounces / 128 g)
8 slices center-cut bacon, cut crosswise into thirds
¼ cup crumbled blue cheese, divided

1. Preheat the air fryer oven to 400ºF (204ºC).
2. Halve the prunes lengthwise, but don't cut them all the way through. Put ½ tsp. of cheese in the center of each prune. Wrap a piece of bacon around each prune and secure the bacon tightly with a toothpick.
3. Working in batches, place a single layer of the prunes in air fryer basket. Then put the air fryer basket onto the baking pan, and slide the baking pan into Rack Position 2, select Air Fry and set time to 7 minutes, flipping halfway.
4. Allow to cool slightly and serve immediately.

## Baked Halloumi Cheese with Greek Salsa

Prep time: 15 minutes | Cook time: 6 minutes | Serves 4

| | |
|---|---|
| **Salsa:** | 1 tsp. freshly cracked black pepper |
| ½ cup finely diced English cucumber | 1 tsp. snipped fresh dill |
| 1 plum tomato, deseeded and finely diced | 1 tsp. snipped fresh oregano |
| 1 small shallot, finely diced | Pinch of kosher salt |
| 3 garlic cloves, minced | **Cheese:** |
| 2 tbsps. fresh lemon juice | 1 tbsp. extra-virgin olive oil |
| 2 tbsps. extra-virgin olive oil | 8 ounces (227 g) Halloumi cheese, sliced into ½-inch-thick pieces |
| 2 tsps. chopped fresh parsley | |

1. Preheat the air fryer oven to 375ºF (191ºC).
2. For the salsa: In a medium bowl, combine the shallot, garlic, lemon juice, olive oil, pepper, and salt. Place the cucumber, tomato, parsley, dill, and oregano. Toss to combine well and set aside.
3. For the cheese: In a medium bowl, place the cheese slices. Drizzle with the olive oil. Toss gently to coat. Spread the cheese in a single layer in the baking pan. Slide the baking pan into Rack Position 1, select Convection Bake and set time to 6 minutes.
4. Distribute the cheese among four serving plates. Top with the salsa and serve right away.

## Chile Mexican Street Corn

Prep time: 5 minutes | Cook time: 7 minutes | Serves 4

| | |
|---|---|
| Cooking spray | cilantro |
| 4 medium ears corn, husked | 2 tbsps. mayonnaise |
| | 1 tbsp. fresh lime juice |
| 2 ounces (57 g) crumbled Cotija or feta cheese | ½ tsp. ancho chile powder |
| 2 tbsps. chopped fresh | ¼ tsp. kosher salt |

1. Preheat the air fryer oven to 375ºF (191ºC).
2. Spray the corn lightly with cooking spray. Working in batches, place the ears of corn in the air fryer basket in a single layer. Put the air fryer basket onto the baking pan, and slide the baking pan into Rack Position 2, select Air Fry and set time to 7 minutes, flipping halfway. When cool enough to handle, cut the corn kernels off the cob.
3. Mix together mayonnaise, lime juice, ancho powder, and salt in a large bowl. Place the corn kernels and mix to combine well. Take to a serving dish and place the Cotija and cilantro on top. Serve hot.

## Cheddar Bacon-Wrapped Jalapeño Poppers

Prep time: 5 minutes | Cook time: 12 minutes | Serves 6

| | |
|---|---|
| 6 large jalapeños | ¼ cup shredded reduced-fat sharp Cheddar cheese |
| 4 ounces (113 g) ⅓-less-fat cream cheese | |
| 6 slices center-cut bacon, halved | 2 scallions, green tops only, sliced |

1. Preheat the air fryer oven to 325ºF (163ºC).
2. Wearing rubber gloves, halve the jalapeños lengthwise to make 12 pieces. Spoon out the seeds and membranes and discard.
3. Combine the cream cheese, Cheddar, and scallions in a medium bowl. Fill the jalapeños with the cream cheese filling with a small spoon or spatula. Wrap a bacon strip around each pepper and secure tightly with a toothpick.
4. Working in batches, put the stuffed peppers in a single layer in the baking pan. Slide the baking pan into Rack Position 1, select Convection Bake and set time to 12 minutes, until the peppers are soft, the bacon is browned and crisp, and the cheese is melted.
5. Serve hot.

## Parmesan Shrimps

Prep time: 10 minutes | Cook time: 16 minutes | Serves 4 to 6

| | |
|---|---|
| Cooking spray | 1 tsp. onion powder |
| 2 tbsps. olive oil | 1 tsp. basil |
| 2 pounds (907 g) cooked large shrimps, peeled and deveined | Lemon wedges, for topping |
| ⅔ cup grated Parmesan cheese | ½ tsp. oregano |
| 4 minced garlic cloves | 1 tsp. ground black pepper |

1. Preheat the air fryer oven to 350ºF (177ºC). Spray a baking pan lightly with cooking spray.
2. In a large bowl, combine all the ingredients, except for the shrimps. Stir to mix well.
3. Dip the shrimps in the mixture and toss to coat evenly. Shake the excess off.
4. Place the shrimps in the baking pan. Slide the baking pan into Rack Position 2, select Roast and set time to 8 minutes. Turn the shrimps halfway through. You may need to cook in batches to avoid overcrowding.
5. Take the cooked shrimps on a large plate and squeeze the lemon wedges over before serving.

## Cheesy Jalapeño Poppers with Bacon

Prep time: 5 minutes | Cook time: 25 minutes | Serves 6

| | |
|---|---|
| 6 large jalapeños, halved lengthwise and deseeded | Cheddar cheese |
| ¾ cup whole milk ricotta cheese | ½ cup finely crushed potato chips |
| 2 slices bacon, halved | 1 green onion, finely chopped |
| ½ cup shredded sharp | ¼ tsp. salt |

1. Preheat the air fryer oven to 400ºF (204ºC).
2. Put the bacon in single layer in the air fryer basket. Place the air fryer basket onto the baking pan, and slide the baking pan into Rack Position 2, select Air Fry and set time to 5 minutes. Remove bacon and put on paper towels to drain. When cool, finely chop.
3. In a medium bowl, stir together ricotta, Cheddar, green onion, bacon, and salt. Scoop into jalapeños and top with potato chips.
4. Arrange half the jalapeños in the air fryer basket and air fry for 8 minutes, or until soft. Repeat this process with the remaining jalapeños.
5. Serve warm.

## Authentic Queso Fundido

Prep time: 10 minutes | Cook time: 25 minutes |
Serves 4

2 cups shredded Oaxaca
or Mozzarella cheese
1 cup chopped tomato
4 ounces (113 g) fresh
Mexican chorizo, casings
removed
1 medium onion,
chopped

2 jalapeños, deseeded
and diced
½ cup half-and-half
3 cloves garlic, minced
2 tsps. ground cumin
Celery sticks or tortilla
chips, for serving

1. Preheat the air fryer oven to 400ºF (204ºC).
2. Combine the chorizo, onion, garlic, tomato,
   jalapeños, and cumin in the air fryer basket. Stir to
   combine well.
3. Place the air fryer basket onto the baking pan, and
   slide the baking pan into Rack Position 2, select
   Air Fry and set time to 15 minutes, stirring halfway
   through the cooking time to break up the sausage.
4. Put the cheese and half-and-half and stir to combine
   well. Air fry for about 10 minutes, or until the cheese
   has melted.
5. Serve hot with celery sticks or tortilla chips.

## Healthy Sweet Potato Soufflé

Prep time: 10 minutes | Cook time: 30 minutes |
Serves 4

1 sweet potato, baked
and mashed
1 large egg, separated
¼ cup whole milk

2 tbsps. unsalted butter,
divided
½ tsp. kosher salt

1. Preheat the air fryer oven to 330ºF (166ºC).
2. Combine the sweet potato, 1 tbsp. of melted butter,
   egg yolk, milk, and salt in a medium bowl. Keep
   aside.
3. Whisk the egg white in a separate medium bowl,
   until stiff peaks form.
4. With a spatula, carefully fold the egg white into the
   sweet potato mixture.
5. Brush the inside of four 3-inch ramekins with the
   remaining 1 tbsp. of butter, then fill each ramekin
   halfway full. Put 2 ramekins in a baking pan. Slide the
   baking pan into Rack Position 1, select Convection
   Bake and set time to 15 minutes. Repeat with the
   remaining ramekins.
6. Transfer the ramekins from the air fryer oven and
   let cool on a wire rack for about 10 minutes before
   serving.

## Quick Baked Green Beans

Prep time: 5 minutes | Cook time: 10 minutes |
Makes 2 cups

1 tbsp. olive oil
2 cups fresh green
beans, trimmed and
snapped in half

2 tsps. granulated garlic
½ tsp. lemon pepper
½ tsp. salt

1. Preheat the air fryer oven to 370ºF (188ºC).
2. In a bowl, combine the lemon pepper, garlic, salt, and
   olive oil. Stir to mix well.
3. Place the green beans to the bowl of mixture and
   toss to coat well.
4. Put the green beans in the baking pan. Slide the
   baking pan into Rack Position 1, select Convection
   Bake and set time to 10 minutes, until tender and
   crispy. Flip halfway through to make sure the green
   beans are cooked evenly.
5. Serve hot.

## Garlicky Zoodles with Basil

Prep time: 10 minutes | Cook time: 10 minutes |
Serves 4

Cooking spray
1 tbsp. olive oil, divided
2 large yellow summer
squashes, peeled and
spiralized
2 large zucchinis, peeled

and spiralized
1 garlic clove, whole
2 tbsps. fresh basil,
chopped
½ tsp. kosher salt

1. Preheat the air fryer oven to 360ºF (182ºC). Spray
   the air fryer basket lightly with cooking spray.
2. In a large bowl, combine the zucchini and summer
   squash with 1 tsp. olive oil and salt. Toss to coat
   evenly.
3. Take the zucchini and summer squash in the air fryer
   basket and put the garlic.
4. Place the air fryer basket onto the baking pan, and
   slide the baking pan into Rack Position 2, select Air
   Fry and set time to 10 minutes, until tender and
   fragrant. Toss the spiralized zucchini and summer
   squash halfway through the cooking time.
5. Remove the cooked zucchini and summer squash
   onto a plate and keep aside.
6. Remove the garlic from the air fryer oven and let cool
   for a few minutes. In a small bowl, mince the garlic
   and combine with remaining olive oil. Stir to mix well.
7. Pour the garlic oil over the spiralized zucchini and
   summer squash and sprinkle with basil. Toss to serve
   warm.

Fried Chicken Wings, page 155

Parsley Knots, page 151

Indian Sweet Potato Fries, page 154

Baked Cherry Tomatoes with Basil, page 152

## Parsley Knots

Prep time: 10 minutes | Cook time: 10 minutes |
Makes 8 knots

1 (11-ounce / 312-g) tube
refrigerated French bread
dough, cut into 8 slices

¼ cup melted butter
2 tsps. garlic powder
1 tsp. dried parsley

1. Preheat the air fryer oven to 350ºF (177ºC).
2. In a bowl, combine the parsley, butter, and garlic
   powder. Stir to mix well.
3. On a clean work surface, place the French bread
   dough slices, then roll each slice into a 6-inch long
   rope. Tie the ropes into knots and put them on a
   plate. Coat the knots with butter mixture.
4. Take the knots into the baking pan. You need to cook
   in batches to avoid overcrowding.
5. Slide the baking pan into Rack Position 1, select
   Convection Bake and set time to 10 minutes, until
   the knots are golden brown. Gently flip the knots
   halfway through the cooking time.
6. Serve hot.

## Breaded Green Tomatoes

Prep time: 5 minutes | Cook time: 6 to 8 minutes |
Serves 4

2 tsps. olive oil
4 medium green
tomatoes
1 cup ground almonds
2 egg whites
½ cup panko bread

crumbs
⅓ cup all purpose flour
¼ cup almond milk
1 clove garlic, minced
1 tsp. paprika

1. Preheat the air fryer oven to 400ºF (204ºC).
2. Rinse the tomatoes and pat dry with paper towels.
   Cut the tomatoes into ½-inch slices, discarding the
   thinner ends.
3. Place the flour on a plate. Beat the egg whites with
   the almond milk in a shallow bowl, until frothy.
   And combine the almonds, bread crumbs, olive oil,
   paprika, and garlic on another plate, and mix well.
4. Dunk the tomato slices into the flour, then into the
   egg white mixture, then into the almond mixture to
   coat.
5. Arrange four of the coated tomato slices in the air
   fryer basket. Then place the air fryer basket onto
   the baking pan, and slide the baking pan into Rack
   Position 2, select Air Fry and set time to 7 minutes.
   Repeat this process with remaining tomato slices and
   serve hot.

## Garlicky Veggie Mix

Prep time: 10 minutes | Cook time: 15 minutes |
Serves 4

1 Yukon Gold potato,
thinly sliced
1 medium carrot, thinly
sliced
1 small sweet potato,
peeled and thinly sliced

¾ cup 2 percent milk
¼ cup minced onion
3 garlic cloves, minced
2 tbsps. cornstarch
½ tsp. dried thyme

1. Preheat the air fryer oven to 380ºF (193ºC).
2. Layer the potato, sweet potato, carrot, onion, and
   garlic in a baking pan.
3. Whisk the milk, cornstarch, and thyme in a small
   bowl until blended. Place the milk mixture evenly
   over the vegetables in the pan.
4. Slide the baking pan into Rack Position 2, select Roast
   and set time to 15 minutes. Check the casserole—it
   should be golden brown on top, and the vegetables
   should be soft.
5. Serve hot.

## Southwest Corn, Bell Pepper and Onion Roast

Prep time: 10 minutes | Cook time: 10 minutes |
Serves 4

**For the Corn:**
Cooking spray
1½ cups thawed frozen
corn kernels
1 cup mixed diced bell
peppers
1 cup diced yellow onion
1 jalapeño, diced
1 tbsp. fresh lemon juice

1 tsp. ground cumin
½ tsp. ancho chile
powder
½ tsp. kosher salt
**For Serving:**
¼ cup chopped fresh
cilantro
¼ cup feta cheese
1 tbsp. fresh lemon juice

1. Preheat the air fryer oven to 375ºF (191ºC). Spray
   the air fryer basket lightly with cooking spray.
2. In a large bowl, combine the ingredients for the corn.
   Stir to mix well.
3. Pour the mixture into the air fryer basket. Then place
   the air fryer basket onto the baking pan, and slide
   the baking pan into Rack Position 2, select Air Fry and
   set time to 10 minutes, flipping halfway through the
   cooking time.
4. Take them onto a large plate, then sprinkle with feta
   cheese and cilantro. Drizzle with lemon juice and
   serve hot.

## Simple Hot Wings

Prep time: 5 minutes | Cook time: 30 minutes | Makes 16 wings

3 tbsps. hot sauce    Cooking spray
16 chicken wings

1. Preheat the air fryer oven to 360ºF (182ºC). Spray the air fryer basket lightly with cooking spray.
2. Place the chicken wings in the air fryer basket. You need to cook in batches to avoid overcrowding.
3. Put the air fryer basket onto the baking pan, and slide the baking pan into Rack Position 2, select Air Fry and set time to 15 minutes, flipping at lease three times during the cooking time.
4. Take the air fried wings on a plate and serve warm with hot sauce.

## Broiled Carrot Chips with Parsley

Prep time: 5 minutes | Cook time: 15 minutes | Makes 3 cups

1 tbsp. olive oil    fresh parsley
3 large carrots, peeled  1 tbsp. granulated garlic
and sliced into long and  1 tsp. salt
thick chips diagonally  ¼ tsp. ground black
1 tbsp. finely chopped  pepper

1. Preheat the air fryer oven to 360ºF (182ºC).
2. In a large bowl, toss the carrots with garlic, salt, ground black pepper, and olive oil to coat well.
3. Arrange the carrots in the air fryer basket. Then place the air fryer basket onto the baking pan, and slide the baking pan into Rack Position 2, select Convection Broil and set time to 15 minutes, flipping halfway through.
4. Sprinkle with parsley on top and serve warm.

## Fast Cheesy Chile Toast

Prep time: 5 minutes | Cook time: 5 minutes | Serves 1

10 to 15 thin slices  2 tbsps. grated Parmesan
serrano chile or jalapeño  cheese
2 slices sourdough bread  2 tsps. salted butter, at
2 tbsps. grated  room temperature
Mozzarella cheese  ½ tsp. black pepper

1. Preheat the air fryer oven to 325ºF (163ºC).
2. Stir together the Parmesan, Mozzarella, butter, and chiles in a small bowl.
3. Spread half the mixture onto one side of each slice of bread. Scatter with the pepper. Arrange the slices, cheese-side up, in the baking pan. Slide the baking pan into Rack Position 2, select Toast and set time to 6 minutes, until the cheese has melted and started to brown slightly.
4. Serve hot.

## Spicy Old Bay Shrimp

Prep time: 7 minutes | Cook time: 10 minutes | Makes 2 cups

1 tbsp. olive oil    pepper
½ pound (227 g) shrimps,  ½ tsp. Old Bay
peeled and deveined  Seasoning
Juice of half a lemon  ½ tsp. paprika
1 tsp. ground cayenne  ⅛ tsp. salt

1. Preheat the air fryer oven to 390ºF (199ºC).
2. In a large bowl, combine the Old Bay Seasoning, cayenne pepper, paprika, olive oil, and salt, then add the shrimps and toss to coat well.
3. Arrange the shrimps in the air fryer basket. Then place the air fryer basket onto the baking pan, and slide the baking pan into Rack Position 2, select Air Fry and set time to 10 minutes. Gently flip the shrimps halfway through.
4. Pour lemon juice over the shrimps and serve warm.

## Baked Cherry Tomatoes with Basil

Prep time: 5 minutes | Cook time: 5 minutes | Serves 2

Cooking spray    sliced
1 tsp. olive oil  1 tbsp. freshly chopped
2 cups cherry tomatoes  basil, for topping
1 clove garlic, thinly  ⅛ tsp. kosher salt

1. Preheat the air fryer oven to 360ºF (182ºC). Spray the baking pan lightly with cooking spray and keep aside.
2. Toss together the cherry tomatoes, sliced garlic, olive oil, and kosher salt in a large bowl. Spread the mixture in an even layer in the prepared pan.
3. Slide the baking pan into Rack Position 1, select Convection Bake and set time to 5 minutes, until the tomatoes become tender and wilted.
4. Take to a bowl and let rest for about 5 minutes. Top with the chopped basil and serve immediately.

## Air Fried Okra Chips

Prep time: 5 minutes | Cook time: 16 minutes | Serves 6

2 tbsps. canola oil
2 pounds (907 g) fresh okra pods, cut into 1-inch
pieces
1 tsp. coarse sea salt

1. Preheat the air fryer oven to 400ºF (204ºC).
2. In a bowl, stir the oil and salt to mix well. Place the okra and toss to coat evenly.
3. Arrange the okra in the air fryer basket. Then place the air fryer basket onto the baking pan, and slide the baking pan into Rack Position 2, select Air Fry and set time to 16 minutes, until lightly browned. Flip at least three times during cooking.
4. Serve hot.

## Appetizing Sweet and Sour Peanuts

Prep time: 5 minutes | Cook time: 5 minutes | Serves 9

3 cups shelled raw peanuts
3 tbsps. granulated white sugar
1 tbsp. hot red pepper sauce

1. Preheat the air fryer oven to 400ºF (204ºC).
2. In a large bowl, put the peanuts, then drizzle with hot red pepper sauce and scatter with sugar. Toss to coat evenly.
3. Place the peanuts in the air fryer basket. Then put the air fryer basket onto the baking pan, and slide the baking pan into Rack Position 2, select Air Fry and set time to 5 minutes, flipping halfway through.
4. Serve hot.

## Easy Frico

Prep time: 5 minutes | Cook time: 5 minutes | Serves 2

1 cup shredded aged Manchego cheese
1 tsp. all-purpose flour
½ tsp. cumin seeds
¼ tsp. cracked black pepper

1. Preheat the air fryer oven to 375ºF (191ºC). Line a baking pan with parchment paper.
2. In a bowl, combine the cheese and flour. Stir to mix well. Spread the mixture in the baking pan into a 4-inch round.
3. In a small bowl, combine the cumin and black pepper.

Stir to mix well. Scatter the cumin mixture over the cheese round.
4. Slide the baking pan into Rack Position 1, select Convection Bake and set time to 5 minutes, until the cheese is lightly browned and frothy.
5. Transfer the cheese wafer onto a plate with tongs and slice to serve.

## Healthy Baked Cheese and Grits

Prep time: 10 minutes | Cook time: 12 minutes | Serves 6

1 tbsp. butter, melted
1 cup shredded Cheddar cheese or jalapeño Jack cheese
1 large egg, beaten
2 (1-ounce / 28-g)
packages instant grits
¾ cup hot water
2 cloves garlic, minced
½ to 1 tsp. red pepper flakes

1. Preheat the air fryer oven to 400ºF (204ºC).
2. Combine the water, grits, egg, butter, garlic, and red pepper flakes in a baking pan. Stir until combined well. Stir in the shredded cheese.
3. Slide the baking pan into Rack Position 1, select Convection Bake and set time to 12 minutes, until the grits have cooked through and a knife inserted near the center comes out clean.
4. Let sit for about 5 minutes before serving.

## Broiled Mushroom and Green Beans

Prep time: 10 minutes | Cook time: 16 minutes | Serves 4

1 tsp. olive oil
1 (8-ounce / 227-g) package sliced mushrooms
1 cup green beans, cut into 2-inch pieces
1 red bell pepper, sliced
⅓ cup diced red onion
3 garlic cloves, sliced
½ tsp. dried basil
½ tsp. dried tarragon

1. Preheat the air fryer oven to 350ºF (177ºC).
2. Mix the red bell pepper, mushrooms, green beans, red onion, and garlic in a medium bowl. Drizzle with the olive oil. Toss to coat well.
3. Put the herbs and toss again.
4. Arrange the vegetables in the air fryer basket. Then place the air fryer basket onto the baking pan, and slide the baking pan into Rack Position 2, select Convection Broil and set time to 16 minutes. Serve hot.

## Lemony Asparagus

Prep time: 5 minutes | Cook time: 10 minutes | Makes 10 spears

Cooking spray
10 spears asparagus (about ½ pound / 227 g in total), snap the ends off

1 tbsp. lemon juice
2 tsps. minced garlic
½ tsp. salt
¼ tsp. ground black pepper

1. Preheat the air fryer oven to 400ºF (204ºC). Line a parchment paper in the air fryer basket.
2. Place the asparagus spears in a large bowl. Drizzle with lemon juice and season with minced garlic, salt, and ground black pepper. Toss to coat evenly.
3. Place the asparagus in the air fryer basket and spray lightly with cooking spray. Put the air fryer basket onto the baking pan, and slide the baking pan into Rack Position 2, select Air Fry and set time to 10 minutes, until wilted and tender. Flip the asparagus halfway through.
4. Serve hot.

## Indian Sweet Potato Fries

Prep time: 5 minutes | Cook time: 8 minutes | Makes 20 fries

**Fries:**
2 tsps. olive oil
2 large sweet potatoes, peeled
**Seasoning Mixture:**
¾ tsp. ground coriander

½ tsp. garlic powder
½ tsp. ground cumin
½ tsp. garam masala
¼ tsp. ground cayenne pepper

1. Preheat the air fryer oven to 400ºF (204ºC).
2. Combine all the ingredients of seasoning mixture in a small bowl.
3. Cut the sweet potatoes into ¼-inch-thick fries.
4. Toss the sliced sweet potatoes with the olive oil and the seasoning mixture in a large bowl.
5. Put the seasoned sweet potatoes in the air fryer basket. Then place the air fryer basket onto the baking pan, and slide the baking pan into Rack Position 2, select Air Fry and set time to 8 minutes.
6. Serve hot.

## Honey Pears with Lemony Ricotta

Prep time: 10 minutes | Cook time: 8 minutes | Serves 4

2 large Bartlett pears, peeled, cut in half, cored
½ cup whole-milk ricotta cheese
3 tbsps. melted butter
3 tbsps. brown sugar
1 tbsp. honey, plus

additional for drizzling
1 tsp. pure lemon extract
1 tsp. pure almond extract
½ tsp. ground ginger
¼ tsp. ground cardamom

1. Preheat the air fryer oven to 375ºF (191ºC).
2. In a large bowl, toss the pears with butter, ginger, cardamom, and sugar. Toss to coat well.
3. Place the pears in the air fryer basket, cut side down. Then put the air fryer basket onto the baking pan, and slide the baking pan into Rack Position 2, select Air Fry and set time to 5 minutes. Air fry for about 5 minutes. Flip the pears and air fry for another 3 minutes or until the pears are tender and browned.
4. At the same time, mix the remaining ingredients in a separate bowl. With a hand mixer, whip for 1 minute until the mixture is puffed.
5. Distribute the mixture evenly into four bowls, then place the pears over the mixture and drizzle with more honey to serve.

## Brown Rice and Carrot Fritters

Prep time: 10 minutes | Cook time: 8 minutes | Serves 4

2 tsps. olive oil
1 (10-ounce / 284-g) bag frozen cooked brown rice, thawed
1 egg
⅓ cup finely grated carrots

⅓ cup minced red bell pepper
3 tbsps. grated Parmesan cheese
3 tbsps. brown rice flour
2 tbsps. minced fresh basil

1. Preheat the air fryer oven to 380ºF (193ºC).
2. Combine the thawed rice, egg, and flour in a small bowl, and mix to blend well.
3. Stir in the bell pepper, carrots, basil, and Parmesan cheese.
4. Shape the mixture into 8 fritters and drizzle with the olive oil.
5. Place the fritters carefully in the air fryer basket. Then put the air fryer basket onto the baking pan, and slide the baking pan into Rack Position 2, select Air Fry and set time to 8 minutes, until the fritters are golden brown and cooked through.
6. Serve hot.

# Fried Chicken Wings

Prep time: 5 minutes | Cook time: 19 minutes | Serves 6

2 pounds (907 g) chicken wings, tips removed
⅛ tsp. salt

1. Preheat the air fryer oven to 400ºF (204ºC). Season the wings with salt.
2. Working in 2 batches, put half the chicken wings in the air fryer basket. Then place the air fryer basket onto the baking pan, and slide the baking pan into Rack Position 2, select Air Fry and set time to 15 minutes, turning the wings by using tongs halfway through the cooking time.
3. Combine both batches in the air fryer oven and air fry for another 4 minutes. Transfer to a large bowl and serve hot.

# Classic Indian Masala Omelet

Prep time: 10 minutes | Cook time: 12 minutes | Serves 2

Olive oil, for greasing the pan
4 large eggs
½ cup diced tomato
½ cup diced onion
1 jalapeño, deseeded and finely chopped

¼ cup chopped fresh cilantro
½ tsp. ground turmeric
½ tsp. kosher salt
½ tsp. cayenne pepper

1. Preheat the air fryer oven to 250ºF (121ºC). Generously grease a 3-cup Bundt pan with olive oil.
2. Beat the eggs. Stir in the onion, tomato, cilantro, jalapeño, turmeric, salt, and cayenne in a large bowl.
3. Place the egg mixture into the prepared pan. Slide the Bundt pan into Rack Position 1, select Convection Bake and set time to 6 minutes, until the eggs are cooked through. Carefully unmold and cut the omelet into four pieces.
4. Serve hot.

# Chapter 12 Holiday Specials

## Parmesan Potatoes

Prep time: 5 minutes | Cook time: 50 minutes | Serves 4

Cooking spray
4 russet potatoes, peeled
¼ cup grated Parmesan
cheese
Salt and freshly ground black pepper, to taste

1. Preheat the air fryer oven to 400ºF (204ºC).
2. Spritz the air fryer basket with cooking spray.
3. Make thin parallel cuts into each potato, ⅛-inch to ¼-inch apart, stopping at about ½ of the way through. The potato needs to stay intact along the bottom.
4. Spritz the potatoes lightly with cooking spray and use the hands or a silicone brush to completely coat the potatoes lightly in oil.
5. Arrange the potatoes, sliced side up, in the air fryer basket in a single layer. Leave a little room between each potato. Scatter the potatoes lightly with salt and black pepper.
6. Place the air fryer basket onto the baking pan, and slide the baking pan into Rack Position 2, select Air Fry and set time to 20 minutes. Reposition the potatoes and spray with cooking spray again. Air fry for another 20 to 30 minutes until the potatoes are fork-tender and crispy and browned.
7. Scatter the potatoes with Parmesan cheese and serve warm.

## Pecan Monkey Bread

Prep time: 15 minutes | Cook time: 25 minutes | Serves 6 to 8

1 (16.3-ounce / 462-g) can store-bought refrigerated biscuit dough
½ cup powdered sugar
¼ cup packed light brown sugar
4 tbsps. (½ stick) unsalted butter, melted
2 tbsps. chopped candied cherries
2 tbsps. chopped pecans
2 tsps. bourbon
1 tsp. ground cinnamon
½ tsp. ground ginger
½ tsp. freshly grated nutmeg
½ tsp. kosher salt
¼ tsp. ground allspice
⅛ tsp. ground cloves

1. Preheat the air fryer oven to 310ºF (154ºC).
2. Open the can and separate the biscuits, then cut each into quarters. In a large bowl, toss the biscuit quarters with the brown sugar, cinnamon, nutmeg, ginger, salt, allspice, and cloves until evenly coated. Take the dough pieces and any sugar left in the bowl to a round cake pan, metal cake pan, or foil pan and drizzle evenly with the melted butter. Slide the cake pan into Rack Position 1, select Convection Bake and set time to 25 minutes, until the monkey bread is golden brown and cooked through in the middle. Take the bread to a wire rack and allow to cool completely. Unmold from the pan.
3. Whisk the powdered sugar and the bourbon into a smooth glaze in a small bowl. Drizzle the glaze over the cooled monkey bread and, when the glaze is still wet, scatter with the cherries and pecans to serve.

## Crunchy Golden Nuggets

Prep time: 15 minutes | Cook time: 4 minutes per batch | Makes 20 nuggets

Cooking spray
1 cup all-purpose flour, plus more for dusting
¼ cup water
1 tsp. baking powder
½ tsp. butter, at room
temperature, plus more for brushing
¼ tsp. garlic powder
¼ tsp. salt
⅛ tsp. onion powder
⅛ tsp. seasoning salt

1. Preheat the air fryer oven to 370ºF (188ºC). Line the air fryer basket with parchment paper.
2. In a large bowl, mix the flour, baking powder, butter, and salt. Stir to mix well. Slowly whisk in the water until a sanity dough forms.
3. Place the dough on a lightly floured work surface, then roll it out into a ½-inch thick rectangle with a rolling pin.
4. Slice the dough into about twenty 1- or 2-inch squares, then place the squares in a single layer in the air fryer basket. Spray lightly with cooking spray. You need to cook in batches to avoid overcrowding.
5. In a small bowl, combine onion powder, garlic powder, and seasoning salt. Stir to mix well, then sprinkle the squares with the powder mixture.
6. Put the air fryer basket onto the baking pan, and slide the baking pan into Rack Position 2, select Air Fry and set time to 4 minutes. Flip the squares halfway through the cooking time.
7. Transfer the golden nuggets from the air fryer oven and coat with more butter immediately. Serve hot.

## Risotto Croquettes with Tomato Sauce

Prep time: 1 hour 40 minutes | Cook time: 1 hour | Serves 6

**Risotto Croquettes:**
Cooking spray
1½ cups panko breadcrumbs
3 eggs
1 cup Arborio rice
3½ cups chicken stock
1 small yellow onion, minced
½ cup all-purpose flour
½ cup dry white wine
½ cup grated Parmesan cheese
¼ cup peas
2 ounces (57 g) fresh Mozzarella cheese

4 tbsps. unsalted butter
Zest of 1 lemon
2 tbsps. water
Kosher salt and ground black pepper, to taste
**Tomato Sauce:**
2 tbsps. extra-virgin olive oil
1 (28-ounce / 794-g) can crushed tomatoes
4 cloves garlic, minced
2 tsps. granulated sugar
¼ tsp. red pepper flakes
Kosher salt and ground black pepper, to taste

1. In a pot over medium heat, melt the butter, then add the onion and salt to taste. Sauté for about 5 minutes or until the onion in translucent.
2. Place the rice and stir to coat well. Cook for about 3 minutes or until the rice is lightly browned. Add the chicken stock and wine.
3. Bring to a boil. Then cook for about 20 minutes or until the rice is soft and liquid is almost absorbed.
4. Make the risotto: When the rice is cooked, break the egg into the pot. Place the lemon zest and Parmesan cheese. Season with salt and ground black pepper to taste. Stir to mix well.
5. Pour the risotto in the baking pan, then level by using a spatula to spread the risotto evenly. Wrap the baking pan in plastic and refrigerate for 1 hour.
6. At the same time, heat the olive oil over medium heat in a saucepan until shimmering.
7. Add the garlic and scatter with red pepper flakes. Sauté for a minute or until fragrant.
8. Place the crushed tomatoes and scatter with sugar. Stir to mix well. Bring to a boil. Lower the heat and simmer for 15 minutes or until lightly thickened. Season with salt and pepper to taste. Keep aside until ready to serve.
9. Transfer the risotto from the refrigerator. Spoon the risotto into twelve 2-inch balls, then flatten the balls with your hands.
10. Put a about ½-inch piece of Mozzarella and 5 peas in the center of each flattened ball, then wrap them back into balls.
11. Take the balls in the baking pan lined with parchment paper, then refrigerate for 15 minutes or until firm.
12. Preheat the air fryer oven to 400ºF (204ºC).
13. In a bowl, whisk the remaining 2 eggs with 2 tbsps. of water. Place the flour in a second bowl and put the panko in a third bowl.
14. Dredge the risotto balls in the bowl of flour first, then into the eggs, and then into the panko. Shake the excess off.
15. Take the balls in the baking pan and spray lightly with cooking spray. You may need to cook in batches to avoid overcrowding.
16. Slide the baking pan into Rack Position 1, select Convection Bake and set time to 10 minutes, until golden brown. Flip the balls halfway through.
17. Serve the risotto balls with the tomato sauce.

## Breaded Kale Sushi Rolls with Sriracha Mayonnaise

Prep time: 10 minutes | Cook time: 10 minutes | Serves 12

**Kale Salad:**
¾ tsp. toasted sesame oil
1½ cups chopped kale
1 tbsp. sesame seeds
¾ tsp. soy sauce
½ tsp. rice vinegar
¼ tsp. ginger
⅛ tsp. garlic powder
**Sushi Rolls:**

1 batch cauliflower rice
3 sheets sushi nori
½ avocado, sliced
**Sriracha Mayonnaise:**
¼ cup vegan mayonnaise
¼ cup Sriracha sauce
**Coating:**
½ cup panko breadcrumbs

1. Preheat the air fryer oven to 390ºF (199ºC).
2. Toss all the ingredients for the salad together in a medium bowl until well coated and keep aside.
3. On a clean work surface, place a sheet of nori and spread the cauliflower rice in an even layer on the nori. Spoon 2 to 3 tbsp. of kale salad on the rice and spread over. Put 1 or 2 avocado slices on top. Roll up the sushi, pressing gently to get a nice, tight roll. Repeat this process to make the remaining 2 rolls.
4. Stir together the Sriracha sauce and mayonnaise in a bowl until smooth. Add breadcrumbs to a separate bowl.
5. Dredge the sushi rolls in Sriracha Mayonnaise, then roll in breadcrumbs till well coated.
6. Put the coated sushi rolls inthe air fryer basket. Then place the air fryer basket onto the baking pan, and slide the baking pan into Rack Position 2, select Air Fry and set time to 10 minutes. Flip the sushi rolls gently halfway through to ensure even cooking.
7. Take to a platter and let rest for about 5 minutes before slicing each roll into 8 pieces. Serve immediately.

## Butter Cake

Prep time: 25 minutes | Cook time: 20 minutes | Serves 8

Cooking spray
1 cup all-purpose flour
2 large eggs
1 large egg yolk
½ cup plus 1½ tbsps. granulated white sugar

9½ tbsps. butter, at room temperature
2½ tbsps. milk
1¼ tsps. baking powder
1 tsp. vanilla extract
¼ tsp. salt

1. Preheat the air fryer oven to 325ºF (163ºC). Spray a cake pan lightly with cooking spray.
2. In a large bowl, combine the flour, baking powder, and salt. Stir to mix well.
3. In a separate bowl, whip the sugar and butter with a hand mixer on medium speed for 3 minutes.
4. Whip the milk, eggs, egg yolk, and vanilla extract into the sugar and butter mix with a hand mixer.
5. Add the flour mixture and whip with hand mixer until sanity and smooth.
6. Scrape the batter into the cake pan and level the batter by using a spatula.
7. Slide the baking pan into Rack Position 1, select Convection Bake and set time to 20 minutes, until a toothpick inserted in the center comes out clean. Check the doneness during the last 5 minutes of the baking.
8. Invert the cake on a cooling rack and let cool for 15 minutes before slicing to serve.

## Sriracha Shrimp

Prep time: 15 minutes | Cook time: 10 minutes per batch | Serves 4

Cooking spray
1 pound (454 g) raw shrimp, shelled and deveined, rinsed and drained
1 cup panko breadcrumbs

¾ cup mayonnaise
1 egg, beaten
2 tbsps. sweet chili sauce
1 tbsp. Sriracha sauce
1 tsp. Worcestershire sauce
Lime wedges, for serving

1. Preheat the air fryer oven to 360ºF (182ºC). Spray the air fryer basket lightly with cooking spray.
2. In a bowl, combine the Sriracha sauce, Worcestershire sauce, chili sauce, and mayo. Stir to mix well. Reserve ⅓ cup of the mixture as the dipping sauce.
3. Mix the remaining sauce mixture with the beaten egg. Stir to combine well. Place the panko in a separate bowl.
4. Dredge the shrimp in the sauce mixture first, then into the panko. Roll the shrimp to coat well. Shake the excess off.
5. Arrange the shrimp in the air fryer basket and spray lightly with cooking spray. You may need to cook in batches to avoid overcrowding.
6. Place the air fryer basket onto the baking pan, and slide the baking pan into Rack Position 2, select Air Fry and set time to 10 minutes, until opaque. Gently flip the shrimp halfway through the cooking time.
7. Transfer the shrimp from the oven and squeeze the lime wedges over. Serve hot with reserve sauce mixture.

## Maple Pecan Tart

Prep time: 2hours 25 minutes | Cook time: 30 minutes | Serves 8

**Tart Crust:**
1 cup all-purpose flour
⅓ cup butter, softened
¼ cup firmly packed brown sugar
¼ tsp. kosher salt
**Filling:**
1½ cups finely chopped

pecans
½ cup packed brown sugar
¼ cup pure maple syrup
¼ cup whole milk
4 tbsps. butter, diced
¼ tsp. pure vanilla extract
¼ tsp. sea salt

1. Preheat the air fryer oven to 350ºF (177ºC). Line a baking pan with aluminum foil, then spray the pan lightly with cooking spray.
2. In a bowl, stir the brown sugar and butter with a hand mixer until puffed, then place the flour and salt and stir until crumbled.
3. Pour the mixture in the prepared baking pan and tilt the pan to coat the bottom well.
4. Slide the baking pan into Rack Position 1, select Convection Bake and set time to 13 minutes, until the crust is golden brown.
5. At the same time, pour the milk, butter, sugar, and maple syrup in a saucepan. Stir to mix well. Bring to a simmer, then cook for another minute. Stir frequently.
6. Turn off the heat and place the pecans and vanilla into the filling mixture.
7. Add the filling mixture over the golden crust and spread by using a spatula to coat the crust evenly.
8. Bake for another 12 minutes or until the filling mixture is set and frothy.
9. Transfer from the air fryer oven and season with salt to taste. Let sit for about 10 minutes or until cooled.
10. Take the tart to the refrigerator to chill for at least 2 hours, then remove the aluminum foil and slice to serve.

Parmesan Potatoes, page 157

Crunchy Golden Nuggets, page 157

Pão de Queijo, page 161

Butter Cake, page 159

## Classic Jewish Blintzes

Prep time: 5 minutes | Cook time: 10 minutes | Makes 8 blintzes

4 tbsps. butter, melted
2 (7½-ounce / 213-g) packages farmer cheese, mashed
8 egg roll wrappers
¼ cup granulated white sugar
¼ cup cream cheese
¼ tsp. vanilla extract

1. Preheat the air fryer oven to 375ºF (191ºC).
2. In a bowl, combine the farmer cheese, cream cheese, vanilla extract, and sugar. Stir to mix well.
3. On a clean work surface, unfold the egg roll wrappers, spread ¼ cup of the filling at the edge of each wrapper and leave a ½-inch edge uncovering.
4. Wet the edges of the wrappers with water and gently fold the uncovered edge over the filling. Fold the left and right sides in the center, then tuck the edge under the filling and fold to wrap the filling.
5. Coat the wrappers with melted butter, then place the wrappers in a single layer in the air fryer basket, seam side down. Leave a little space between each two wrappers. Work in batches to avoid overcrowding.
6. Place the air fryer basket onto the baking pan, and slide the baking pan into Rack Position 2, select Air Fry and set time to 10 minutes.
7. Serve warm.

## Pão de Queijo

Prep time: 37 minutes | Cook time: 24 minutes | Makes 12 balls

2 tbsps. butter, plus more for greasing
1½ cups tapioca flour
1 large egg
⅔ cup finely grated aged Asiago cheese
½ cup milk
½ tsp. salt

1. In a saucepan, put the butter and pour in the milk, heat over medium heat until the liquid boils. Keep stirring.
2. Transfer from the heat and mix in the tapioca flour and salt to form a soft dough. Take the dough in a large bowl, then wrap the bowl in plastic and allow to sit for 15 minutes.
3. Break the egg in the bowl of dough and whisk with a hand mixer for about 2 minutes or until a sanity dough forms. Gently fold the cheese in the dough. Cover the bowl in plastic again and let sit for 10 more minutes.
4. Preheat the air fryer oven to 375ºF (191ºC). Grease a cake pan lightly with butter.

5. Spoon 2 tbsps. of the dough into the cake pan. Repeat this process with the remaining dough to make dough 12 balls. Keep a little distance between each two balls. You may need to cook in batches to avoid overcrowding.
6. Slide the cake pan into Rack Position 1, select Convection Bake and set time to 12 minutes, until the balls are golden brown and fluffy. Gently flip the balls halfway through the cooking time.
7. Transfer the balls from the air fryer oven and let cool for 5 minutes before serving.

## Garlicky Olive and Basil Stromboli

Prep time: 25 minutes | Cook time: 25 minutes | Serves 8

Cooking spray
½ pound (227 g) pizza dough, at room temperature
½ cup marinated, pitted green and black olives
½ cup packed fresh basil leaves
4 large cloves garlic,
unpeeled
4 ounces (113 g) sliced provolone cheese (about 8 slices)
3 tbsps. grated Parmesan cheese
¼ tsp. crushed red pepper

1. Preheat the air fryer oven to 370ºF (188ºC). Spray the air fryer basket lightly with cooking spray.
2. Place the unpeeled garlic in the air fryer basket.
3. Put the air fryer basket onto the baking pan, and slide the baking pan into Rack Position 2, select Air Fry and set time to 10 minutes. Transfer the garlic from the oven and let cool until you can handle.
4. Peel the garlic and place into a food processor with 2 tbsps. of Parmesan, olives, basil, and crushed red pepper. Pulse to mix well. Keep aside.
5. Put the pizza dough on a clean work surface, then roll it out with a rolling pin into a rectangle. Cut the rectangle in half.
6. Scatter half of the garlic mixture over each rectangle half, and leave ½-inch edges uncover. Place the provolone cheese on top.
7. Brush one long side of each rectangle half with water, then roll them up. Spray the baking pan lightly with cooking spray. Place the rolls in the baking pan and take to the preheated air fryer oven. Spray lightly with cooking spray and scatter with remaining Parmesan.
8. Slide the baking pan into Rack Position 1, select Convection Bake and set time to 15 minutes. Flip the rolls halfway through.
9. Transfer the rolls from the air fryer oven and let cool for a few minutes before serving.

## Pigs in a Blanket with Sesame Seeds

Prep time: 10 minutes | Cook time: 8 minutes per batch | Makes 16 rolls

1 small package mini smoked sausages, patted dry
1 can refrigerated crescent roll dough
2 tbsps. melted butter
2 tsps. sesame seeds
1 tsp. onion powder

1. Preheat the air fryer oven to 330ºF (166ºC).
2. On a clean work surface, place the crescent roll dough and separate into 8 pieces. Cut each piece in half and you will have 16 triangles.
3. Make the pigs in the blanket: Place each sausage on each dough triangle, then roll the sausages up.
4. Coat the pigs with melted butter and place half of the pigs in the blanket in the baking pan. Scatter with sesame seeds and onion powder.
5. Slide the baking pan into Rack Position 1, select Convection Bake and set time to 8 minutes, until the pigs are fluffy and golden brown. Gently flip the pigs halfway through.
6. Serve warm.

## Panko Shrimp Skewers

Prep time: 10 minutes | Cook time: 6 minutes | Makes 12 skewered shrimp

Cooking spray
12 large shrimp (about 20 shrimps per pound), peeled and deveined
1 large egg
¾ cup panko breadcrumbs
1½ tbsps. mirin
1½ tbsps. soy sauce
1½ tsps. ginger juice

1. In a large bowl, combine the mirin, ginger juice, and soy sauce. Stir to mix well.
2. Dip the shrimp in the bowl of mirin mixture, then wrap the bowl in plastic and refrigerate for 1 hour to marinate.
3. Preheat the air fryer oven to 400ºF (204ºC). Spray the air fryer basket lightly with cooking spray.
4. Run twelve 4-inch skewers through each shrimp.
5. Whisk the egg in the bowl of marinade to combine well. Place the breadcrumbs on a plate.
6. Dredge the shrimp skewers in the egg mixture, then shake the excess off and roll over the breadcrumbs to coat well.
7. Put the shrimp skewers in the air fryer basket and spray lightly with cooking spray. You need to cook in batches to avoid overcrowding.
8. Place the air fryer basket onto the baking pan, and slide the baking pan into Rack Position 2, select Air Fry and set time to 6 minutes, until the shrimp are opaque and firm. Gently flip the shrimp skewers halfway through.
9. Serve warm.

## Hearty Honey Yeast Rolls

Prep time: 10 minutes | Cook time: 20 minutes | Makes 8 rolls

2 tbsps. unsalted butter, at room temperature, plus more for greasing
⅔ cup all-purpose flour, plus more for dusting
¼ cup whole milk, heated
to 115ºF (46ºC) in the microwave
1 tbsp. honey
½ tsp. kosher salt
½ tsp. active dry yeast
Flaky sea salt, to taste

1. Whisk together the milk, yeast, and honey in a large bowl and let stand until foamy, about 10 minutes.
2. Stir in the flour and salt until just combined. Stir in the butter until absorbed. Scrape the dough onto a lightly floured work surface and knead for about 6 minutes until smooth. Take the dough to a lightly greased bowl, cover loosely with a sheet of plastic wrap or a kitchen towel, and allow to sit until nearly doubled in size, about 1 hour.
3. Uncover the dough, lightly press it down to expel the bubbles, then divide it into 8 equal pieces. Prep the work surface by wiping it clean with a damp paper towel (if there is flour on the work surface, it will prevent the dough from sticking lightly to the surface, which helps it form a ball). Roll each piece into a ball by cupping the palm of the hand around the dough against the work surface and moving the heel of the hand in a circular motion while contain the dough with the thumb and tighten it into a perfectly round ball. When all the balls are formed, nestle them side by side in the air fryer basket.
4. Use a kitchen towel or a sheet of plastic wrap to cover the rolls loosely and let sit until lightly risen and puffed, about 20 to 30 minutes.
5. Preheat the air fryer oven to 270ºF (132ºC).
6. Uncover the rolls and gently brush with more butter, being careful not to press the rolls too hard. Place the air fryer basket onto the baking pan, and slide the baking pan into Rack Position 2, select Air Fry and set time to 12 minutes.
7. Transfer the rolls from the air fryer oven and brush liberally with more butter, if you like, and scatter each roll with a pinch of sea salt. Serve hot.

## Spicy Breaded Olives

Prep time: 10 minutes | Cook time: 5 minutes | Serves 4

Vegetable oil for spraying
12 ounces (340 g) pitted black extra-large olives
1 cup panko bread crumbs
¼ cup all-purpose flour

1 egg beaten with 1 tbsp. water
2 tsps. dried thyme
1 tsp. smoked paprika
1 tsp. red pepper flakes

1. Preheat the air fryer oven to 400ºF (204ºC).
2. Drain the olives and put them on a paper towel–lined plate to dry.
3. Place the flour on a plate. On a separate plate, combine the panko, thyme, red pepper flakes, and paprika. Dunk an olive in the flour, shaking off any excess, then coat with egg mixture. Dredge the olive in the panko mixture, pressing to make the crumbs adhere, and put the breaded olive on a platter. Repeat this with the remaining olives.
4. Spritz the olives lightly with oil and arrange them in a single layer in the air fryer basket. Work in batches if necessary, so as not to overcrowd the air fryer basket. Place the air fryer basket onto the baking pan, and slide the baking pan into Rack Position 2, select Air Fry and set time to 5 minutes, until the breading is browned and crispy. Serve hot.

# Chapter 13 Sauces for Air Fryer Recipes

## Easy Pico de Gallo

Prep time: 5 minutes | Cook time: 0 minutes | Serves 2

3 large tomatoes, chopped
⅛ cup chopped fresh cilantro
3 garlic cloves, chopped
½ small red onion, diced

2 tbsps. chopped pickled jalapeño pepper
1 tbsp. lime juice
¼ tsp. pink Himalayan salt (optional)

1. Combine all the ingredients in a medium bowl, and mix with a wooden spoon.

## Lemony Almond and Kale Pesto

Prep time: 15 minutes | Cook time: 0 minutes | Makes about 1 cup

3 tbsps. extra-virgin olive oil
2 cups chopped kale leaves, rinsed well and stemmed
½ cup toasted almonds
2 garlic cloves

3 tbsps. freshly squeezed lemon juice
2 tsps. lemon zest
¼ tsp. red pepper flakes
1 tsp. salt
½ tsp. freshly ground black pepper

1. In a food processor, add all the ingredients and pulse until smoothly puréed.
2. It tastes great with the eggs, salads, pasta, soup, cracker, and sandwiches.

## Lime Yogurt Dressing

Prep time: 5 minutes | Cook time: 0 minutes | Makes about 1 cup

8 ounces (227 g) plain coconut yogurt
2 tbsps. freshly squeezed lemon juice
2 tbsps. chopped fresh parsley

1 tbsp. snipped fresh chives
½ tsp. salt
Pinch freshly ground black pepper

1. In a medium bowl, stir together the coconut yogurt, parsley, lemon juice, chives, salt, and pepper until completely mixed.

2. Take to an airtight container and refrigerate until ready to use.
3. You can serve with spring mix greens, grilled chicken or even your favorite salad.

## Lemony Mixed Berry Vinaigrette

Prep time: 15 minutes | Cook time: 0 minutes | Makes about 1½ cups

⅓ cup extra-virgin olive oil
1 cup mixed berries, thawed if frozen
½ cup balsamic vinegar
2 tbsps. freshly squeezed lemon or lime juice
1 tbsp. lemon or lime

zest
1 tbsp. raw honey or maple syrup
1 tbsp. Dijon mustard
1 tsp. salt
½ tsp. freshly ground black pepper

1. In a blender, place all the ingredients and purée until thoroughly mixed and smooth.
2. You can serve it with greens, grilled meat, or fresh fruit salad.

## Traditional Argentinian Chimichurri

Prep time: 15 minutes | Cook time: 0 minutes | Makes 2 cups

1 cup olive oil or avocado oil
1 cup minced fresh parsley
½ cup minced fresh cilantro
½ cup red wine vinegar
¼ cup minced garlic

(about 6 cloves)
¼ cup minced fresh mint leaves
Juice of 1 lemon
2 tbsps. minced fresh oregano leaves
1 tsp. fine Himalayan salt

1. In a medium bowl, thoroughly mix the parsley, cilantro, mint leaves, garlic, oregano leaves, and salt. Pour in the olive oil, vinegar, and lemon juice and whisk to combine well.
2. Store in an airtight container in the refrigerator and shake before using.
3. You can enjoy the chimichurri over vegetables, meats, poultry, and fish. It also can be used as a marinade, dipping sauce, or condiment.

# Quick Hummus

Prep time: 5 minutes | Cook time: 0 minutes | Serves 2

1 (19-ounce / 539-g) can chickpeas, drained and rinsed
¼ cup tahini
1 garlic clove
3 tbsps. cold water
2 tbsps. freshly squeezed lemon juice
½ tsp. turmeric powder
Pinch of pink Himalayan salt
⅛ tsp. black pepper

1. In a food processor, add all the ingredients and blend until smooth.

# Dill Cashew Ranch Dressing

Prep time: 15 minutes | Cook time: 0 minutes | Serves 12

1 cup cashews, soaked in warm water for at least 1 hour
½ cup water
2 tbsps. freshly squeezed
lemon juice
1 tbsp. vinegar
2 tsps. dried dill
1 tsp. onion powder
1 tsp. garlic powder

1. Combine the cashews, water, lemon juice, vinegar, garlic powder, and onion powder in a food processor. Blend until creamy and smooth. Place the dill and pulse a few times until combined well.

# Garlicky Cashew Vodka Sauce

Prep time: 15 minutes | Cook time: 5 minutes | Makes 3 cups

¾ cup raw cashews
¼ cup boiling water
1 tbsp. olive oil
4 garlic cloves, minced
1½ cups unsweetened
almond milk
1 tbsp. arrowroot powder
1 tsp. salt
1 tbsp. nutritional yeast
1¼ cups marinara sauce

1. In a heatproof bowl, place the cashews and add boiling water to cover. Allow to soak for about 10 minutes. Drain the cashews and put them in a blender. Pour in ¼ cup boiling water and blend for about 1 to 2 minutes or until creamy. Keep aside.
2. In a small saucepan over medium heat, heat the olive oil. Place the garlic and sauté for about 2 minutes until golden. Whisk in the almond milk, arrowroot powder, and salt. Bring to a simmer. Continue to simmer, whisking constantly, for 5 minutes or until the sauce thickens.
3. Gently take the hot almond milk mixture to the blender with the cashews. Blend for about 30 seconds to combine, then put the nutritional yeast and marinara sauce. Blend for about 1 minute or until creamy.

# Mustard Balsamic Dressing

Prep time: 5 minutes | Cook time: 0 minutes | Makes 1 cup

¾ cup olive oil
¼ cup balsamic vinegar
2 tbsps. Dijon mustard

1. In a jar, add all the ingredients with a tight-fitting lid. Cover the lid and shake vigorously until well combined. Refrigerate until ready to use and shake well before serving.

# Lemony Mustard Vinaigrette

Prep time: 5 minutes | Cook time: 0 minutes | Makes about 6 tablespoons

¼ cup extra-virgin olive oil
2 tbsps. freshly squeezed lemon juice
1 garlic clove, minced
1 tsp. Dijon mustard
½ tsp. raw honey
¼ tsp. dried basil
¼ tsp. salt

1. Add all the ingredients in a mason jar. Cover and shake vigorously until entirely mixed and well emulsified.
2. Enjoy chilled.

# Coconut Lime and Peanut Dressing

Prep time: 5 minutes | Cook time: 0 minutes | Serves 8

1 cup lite coconut milk
¼ cup creamy peanut butter
¼ cup freshly squeezed lime juice
3 garlic cloves, minced
2 tbsps. low-sodium soy sauce or tamari
1 tbsp. grated fresh ginger

1. In a food processor or blender, place all the ingredients and process until completely mixed and smooth.
2. Serve over grilled chicken or tossed with noodles and green onions.

Easy Pico de Gallo, page 165

Quick Hummus, page 166

Mustard Balsamic Dressing, page 166

Ketchup Sauce, page 168

# Ketchup Sauce

Prep time: 5 minutes | Cook time: 5 minutes | Makes ⅔ cup

3 tbsps. ketchup
2 tbsps. maple syrup
2 tbsps. water
1 tbsp. rice vinegar

2 tsps. soy sauce (or tamari, which is a gluten-free option)
2 tsps. peeled minced fresh ginger root
1 tsp. cornstarch

1.  Combine all the ingredients in a small saucepan over medium heat, and stir continuously for 5 minutes, or until slightly thickened. Serve warm or cold.

# Lime Tahini Dressing

Prep time: 5 minutes | Cook time: 0 minutes | Makes about ¾ cup

⅓ cup tahini
2 tbsps. freshly squeezed lime juice
3 tbsps. filtered water
1 tbsp. apple cider vinegar

1½ tsps. raw honey
1 tsp. lime zest
¼ tsp. garlic powder
¼ tsp. salt

1.  In a small bowl, whisk together the tahini, vinegar, lime juice, water, lime zest, honey, salt, and garlic powder until well emulsified.
2.  Serve right away, or refrigerate in an airtight container for to 1 week.

# Dill Yogurt Ranch Dressing

Prep time: 5 minutes | Cook time: 0 minutes | Serves 8

1 cup plain Greek yogurt
¼ cup chopped fresh dill
1 garlic clove, minced
Zest of 1 lemon

2 tbsps. chopped fresh chives
½ tsp. sea salt
⅛ tsp. freshly cracked black pepper

1.  In a small bowl, mix together the yogurt, dill, chives, lemon zest, garlic, sea salt, and pepper and whisk to combine well.
2.  Serve chilled.

# Cashew-Basil Wheatgrass Pesto

Prep time: 10 minutes | Cook time: 0 minutes | Makes 1 cup

1 tbsp. olive oil
4 cups basil leaves, packed
1 cup wheatgrass
¼ cup raw cashews
⅓ red onion (about 2 ounces / 56 g in total)

¼ cup water
Juice of 1 lemon
2 garlic cloves
¼ tsp. salt

1.  In a heatproof bowl, put the cashews and add boiling water to cover. Let soak for about 5 minutes and then drain.
2.  In a blender, add all the ingredients and blend for about 2 to 3 minutes or until well combined.

# Appendix 1: Measurement Conversion Chart

## Volume Equivalents (Dry)

| US STANDARD | METRIC (APPROXIMATE) |
| --- | --- |
| 1/8 teaspoon | 0.5 mL |
| 1/4 teaspoon | 1 mL |
| 1/2 teaspoon | 2 mL |
| 3/4 teaspoon | 4 mL |
| 1 teaspoon | 5 mL |
| 1 tablespoon | 15 mL |
| 1/4 cup | 59 mL |
| 1/2 cup | 118 mL |
| 3/4 cup | 177 mL |
| 1 cup | 235 mL |
| 2 cups | 475 mL |
| 3 cups | 700 mL |
| 4 cups | 1 L |

## Temperatures Equivalents

| FAHRENHEIT (F) | CELSIUS(C) (APPROXIMATE) |
| --- | --- |
| 225 °F | 107 °C |
| 250 °F | 120 °C |
| 275 °F | 135 °C |
| 300 °F | 150 °C |
| 325 °F | 160 °C |
| 350 °F | 180 °C |
| 375 °F | 190 °C |
| 400 °F | 205 °C |
| 425 °F | 220 °C |
| 450 °F | 235 °C |
| 475 °F | 245 °C |
| 500 °F | 260 °C |

## Volume Equivalents (Liquid)

| US STANDARD | US STANDARD (OUNCES) | METRIC (APPROXIMATE) |
| --- | --- | --- |
| 2 tablespoons | 1 fl.oz. | 30 mL |
| 1/4 cup | 2 fl.oz. | 60 mL |
| 1/2 cup | 4 fl.oz. | 120 mL |
| 1 cup | 8 fl.oz. | 240 mL |
| 1 1/2 cup | 12 fl.oz. | 355 mL |
| 2 cups or 1 pint | 16 fl.oz. | 475 mL |
| 4 cups or 1 quart | 32 fl.oz. | 1 L |
| 1 gallon | 128 fl.oz. | 4 L |

## Weight Equivalents

| US STANDARD | METRIC (APPROXIMATE) |
| --- | --- |
| 1 ounce | 28 g |
| 2 ounces | 57 g |
| 5 ounces | 142 g |
| 10 ounces | 284 g |
| 15 ounces | 425 g |
| 16 ounces (1 pound) | 455 g |
| 1.5 pounds | 680 g |
| 2 pounds | 907 g |

# Appendix 2: Cuisinart Air Fryer Oven Time Table

| Chicken | | | | |
|---|---|---|---|---|
| INGREDIENT | AMOUNT | PREPARATION | AVG.TIME | TEMP.(°F ) |
| Tender | 1-inch | strips | 8 min | 360 |
| Breast | 4 ounces | Boneless | 11 min | 380 |
| Wings | 2 pounds | / | 13 min | 380 |
| Thighs | 1.5 pounds | Boneless | 17 min | 380 |
| Drumsticks | 2.5 pounds | / | 19 min | 370 |
| Thighs | 2 pounds | Bone-in | 21 min | 380 |
| Breast | 1.25 pounds | Bone-in | 24 min | 370 |
| Legs | 1.75 pounds | Bone-in | 30 min | 380 |
| Cornish Hen | 2 pounds | Whole | 32 min | 370 |
| Roast Chicken | 4 pounds | Whole | 55 min | 350 |

| Seafood | | | | |
|---|---|---|---|---|
| INGREDIENT | AMOUNT | PREPARATION | AVG.TIME | TEMP.(°F ) |
| Calamari | 8 ounces | / | 4 min | 400 |
| Shrimp | 1 pound | Whole | 4 min | 400 |
| Lobster Tails | 1 | Whole | 5 min | 370 |
| Scallops | 1 pound | Whole | 6 min | 400 |
| Tuna Steak | 2 inches | thick | 6 min | 400 |
| Fish Fillet | 8 ounces | / | 9 min | 400 |
| Swordfish Steak | 2 inches | thick | 9 min | 400 |
| Crab Cakes | 1-2 inches | thick | 9 min | 400 |
| Salmon Fillet | 12 ounces | / | 10 min | 380 |

| Beef | | | | |
|---|---|---|---|---|
| INGREDIENT | AMOUNT | PREPARATION | AVG.TIME | TEMP.(°F ) |
| Meatballs | 2-inch | / | 8 min | 380 |
| Flank Steak | 1.5 pounds | / | 11 min | 400 |
| Ribeye | 8 ounces | Bone-in | 11 min | 400 |
| Sirloin Steak | 12 ounces | / | 11 min | 400 |
| Burger | 4 ounces | / | 14 min | 370 |
| Filet Mignon | 8 ounces | / | 16 min | 400 |
| London Broil | 2 pounds | / | 18 min | 400 |
| Beef Eye Round | 4 pounds | / | 45 min | 380 |

## Vegetable

| INGREDIENT | AMOUNT | PREPARATION | AVG.TIME | TEMP.($^{o}$F ) |
|---|---|---|---|---|
| Brussels Sprouts | / | Halved | 15 min | 380 |
| Eggplant | 1-inch | Chopped | 15 min | 400 |
| Fennel | / | Quartered | 15 min | 370 |
| Parsnips | 1/2-inch | Chopped | 15 min | 380 |
| Peppers | 1/2-inch | Chopped | 15 min | 400 |
| Baby Potatoes | 1.5 pounds | Small | 16 min | 400 |
| Cherry Tomatoes | / | Whole | 20 min | 340 |
| Carrots | / | Whole | 20 min | 380 |
| Sweet Potato | / | Whole | 35 min | 380 |
| Beets | / | Whole | 40 min | 400 |
| Potatoes | / | Whole | 40 min | 400 |

## Frozen

| INGREDIENT | AMOUNT | PREPARATION | AVG.TIME | TEMP.($^{o}$F ) |
|---|---|---|---|---|
| Onion Rings | 12 ounces | / | 7 min | 370 to 400 |
| Mozzarella Sticks | 12 ounces | / | 7 min | 370 to 400 |
| Pot Stickers | 10 ounces | / | 7 min | 370 to 400 |
| Breaded Shrimp | 12 ounces | / | 9 min | 370 to 400 |
| Fish Sticks | 10 ounces | / | 9 min | 370 to 400 |
| Chicken Nuggets | 12 ounces | / | 10 min | 370 to 400 |
| Thin Fries | 20 ounces | / | 14 min | 370 to 400 |
| Fish Fillet | 10 ounces | / | 14 min | 370 to 400 |
| Chicken Wings | 6 ounces | Precooked | 17 min | 370 to 400 |
| Thick Fries | 20 ounces | / | 17 min | 370 to 400 |

# Appendix 3: Recipes Index

Made in the USA
Coppell, TX
02 December 2023

25177101R00105